CRIMINOLOGY BETWEEN THE RULE OF LAW AND THE OUTLAWS

CRIMINOLOGY BETWEEN THE RULE OF LAW AND THE OUTLAWS

Volume in honour of
Willem H. Nagel

Springer-Science+Business Media, B.V. 1976

ISBN 978-90-268-0844-9 ISBN 978-94-017-4988-6 (eBook)
DOI 10.1007/978-94-017-4988-6
ISBN 90 268 0844 5

Originally published by Kluwer B.V. - Deventer (The Netherlands) in 1976

BIOGRAPHY OF WILLEM H. NAGEL

Willem Nagel was born in 1910 in Zwolle, the Netherlands, and grew up in Groningen, where he studied law at the State University. He started his career as a public prosecutor but was relieved of this task in 1941 by the German occupying forces because of 'political and anti-German attitudes.'

In fact, he never was anti-German, as he demonstrated shortly after the war when he was one of the first eight Dutch professors who visited German universities to lecture in criminology. Some of his postwar articles appeared in German periodicals and in 1965 he was awarded the golden Beccaria Medal by the Deutsche Kriminologische Gesellschaft of which he is an honorary member. He has good friends in both Germanies.

Nevertheless he always has been and still is an anti-fascist, with a fine nose for fascism wherever it exists.

Although in a way he is an anti-militarist as well – he considers every war to be unjustifiable and at best excusable under certain circumstances – he volunteered to join the armed wing of the Dutch Resistance Forces operating against the German occupiers during World War II. After the war, however, he refused to be sent as a soldier to Indonesia to assist with its so-called pacification.

After the liberation of the Netherlands he served as a court justice until 1949 when he earned a Doctor of Laws degree *cum laude* with his dissertation: *De Kriminaliteit van Oss* (Criminality in Oss). Shortly thereafter he accepted a position at the State University of Leiden as assistant to Dr. J. M. van Bemmelen, Professor of Criminal Law and Criminology. The subject of his inaugural address was *Perjury*. With his appointment as lecturer in the sociology of criminal law in 1950 he became the first lecturer in the sociology of law in the Netherlands. His interest in this discipline continued to increase even though he was appointed Professor of Criminology in 1953. On this occasion his inaugural address dealt with *Het Strafrecht en de Onmens* (Criminal Law and the Monster).

Some of Nagel's most amazing characteristics, which make him a paradox to many outsiders, is his ability to devote himself entirely to scholarly study behind the closed doors of his office working hard, regularly, and in deep concentration behind his desk for weeks and months at a time, until the globe-trotter in him puts his desk production under his arm, books a plane and travels abroad.

He has been a visiting professor in the United States, Jerusalem, Djakarta, and Thailand, where he served for one year as a UN-advisor, and he has regularly attended international criminological congresses. He is vice-president of the International Society for Criminology. He is the founder of *Abstracts on Police Science* and the father of two well-known criminological periodicals: *Abstracts on Criminology and Penology* (formerly *Excerpta Criminologica*) and the *International Journal of Criminology and Penology*, and is still editor-in-chief of both. Last but not least, he has contributed to criminology a great number of studies, articles, and papers, as his impressive bibliography (printed elsewhere in this book) shows.

Outsiders may find the desk-scholar and globe-trotter contradictory characteristics in one man. However, insiders, especially his colleagues, know that both these activities are sides of the criminological medal as Nagel sees it.

Criminology is theory *and* practice, demanding interaction between both on a worldwide level, and criminology must be a criminology of relationships. In his lectures Nagel has repeatedly stressed that criminology might be called micro-polemology and he is strongly convinced that it may not derive its subject matter from criminal law alone. The criminologist is more than merely the 'dermatologist of society'.

This conception of criminology and his manifold international activities have influenced criminology at home and abroad. This 'Festschrift' dedicated to Willem H. Nagel contains a collection of articles written spontaneously by friends and colleagues from several countries and is an expression both of their appreciation and admiration.

His literary activities – under his penname J. B. Charles he has received several awards – and his scientific work seem to be merging increasingly. Is it perhaps possible that he will cease to separate his literary identity and his scientific identity after retirement as professor? About one thing there need be little doubt: in any case he will continue to signalize evil in whatever shape or form he meets it.

Leiden, December 1975 *C. W. G. Jasperse*

CONTRIBUTORS

Inkeri Anttila, Professor of Criminal Law and Criminology, Director of the Criminological Institute, University of Helsinki, and Minister of Justice, Finland.

J. M. van Bemmelen, Retired Professor of Penal Law and Criminology, State University of Leiden, The Netherlands.

H. H. Bloembergen, Lecturer in Criminology, State University of Leiden, The Netherlands.

Dennis Chapman, Professor of Sociology, University of Liverpool, Great Britain.

Karl O. Christiansen, Professor of Criminology, University of Copenhagen, Denmark.

Marshall B. Clinard, Professor of Sociology, University of Wisconsin, Madison, U.S.A.

C. I. Dessaur, Professor of Criminology, Catholic University of Nijmegen, The Netherlands.

A. R. Hauber, Lecturer in Criminology, State University of Leiden, The Netherlands.

Stuart C. Hadden, Sonoma State College, Rohnert Park, U.S.A.

Len Herkomer, Sonoma State College, Rohnert Park, U.S.A.

Hans Hinderer, Professor of Penal Law, Martin-Luther Universität, Halle-Wittenberg, G.D.R.

C. W. G. Jasperse, Lecturer in Sociology, State University of Leiden, The Netherlands.

Günther Kaiser, Professor of Criminology, Director of the Max-Planck-Institute for Foreign and International Criminal Law, Freiburg i.Br., F.R.G.

A. L. Melai, Professor of Penal Law, State University of Leiden, The Netherlands.

Paul Moedikdo, Lecturer in Criminology, State University of Utrecht, The Netherlands.

A. Mergen, Professor of Criminology, Johannes Gutenberg Universität, Mainz, F.R.G.

Kees Schuyt, Professor of Sociology of Law, Catholic University of Nijmegen, The Netherlands.

John M. Steiner, Professor of Sociology, Sonoma State College, Rohnert Park, U.S.A.

Denis Szabo, Professor of Criminology, University of Montreal, Canada.

L. G. Toornvliet, Lecturer in Criminology, State University of Leiden, The Netherlands.

Jac. van Weringh, Professor of Criminology, University of Amsterdam, The Netherlands.

Katja Vodopivec, Professor of Criminology, University of Ljubljana, Jugoslavia.
H. M. Willemse, Lecturer in Criminology, State University of Leiden, The Netherlands.

CONTENTS

Dennis Chapman

THE PROBLEMS WHICH HAVE DEVELOPED IN THE LEGAL SYSTEM OUT OF THE CONFLICT IN NORTHERN IRELAND AND ITS EXTENSION TO THE REST OF THE UNITED KINGDOM

One theoretical position views the penal system as designed to create social harmony and equality of power between individuals and groups. From this position transgressors of the law are seen as evil, sick or ignorant and policies of prevention, punishment or reform are justified. An alternative approach sees the penal system as a means of regulating society in general but particularly as the apparatus by which the interests of the property owning class are protected. The degree to which the penal system operates in the general or in the 'class' interest changes with changes in the economic system and in times of crisis the monopoly of violence legitimized in the penal system is reinforced by military power. In this analysis transgressors appear as victims, scapegoats or martyrs, or as enemies and the solution to social conflict is seen in a radical transformation of society by one side or the destruction of the enemy by the other.

The situation is complicated in colonial dependencies where the power structure is alien to the majority of the population, although some part of the privileged 'middle' and 'upper' native class may be identified with the colonial power. This may be further complicated by the acceptance by these classes of the culture and religion of the colonial power as in the former French colonies of Southeast Asia.

The ritual, formality and bureaucracy of police and military organizations which ensure the predictability of the behavior of antagonists give to conflict a rational form like that of organized sport or a game of skill – chess for example. Advantage or disadvantage lies in skill or in the quantity of resources. The manifest activities of police and military forces are supported marginally by the latent activities of espionage and other 'special' agencies, the departments of 'dirty tricks,' but these are directed to 'political' objectives rather than military. The emergence of urban guerrilla movements presents the military and the police with problems which are outside their normal expertise. The urban guerrilla movement is weak in manpower and firepower but has the advantage of invisibility and surprise. The urban guerrilla movement is vulnerable to treachery and infiltration, for up to the threshold where its success seems assured there will be advantages for those who support the ruling power. Moreover, colonial powers and military conquerors either establish a new apparatus of government or leave intact existing bureaucracies which gives them substantial support from the middle and upper classes. The urban guerrilla will in many situations be, working class or intellectual, of a minority indigenous religion, of left-wing politics and young. The movement may be supported by a foreign power or powers and by expatriates.

The objectives of the guerrilla cannot be military victory but to change the political policies of the 'colonial' power by directly affecting the civilian population or by imposing intolerable financial burdens on the government of the colonial power. There is a continuity from guerrilla movements to wars of liberation in which these processes may be observed.

The classic examples of guerrilla successes are the defeat of the United Kingdom by Jewish guerrillas in Palestine, or by Arab guerrillas in Aden. Guerrilla movements were important in the 'liberation' of the United Kingdom's Central and East African colonies.

The response of the military and police bureaucracies to urban guerrilla movements are characteristic of the frustration-aggression pattern. Normal military action is unemotional, the casualties inflicted upon the enemy are calculated in statistical form, no hatred is involved and in the more civilized forms of war there need be no contact between personnel. In guerrilla warfare the opposite is found; the guerrilla is not protected by the rules of war, he is identified as a personal enemy presented in stereotype form and is dealt with by the taking of hostages, the killing of hostages, the destruction of villages or districts where the guerrilla finds support, massacres and torture, both gratuitous and under interrogation. Inevitably these activities become regularized and specialist units are developed to carry them out. This process is part of the development of all organizations. It has two valuable characteristics; it preserves intact the moral character of the traditional military and police bureaucracy and makes it possible to sacrifice the 'special' units if their activities become politically unacceptable.

To understand the influence of the urban guerrilla activities of the Irish on the penal system in the United Kingdom requires a consideration of the way in which the penal system is changed, the nature of the conflict between organizations of Irish men and women and the governments of the United Kingdom and Eire, and the nature of the conflicts in Northern Ireland between different groups of Irish men and women.

The conflict which manifests itself as an attempt to persuade the government of the United Kingdom to withdraw its armed forces from Northern Ireland, to change the character of the Royal Ulster Constabulary and to create a politically united Ireland independent of Great Britain conceals underlying social, economic and religious conflicts which have their origin in a continuous history beginning with the Anglo-Norman conquest of Ireland in 1169. It is unlikely that the conflict can be ended by political or administrative measures of a kind which would be acceptable to any British Parliament in any short period.

The guerrilla campaign is trivial in its material effects. It involves the murder of police, soldiers and members of rival religions and political organizations, some attempts at mass killings by bombing public houses, bars and shops, especially those used by soldiers or members of rival organizations, attacks on individuals with letter bombs, some directed and some at random, and arson in large stores and in some factories. Most of the activity takes place in Belfast and other towns in Northern Ireland but there has been some in London, Birmingham, Manchester and in English garrison towns.

Before describing in more detail the nature of the conflict some account must be given of the process of change in the penal system of the United Kingdom since the subjects are closely interrelated.

To describe the complexity of the English penal system even in outline would be impossible in a short essay but mention must be made of some of the salient issues relevant to the present crisis.

The parliamentary system in Britain is essentially a two-party system in which power is operated by either a Labour Government or a Government of the Conservative and Unionist Parties. Northern Ireland sends members to the British Parliament at Westminster. In most situations a Conservative administration can rely on the support of the Unionist Members of Parliament from Northern Ireland and the Labour administration upon the representatives of the Social Democratic and Labour Party from the 'province,' a term significant in itself. The Unionist Members of Parliament are invariably Protestant and those of the Social Democratic and Labour Party Roman Catholic.

Roman Catholic influence in the Conservative and Unionist Parties has a somewhat different character from that in the Labour Party, as it is indigenous and has pre-Reformation roots as exemplified in the person of the late Duke of Norfolk, the Earl Marshal of England who was responsible for all great state ceremonials. The Roman Catholic influence in the Labour Party derives entirely from the large populations of Irish descent concentrated in a number of towns and cities in England and Scotland and in certain districts in some cities.

Large-scale Irish migration to England has its origin in the famines in Ireland in the mid-nineteenth century which were allowed to continue without a serious attempt by the British Government to relieve the starvation and death of a major part of the population. The result is that in Glasgow, Dundee, Manchester, Liverpool and south Lancashire there are very large populations of Irish origin, sentiment, culture and of Roman Catholic religion. These populations have been reinforced by large new migrations in the last 20 years and there have been new areas of settlement in London and Birmingham. The poverty of the rural population in Eire is an influence which encourages many men and women to enter the priesthood or to enter religious orders. This is a means of moving into the middle class and a high proportion of Roman Catholic clergy and teachers in Roman Catholic schools and colleges in the United Kingdom are from the Irish Republic. Denominational schools now receive most of their support from public funds so that the religious and cultural links with Ireland are maintained by the flow of personnel on the one hand and by financial support on the other. The presence of this minority in England and Scotland has an important influence in the Labour Party and has affected its domestic and foreign policies and has determined the composition of its cabinets. The Irish influence on the Labour movement is also influential in the trade union movement where in many cases the struggle for leadership is between left-wing, broadly communist influence and the right-wing, often Roman Catholic of Irish origin. In drawing attention to this influence in the Labour Party it should be emphasized that it is Irish and Roman Catholic and not Republican. It is likely therefore to be directed to ends of social justice rather than the political unification of Ireland. There is evidence of this in some of the recent actions of the British Government.

In contrast, the Irish influence on the Conservative Party is Protestant. It represents the organized and particularly the skilled working class, the business community and the landed aristocratic class with its traditional connection with the armed forces. The attitudes which derive from this situation are intense loyalty to the Crown and the flag and attitudes to the Roman Catholic population which range from extreme hostility to feudal patronage.

The crisis over Northern Ireland has superimposed its influence on other forces for change in the British penal system. Although the British system is very punitive by Dutch standards, there has been a long-term process of liberalization interrupted by events like prison escapes, the growth of marijuana smoking and the hysteria over communism at the height of the cold war.

There is, especially in middle class conservative circles, a widespread belief in a number of interlocking and supportive conspiracies. One is the movement to destroy morality by the liberalization of drug use, by pornography in literature, illustration, film, theater and television, and the liberalization of contraception and abortion. The other conspiracy is believed to be the control of trade unions and subversion by left-wing groups.

These beliefs made it possible to extend investigatory procedures which invade privacy by granting new powers of search which could be used for purposes other than those intended in legislation.

Thus the Dangerous Drugs Act of 1967 which gave the police the power to stop and search any person in the street was followed by the widespread harrassment of young people with long hair and colored juveniles who fitted the popular stereotype. The Criminal Damage Act 1971 which was a response to Irish Republican Army (IRA) bombings and the activities of the 'Angry Brigade'; a tiny group of young people who attempted to exercise political influence by explosions designed to do minor damage rather than to endanger life; contained clauses which extended police power of search and seizure. On the occasion of the IRA bomb attack on the army barracks at Aldershot in which seven people were killed, the police used these powers to raid many homes in London, using warrants executed under this Act, including those of members of the International Socialist Group, who could not have been involved.

The Home Office in the person of the Home Secretary acts to control police behavior and a succession of Home Secretaries have been liberal, Mr Reginald Maudling, Mr Robert Carr, Conservatives, and Mr Roy Jenkins in two Labour administrations. An example of their countervailing influence was the establishment of a committee to study police powers under the chairmanship of a Conservative Member of Parliament who had been much concerned with race relations, Sir William Deedes.

A reflection of the interest of the Home Office may be seen in the appointment of Sir Robert Mark as Chief Commissioner of the Metropolitan Police. Sir Robert Mark might be described as introducing a puritan austerity into the administration of the police in the metropolis and having an influence throughout the United Kingdom. He is convinced that the jury system results in the acquittal of many guilty persons and has therefore exercised his influence to change the English requirement of unanimous jury verdicts to the Scottish pattern of majority verdicts. He is convinced that in the adversary system of the British courts the forensic skill of some lawyers in exploiting technicalities or discrediting police evidence also results in the acquittal of persons *known* by the police to be guilty. His attitude to barristers has been reflected in the comments and acts of one judge in an IRA case when he attacked them in his summing up for attempting to discredit police witnesses and ruled that their fees be 'taxed.'[1] This had the effect of greatly reducing them. Sir Robert Mark has a ruthless determination to eliminate all corruption and malpractice from the conduct of the Metropolitan Police. His philosophy is summarized thus: 'I believe that in a free society a small unarmed Police Force with limited legal powers depends for its effectiveness on public acceptance. That acceptance depends on integrity, which in turn depends on quality of manpower, supervision and accountability. The more open and accountable the Police are, the more likely they are to be respected and supported.'[2]

Unlike his predecessor and almost all other senior police officers in the United Kingdom, Sir Robert Mark maintains a continuous dialogue with the general public through press, radio and television.

The main reason for the introduction of the Army into Northern Ireland was a failure of the Royal Ulster Constabulary to either command confidence or to cope with the disturbances. Sir Robert Mark's influence is seen in the report of the Hunt Committee on the Police in Northern Ireland of which he was a member. This will be discussed later.[3]

The legislative and penal practice which has developed in reference to the crisis has had the effect, as will be shown, of increasing the powers of the police and courts and increasing the activities of the security services. The legislation has also confirmed the widespread but illegal practices of the police in arresting and detaining persons for questioning without charging them, holding them incommunicado and searching them and their homes; practices which have been challenged on many occasions by civil rights organizations.

The influences which control and moderate the effects of new legislation are first, Parliament. Any member can question any minister on any subject and receive a reasoned reply which is made public. This applies to all matters except those where the information would be of value to an enemy. Persistent questioning which reveals serious problems may invoke proposals for new legislation, the amendment of existing law, the issue of orders provided for in law, and, in circumstances like the present, advice to chief constables on the administration of the law. Parliament also responds by debating issues as they arise. This allows the Government to test the extent to which its policies have support. It allows a wide expression of opinion in

Parliament, in the press and on radio and television. An example of this was a debate on the death penalty for terrorism which followed the Birmingham bombings of November 1974 which killed 19 persons and injured 200. An amendment which would have allowed the reintroduction of the death penalty was defeated by 369 votes to 217.

While the discussion rehearsed many of the issues of previous debates, it was remarkable for the understanding displayed in some speeches of the underlying causes of conflict in Northern Ireland and the role of martyrdom in the Republican movement which is deeply involved in Roman Catholicism.

The funeral of a Republican or a Roman Catholic killed in the conflict is dramatic, with Irish pipes and laments, with Roman Catholic ritual and, where appropriate, military honors.

Within the ranks of the Provisional IRA martyrdom by fasting in prison has been legitimized by being undertaken on the orders of superior officers.

The third method by which Parliament responds is by setting up a committee of inquiry. These have many forms from simple advisory committees to tribunals with the powers of a High Court. Although such committees may to some extent reflect the interests of the Government of the day, they are led by distinguished public figures, often judges of the High Court, and are balanced with experts and holders of different views. Every aspect of the Irish situation has been examined by committees in the last 10 years and reference will be made to the more important of them. Such committees sometimes appear to be face-saving devices, to offer symbolic gestures rather than real solutions or to defend policies which are indefensible by specious or naïve arguments. In spite of such criticisms, on balance the reports of the committees on the crisis in Northern Ireland have identified the fundamental problems, have offered a perceptive sociological analysis and have suggested policies of social justice which have been initiated. On the other side the force of events has produced military and legislative responses which give cause for much concern.

Outside Parliament there are two categories of influence which have effects on the general public and on Members of Parliament. These are the organizations concerned with civil liberties and the investigative journalist.

There are many charities and other organizations concerned with the interests of minorities but these are outside the interest of this account. Relevant are Justice, an all party organization of lawyers, Amnesty International and above all the National Council for Civil Liberties (NCCL) and its associated research organization, the Cobden Trust. The NCCL has been active in many issues concerned with civil rights as they have been affected by the Northern Irish crisis and has published many critical examinations of reports, legislation and practices. It is perhaps a measure of the Council's activity that in a survey made of 1000 Metropolitan policemen conducted by Dr William Belson the NCCL was named by 50% as the organization doing the police most harm, followed by immigrant organizations 23%, the National Union of Students 16% and the courts 12%.[4]

The seriousness with which the Government views the criticism of the NCCL and the associated Cobden Trust is shown by the response of the Law Officers' Department to a report by the Cobden Trust entitled *Justice in Northern Ireland* which made imputations against the impartiality of the prosecuting authority.[5] The Law Officers' Department published a detailed and exhaustive reply, *Prosecutions in Northern Ireland, a Study of the Facts*.[6]

The interest of the NCCL in the Northern Ireland situation dates from 1936 when it published the report of a commission of inquiry appointed to examine the purpose and effect of the Civil Authorities (Special Powers) Acts (Northern Ireland) 1922 and 1933.[7]

Investigative journalism in the United Kingdom has influence within the limits of the laws of libel and the Official Secrets Acts. Both television channels have regular programs which expose injustice and social problems. The quality newspapers likewise give detailed and critical accounts of the Northern Ireland crisis. The 'Insight Team' of the *Sunday Times* has published accounts of the situation which have been brought out in book form under the title *Ulster*.[8] This study, which covers much of the same ground as the reports of official committees and tribunals, uses their data and adds new material drawn from Republican sources.

So much for the general picture, now it remains to briefly describe the origins of the conflict and its present effect on the penal system.

The influences which have contributed through some hundreds of years to the present conflict are war, civil war, genocide, massacres, famine, economic discrimination and religious persecution. In this there have been complex interactions between religion, politics and social and economic forces.

The present division in the six counties of Ulster (Ulster is one of the four divisions of Ireland of which six of the eight counties are part of the United Kingdom of Great Britain and Northern Ireland. Two counties are in the Republic of Ireland) dates from a rebellion of Irish chieftains and their clans in the reign of James I of England (1603-1625) as a result of which the Irish were expelled and in 1611 their lands were confiscated and given to colonists mainly from the lowlands of Scotland but also some from England. These were foreigners speaking a different language and belonging to a different religion, either the Presbyterian or Anglican Protestant faith. Two other remote events are still powerful symbolically, the Siege of Londonderry in August 1689 and the Battle of the Boyne in 1690. Both resulted in defeats of the Roman Catholic forces of James II by those of William III of Orange (King Billy). The principal political society of Northern Ireland Protestants is the Royal Orange Order which has pervaded all institutions of political power and influence from the Ulster Unionist Party to the Royal Ulster Constabulary. On the anniversary of the Battle of the Boyne the Order parades to the music of Scottish drum and pipe bands in all towns in Northern Ireland and in some English and Scottish towns, wearing city suits with bowler hats and orange sashes and carrying rolled umbrellas. These processions, which appear as demonstrations of power and superiority, have on many occasions given rise to riots which in turn involve the Royal Ulster Constabulary.

The constitutional status of Northern Ireland was established by the Government of Ireland Act 1920 which gave power to the local parliament over domestic matters but reserved other powers to the Parliament of the United Kingdom in which it is represented. Southern Ireland became a free state within the Commonwealth in 1922 and a republic in 1948. Politics within Southern Ireland has a considerable bearing on events in the North. For example, although the IRA is banned in the South as it is in the North it is treated with ambivalence by the Government of the Republic. The role of the Roman Catholic Church in the political events of the early years in the Free State as it then was, resulted in it having a 'special position' in Article 44 of the Constitution of 1937; this was abolished in 1974. The Church has virtual control of primary and secondary education and has been instrumental in preventing the legalization of divorce and contraception (the law is now in an indeterminate state). It prevented the introduction of a state scheme for maternal and child welfare in 1951 on the obscure grounds that it would weaken family life. The contrast between the social and educational services of the North and South are part of the rational basis for the Protestants' opposition to a United Ireland.

The Civil Authorities (Special Powers) Act (Northern Ireland) of 1922 is the crucial legislation from which the continuing crisis of Northern Ireland has developed and which is influencing legislation in the United Kingdom at the present time.

Before discussing some of the provisions of the 1922 Act, the overriding provisions of the Government of Ireland Act 1920 must be stated. The Act specifies some fourteen matters which are reserved to the Central Government and it specially declares any law *void* if: (a) it gives preference, privilege or advantage or imposes disability or disadvantage on account of any religious belief, or (b) it takes any property without compensation.

These provisions can be likened to the provisions of the Treaty of Limerick of 1691 made between William III and the Irish supporters of James II. The violation of the treaty by the Irish Parliament in 1692 is remembered in the traditions of the Roman Catholic population.

The 1922 Act was an emergency measure and was intended to be temporary. Section 12 of the Act provided that 'This Act shall continue in force for one year and no longer unless Parliament otherwise determines' (the reference is to the Parliament of Northern Ireland). It is a general characteristic of all political organizations that emergencies provide the occasions for the taking of power, that power is taken temporarily and is then retained permanently. The Act of 1922 was renewed annually until 1928 when a bill was introduced to make the Act permanent. This was not accepted and the Special Powers Act was renewed for 5 years. In 1933 a new Special Powers Act was passed, in which Section 12 of the 1922 Act was replaced with 'The Act of 1922 shall continue in force until Parliament otherwise determines.'

The Special Powers Acts have two characteristics, first the transfer of power from Parliament to the apparatus of state, the 'Civil Authority' and to the 'Home Minister', and secondly its taking of powers under regulations which were unique in British history, not excluding wartime, which were like those found in fascist regimes. The fact that Protestants outnumbered Roman Catholics by 2 to 1 in the electorate and that the electoral law was framed to favor the Protestant population, and that constituency boundaries had been drawn to favor the Protestant electorate ensured that the Act would remain permanent until the suspension of the Northern Ireland Parliament on Friday, 24 March 1972.

The Act of 1922 delegated all powers necessary 'to preserve peace and maintain civil order' and gave to the Home Minister the power to make, vary or revoke regulations to this end. It gave him the power to delegate any or all of his powers to any officer of police. Whereas in Great Britain the police are primarily under local control the Royal Ulster Constabulary was directly responsible to the Home Minister. The British police are unarmed and the work of the special constabulary is limited to relieving the regular force of routine duties. In contrast, the Royal Ulster Constabulary was a heavily armed force and the B Specials, the volunteer force, had access to arms under the control of their officers.

The forces were originally intended to be made up of Protestants and Catholics in the proportion of 2 to 1 but in practice the Royal Ulster Constabulary was almost entirely Protestant and the B Specials were recruited from members of the Royal Orange Order.

The 1922 Act gave the local authority very wide powers, for example, it had powers to close roads, to take over buildings, to stop, question and search and arrest without warrant, to intern suspects without charge, to exclude suspects from any place, to examine bank accounts, to confiscate property and to prohibit processions or the exhibition of films and the playing of gramophone records – aimed at traditional Irish patriotic songs!

A regulation of 1931 directed against the exploitation of martyrdom gave the power to prohibit, remove or destroy memorials. Another gave power to prohibit meetings or processions including funerals, and yet another regulation directed against martyrdom gave the Civil Authority the power to suspend coroners' inquests as to the cause of death.

Offenses against the Special Powers Acts were punishable by fines and imprisonment but the Acts made special provisions for the prosecution and punishment of offenses against existing law, provided for flogging for firearms offenses, for arson and for malicious damage, and death for offenses relating to the possession of explosives.

The Acts established special courts with two or more 'Resident Magistrates' who sat without a jury and had powers of summary jurisdiction. The appellate tribunal consisted of a recorder or County court judge sitting alone. The 'Resident Magistrate' also conducted private examinations of suspects who were not entitled to legal assistance and who if they refused to answer any question, committed an offense under the Acts.

Most important, however, was the power of the Civil Authority to suspend *habeas corpus*, a power which the House of Lords, the final court of appeal in the United Kingdom, decided it had no jurisdiction to challenge. This power is contained in Regulations 23, 23A and 23B, which provided that a person could be arrested without warrant on suspicion and detained without charge or trial indefinitely. The Acts also provided for the arrest and detention of witnesses.

This account is necessarily brief and incomplete. The way in which the Acts worked over the 50 years since they were first enacted have depended on social and economic factors.

The Roman Catholic population is not evenly spread over the country; it lives in rural areas particularly to the south and west, and in Belfast and Londonderry it is concentrated in distinct areas. This concentration has been increased in some places by the housing policies of local authorities. It has further made it possible to arrange electoral boundaries so that the Roman Catholic population is under-represented in local councils and in the Northern Ireland Parliament (gerrymandering). This in turn has had two consequences, discrimination against Roman Catholics in housing and in local authority employment. This latter is of importance in a country of high unemployment and low wages where there is also much discrimination against Roman Catholics by Protestant employers. (A single example will suffice. In the British Government's Harland and Wolff Shipyard in Belfast, taken over to prevent unemployment, only some 400 of the 10,000 employees were Roman Catholic.)

The uneven distribution of population adds another dimension to the conflict. Wherever the Government intervenes, in the provision of a new factory or, as in the case of the new University of Ulster at Coleraine, it can be argued that one community is favored at the expense of the other.

The continuous border with the Republic inhabited mainly by Roman Catholics makes escape easy for guerrillas, the ghettos provide refuge, and create clear battle lines. Religious education increases the separation of communities through local denominational schools.

The immediate origin of the present conflict was the development of a civil rights movement in the formerly passive Roman Catholic community. As a result of postwar social legislation Northern Ireland had shared in improvements in education, public health, medical treatment, social security, housing and employment. It had shared in prosperity directly and indirectly from the large numbers of workers who migrated temporarily to England and who settled in areas of high prosperity but still made contributions to their families. They found acceptance without discrimination (England had its own second class citizens but they were black or brown).

The Roman Catholic Church, which in Ireland was perhaps the most traditional outside Italy and Spain, was losing some of its influence in both the Republic and the North. Its influence was to oppose violence, to support social equality, to protect its members, to support by implication the unification of Ireland since this would increase Roman Catholic influence and diminish that of the Protestants and might lead to the control of social legislation in the North of the kind which the Church found unacceptable and had prevented in the Republic.

From 1963 the civil rights movement developed from a 'Homeless Citizens' League' to a 'Campaign for Civil Justice' then to a 'Northern Ireland Civil Rights Association' which was founded at Belfast in 1967 with the support of the Irish Republican Army. Its policy was moderate and directed toward the reform of the electoral system on the basis of one man one vote and the redrawing of electoral boundaries, the removal of discrimination in local government and the provision of machinery to deal with complaints, the allocation of public housing on a points system and two major political demands, the repeal of the Special Powers Act and the disbanding of the B Special Constabulary. It is important to recognize that what was *not* demanded was a united Ireland; this represented a change in the IRA away from guerrilla war toward political action.

From then on there were new developments; part of the Protestant community began to take countermeasures against civil rights demonstrations and action and reaction developed with the Civil Authority becoming increasingly compromised. The riots of 1969 were the culmination of this process and the beginning of intervention by the Government of the United Kingdom in Northern Irish affairs.

It would be naïve to assume that the policy of the United Kingdom Government was consistent or directed toward a clearly defined and coherent end. It has been a policy of successive approximation and one in which institutional forces in the police, the penal system and the armed forces have played an important part. The effect of intervention has been mediated by the presence on the border of a Republic with a different political, educational, social and religious system which continuously interacts with the Roman Catholic population of the North. Moreover, policies which appeared reasonable and just were violently rejected by the Protestant majority of the population. Finally the prosperity which could have made change easier has given way to depression which has intensified the divisions in Northern Ireland.

The intervention of the United Kingdom Government has been symbolic, administrative and political.

At the symbolic level there have been the commissions, committees, tribunals and other inquiries. Initially they have been concerned to establish the facts and in the process have offered guarded criticism of the Northern Ireland Government, suggesting a modification of policy and offering some support to the critics. In the second stage the criticism has been radical and has resulted in major changes in administration; finally the growth and extension of conflict has resulted in inquiries which have introduced or reintroduced measures to control violence which correspond to those that led to the confrontation in the first instance, a circular process.

Some critics of the major inquiries have come to different conclusions from the same data; this is to misunderstand the latent function of the inquiries which is to promote change within the limits made possible by the political forces of the time whereas the manifest function is to establish the facts.

At this point it is necessary to introduce some discussion of the nature of the forces in the conflict. There appear to be three levels of activity; first the closely organized, centrally commanded, but loosely controlled groups concerned with bombing, assassination, propaganda and leadership in the Roman Catholic community. These have close connections with organizations in the Republic. Personnel from both the Republic and the North operate in England. The conspiratorial and aggressive activities of such groups are of the same kind as those of branches of intelligence operations, 'special service troops,' paratroopers and other marginal forces.[9] The legitimization of their activities is achieved by having organizational forms like the IRA, the Ulster Volunteer Force and the Ulster Defence Association with political and patriotic objectives. The hierarchy of command relieves the operational members of emotional responsibility for their actions and the recognition of the distinction by the Northern Ireland Government between actions which are political and those that are criminal replaces the sentiment of 'guilt' in the operational members by that of 'duty'. The issue of political status has been of importance in the conflict. Prisoners in the Republic have sustained long hunger strikes to obtain it; it has been refused to prisoners in England but granted to detainees and convicted persons in Northern Ireland. The guerrilla organizations are infiltrated by the security forces; the informer has long been a feature of Irish politics. Internal conflicts occur and torture, mutilation, intimidation and assassination are found on both sides. The populations which give the guerrillas shelter become hostages in the struggle.

The second level of activity is that of boys and young men who participate in open hostility with firearms and improvised weapons. Their action is directed to immediate objectives and is of the same character as the violence of football supporters and like this develops when attempts are made by the police and armed forces to control it.

The third form appears as the mass action of large numbers of people under the influence of an event real or rumored, manipulated by demagogues and infiltrated by guerrilla organizations. In such events the guerrillas can conduct precision military actions and youth the random aggression of the stone, the petrol and the nail bomb within the environment of a riot.

A number of major civil disturbances in Northern Ireland in the summer of 1968 began a process in which the United Kingdom intervened first symbolically then administratively, politically and militarily, in pursuit of a policy of justice and equality for the Roman Catholic population. It will be seen that under the pressure of events and of institutional forces the penal system, now including the British Army, responded in ways opposed to those stated intentions. There has been a process of oscillation the final outcome of which is still in doubt.

This period was investigated by the Cameron Commission set up by the Labour Government – *Disturbances in Northern Ireland* – which not only investigated the conflicts but drew attention to the underlying social, political and economic causes. It also described in detail the Roman Catholics' resentment of the Special Powers Act, under which Republican Clubs had been banned in 1967, and the continuance of the exclusively Protestant B Special Constabulary.[10]

The violence and riots of March to August 1969 were again conflicts in which the civil rights movement and the Protestants were in conflict and these events were investigated by another government body, this time a tribunal under the chairmanship of the Hon Mr Justice Scarman.[11] The Tribunal's report, which was primarily directed to establishing facts, was in its emphasis different from that of the Cameron Commission; it wrote that 'in a very real sense our inquiry was an investigation of police conduct.' The effect of these inquiries on the central interest of this paper is in the establishment of a committee under Lord Hunt to examine the police force of Northern Ireland: The Advisory Committee on the Police in Northern Ireland.[3] This was a committee of three of whom one was Mr Robert Mark (now Sir Robert Mark) who, it may be assumed, as the only police officer in the committee, was very influential in determining its conclusions.

This report which is couched in positive terms is the most critical examination of any part of the penal system of the United Kingdom ever published. Either directly or by implication it recommended changes in every aspect of the force from the leadership, through to the color of the uniform. To list all the reforms proposed would be outside the scope of this account but essentially it recommended the demilitarization and disarming of the police, changes in training and recruitment especially designed to change the almost exclusively Protestant nature of the force and to change their attitudes. It proposed the removal of questions about religion in applications for entry into the force and suggested that membership in sectarian organizations was incompatible with the role of the police. It proposed the disbanding of the B Specials, the repeal of the Special Powers Act and the establishment of an independent public prosecutor on the lines of the Scottish system. The report also recommended that all policemen should wear an identifiable number, that there should be a new procedure for dealing with complaints against the police and that the chief officer of police should be made vicariously liable for wrongful acts committed by members of the force.

The setting up of the Hunt Committee and the establishment of the Scarman Tribunal was accompanied on 19 August 1969 by a statement from the British (Labour) Government that 'in all legislative and executive decisions of Government every citizen of Northern Ireland is entitled to the same equality of treatment and freedom from discrimination as obtains in the rest of the United Kingdom, irrespective of political views or religion.'[12]

To summarize the situation at this watershed: the Cameron Commission had identified and established the underlying causes of Roman Catholic discontent, the Scarman Tribunal had identified the roles of the guerrilla organizations, the youth, the mob and the demagogue, and the Hunt Inquiry had criticized the organization of the police, the prosecution and the law in Northern Ireland as it discriminated against the Roman Catholics, and had shown why because of its structure and its political connections it could not function in a divided society. The Hunt Committee's report can be read in conjunction with other statements made by Sir Robert Mark as giving the conditions under which, if the common view of the criminal is accepted, a police force can operate with the consensus and support of the public. This is a valuable contribution to the sociology of penal organizations.

The Government's declaration confirmed these findings and a beginning was made to translate them into policy. However the situation contained its dialectical antithesis; troops garrisoned in Northern Ireland had earlier that month been called in to assist the Civil Authority and in response to a further request from the Northern Ireland Government, the British Government agreed to send more troops.

It is not possible here to describe the process by which the Army was first greeted with suspicion by the Roman Catholics, then acclaimed by them as protectors, attacked by Protestants and finally identified by the Provisional IRA as enemies. (The Provisional IRA was the guerrilla breakaway from the IRA which had in the course of time largely abandoned violence.) What is important here is that the Army with its experience of 'counterinsurgency' followed the tactics which had been employed in Palestine, Malaya, Kenya, Cyprus, the British Cameroons, Brunei, British Guiana, Aden, Borneo, Malaysia and in the Persian Gulf, under the rubric of the 'Special Powers Act.'

As the Royal Ulster Constabulary was reorganized and the B Specials disbanded, Northern Ireland came under military occupation. There is evidence to suggest that the IRA had little or no influence in Belfast before 1969 but that after that, with support from the Republic, including some 'diverted' government funds designated for relief, local defense organizations and vigilante groups arose behind the barricades that the Roman Catholics erected to protect their ghettos. One tactical blunder was the employment of Scottish regiments that were assumed by Protestants to identify with their cause, they being of Scottish descent, and by the Roman Catholics to be hostile. Some interviews with soldiers on leave from Northern Ireland suggest that many soldiers do not understand nor are they concerned with the nature of the conflict; they are only concerned with their role as a 'peace-keeping force.' They are, however, affected by the 'unfair' character of guerrilla activity and react to it.

Internment of suspects was introduced under the Special Powers Act in August 1971 by which time guerrilla warfare with nail and petrol bombs on one side and rubber bullets and CS gas on the other had developed. Major confrontation with loss of life occurred on 'Bloody Sunday' in January 1972 and 'Bloody Friday' in July 1972. Thus named, these events, with their Roman Catholic martyrs, were added to the ideological calendar.

The leadership of the Provisional IRA was maintained by its capacity to inflict reprisals on the armed forces, on the business community (identified as Protestant) and by its success through hunger strikes in obtaining political status for its members convicted of crimes, including murder, for which political motivation was claimed. The Provisional IRA thus achieved official recognition and legitimization. The IRA was able to argue that this status was a first stage which would be followed after victory or truce by amnesty.

The most remarkable feature of the Northern Ireland prison system is a result of the assumption that the crisis would be of short duration and that temporary expedients would be adequate. Detainees and Special Category prisoners (prisoners convicted of crimes but claiming political motivation) are kept in compounds surrounded by barbed wire and guarded by troops. The prisoners are housed in huts and within the compounds are left to their own devices. Each compound is virtually a self-contained community which keeps the premises it occupies to such a standard as it finds acceptable and engages, if it so wishes, in military drills or lectures on military exercises. Under the pressure of events some of the compounds have become military staff colleges for the Provisional IRA.

Following the experience of other counterinsurgency operations the armed forces have made widespread use of 'intelligence' and 'interrogation,' the former relying on informers either known and rewarded or anonymous, operating via the telephone. On the basis of such information the suspects are identified, detained and interrogated. This has resulted in the most dramatic occurrence in the recent history of the United Kingdom penal system, the systematic torture of suspects in secrecy and without safeguards. The facts are not generally in dispute; suspects were subject to hooding, to continuous exposure to loud and incessant noise, to deprivation of sleep, to deprivation of all but the minimum of bread and water, and were forced to stand spreadeagled against a wall for periods of 6, 7, 8, 9, 10, 11, 12, 13, 14, 15 and 16 hours continuously in different cases and for successive periods up to a total of 43 hours. In specific cases other techniques were employed to exhaust, injure or alarm detainees.[13, 14, 15]

Following allegations in newspapers the Government set up a committee of inquiry under Sir Edmund Compton which published a *Report of the Enquiry Into Allegations Against the Security of Physical Brutality in Northern Ireland Arising Out of Events on the 9th August 1971.*[13] This report ensured that its findings would be only marginally critical of the conduct of the security forces by adopting a definition of brutality which it was impossible to test. The Committee wrote, 'We consider that brutality is an inhuman or savage form of cruelty and that cruelty implies a disposition to inflict suffering, coupled with indifference to, or pleasure in, the victim's pain.'

The Committee naïvely accepted the explanations of the military authorities for their actions and on the basis of its definition reported that there had been no brutality.

In the following year, 1972, a Committee of Privy Councillors was appointed to consider authorized procedures for the interrogation of persons suspected of terrorism under the chairmanship of Lord Parker of Waddington. The report of this committee is in two parts, a majority report by Lord Parker, the former Lord Chief Justice, and Mr A. J. Boyd Carpenter, a former Conservative Minister, and a minority report by Lord Gardner, the former Labour Lord Chancellor. The majority report said that subject to safeguards which they set out 'we have come to the conclusion that there is no reason to rule out these techniques on moral grounds and that it is possible to operate them in a manner consistent with the highest standards of our society.'

The minority report deserves a special place in the history of penal systems; it begins with a devastating examination of the evidence and the proceedings of the Compton Committee and has this to say about its definition of brutality: 'Under the definition which some of our witnesses thought had come from the Inquisition, if an interrogator believed, to his great regret, that it was necessary for him to cut off the fingers of a detainee one by one to get the required information out of him for the sole purpose of saving life, this would not be cruel and, because not cruel, not brutal.' Lord Gardner concluded that 'The Procedures were and are illegal.' He also considered the position under international law but did not express an opinion because among other reasons the Government of the Republic of Ireland had registered a complaint of a breach or breaches of the European Convention for the Protection of Human Rights and Fundamental Freedoms.

The Government (Conservative) immediately accepted Lord Gardner's minority report and these methods of interrogation were ended. The Army however continued to train personnel in these methods, which are nowhere prescribed in any document, at a secret place in order, it is said, to prepare soldiers who might be taken prisoner, to resist interrogation.

Following the recommendations of the Hunt Committee on the police, yet another committee, the MacDermott Committee reported on public prosecutions and a Public Prosecutor was appointed in 1972.

The legislative changes which followed on the taking over of the responsibility for Northern Ireland by the United Kingdom Government show a process of liberalization modified by beliefs concerning the nature of terrorism. It could be argued that the belief about the nature, extent and influence of the Provisional IRA from the late sixties onward was a self-fulfilling prophecy which resulted by a process of action and reaction in creating armed conflict.

The Detention of Terrorist Order (Northern Ireland) 1972 replaced the powers of internment in the Special Powers Act with modified powers of detention, but consistent with the Government's policy of specific inquiries to monitor the effects of legislation on penal practices, a commission was set up under Lord Diplock to consider the legal procedures to deal with terrorist activities in Northern Ireland.[15]

The recommendations of the Diplock Commission reflected the fulfillment of a prophecy, the Provisional IRA had as a result of the presence of the Army become an effective armed force with considerable support from the Roman Catholic population of Northern Ireland, from their leaders in the Republic and from expatriates in Great Britain, Australia and the United States of America. The Irish Roman Catholic community provided very large sums of money for the purchase of arms.

The Commission also identified the role of adolescent youth and the emergence of terrorist organizations on the Protestant side.

The first consideration was of intimidation; this, the Commission argued, made trial by jury ineffective and hampered the normal judicial processes by making it difficult to get witnesses to testify. From this it argued that detention was necessary as an extrapolitical process subject to certain safeguards. It recommended that a schedule of offenses, all in existing law, be tried by a judge of the High Court or a County Court judge sitting alone. In making this recommendation it pointed out, to further support its argument, that juries in Northern Ireland were almost always drawn from the Protestant population and that while a judge could, and on many occasions did, prevent a malicious finding of guilt by dismissing the charge, he had no control over juries which for partisan reasons returned verdicts of not guilty.

Many of the other recommendations restricted liberties and rights: power to arrest and detain persons for questioning (for up to four hours) were to be given to the police, there were to be restrictions on the granting of bail, the onus of proof as to the possession of firearms and explosives was to be altered so that the prisoner had to prove innocence rather than the authorities guilt, confessions by accused persons were to be admissible as evidence, as were signed statements by witnesses who could or would not appear in court.

The Commission was faced with very great difficulties in dealing with the young terrorist. Offenses by children from 10 to 13 years and by young persons 14 to 18 were dealt with under the Children and Young Persons Act (Northern Ireland) 1968. This Act made provision for a variety of institutions, special reception centers and remand homes to which offenders would be sent pending trial, and training schools, remand homes, attendance centers and young offenders' centers for those found guilty. In fact the Commission found that the only provision available was a training school for Catholic boys and a training school for Protestant boys, under 17 years old, neither of which was secure.

The only accommodation for young persons pending trial and the only secure accommodation for those found guilty of serious offenses was an adult prison.

The Commission recommended the establishment of a secure institution to accommodate persons under the age of 17 years who were remanded in or committed to custody having been charged with or convicted of offenses connected with terrorism.

The recommendations of the Commission were incorporated in the Northern Ireland (Emergency Provisions) Act 1973 of the United Kingdom which repealed the Civil Authorities (Special Powers) Acts (Northern Ireland) of 1922 and 1933.

Having taken over government of the province the United Kingdom Government began a series of changes and enforcements to meet the disabilities of the minority thus recognizing that the long-term solutions were social, economic and political. However, having enacted legislation which continued in a modified form some of the features of the Special Powers Acts it set up a Committee to reconsider the situation. Three features of this Committee must be noted, first it was the action of a Labour Government, secondly it considered the matter in the context of civil liberties and human rights, recognizing the influence of civil liberties organizations on the one hand and the intervention of the Government of the Irish Republic on the other, finally there was the choice of Lord Gardner as chairman, the author of the influential minority report of the Parker Committee on interrogation.[16]

The Committee reported at considerable length and under a number of heads. In general it argued that the British Government had acted legitimately and consistently with the terms of the European Convention for the Protection of Human Rights and Fundamental Freedoms but went on to say that the existence of emergency powers should be limited both in scope and duration (the Special Powers Acts lasted 50 years!). It recommended that consideration be given to the enactment of a Bill of Rights, this would be a new development in the United Kingdom.

It recommended that trial by jury for serious cases be restored as soon as possible but in the meantime 'scheduled' offenses should continue to be tried without a jury.

It examined the conduct of the courts in the conditions created by the 1973 Act and noted that the courts had sometimes used discretion in exercising some of their powers and at other times had not done so. The courts had not accepted written evidence and had on occasion disregarded admissions made by the accused under questioning. The Committee therefore recommended that the section of the Act dealing with written statements be repealed and that the courts be given discretion to exclude or disregard admissions made by persons charged, to bring the law into correspondence with practice. On the other hand it recommended that the onus of proof in relation to the possession of firearms and explosives should remain.

The Committee added new offenses, that of being disguised – a unique offense, of advertising on behalf of illegal organizations, and suggested that the broadcasting authorities should receive new 'guidance' on reporting on terrorist organizations.

In the section on the 'Powers of the Security Forces' proposals to increase these powers and make them more consistent were balanced by a proposal like that of the Hunt Committee for the establishment of an independent means of investigating complaints against the police and the army. Similar proposals are under discussion in Great Britain.

The sections which deal with prisons and detention are of great interest. The Committee describes the results of having camp type prison compounds in which the prisoners and detainees control their own affairs, and suggests that the status of political prisoner or, as it had come to be regarded, of prisoner of war, with attendant privileges both legitimized the terrorist organization and gave heroic stature to the terrorist. It therefore suggests that convicted offenders should be treated as ordinary offenders and that new cellular prisons be provided. It also proposes as a matter of urgency that new facilities for young offenders be built.

The Committee faced a number of dilemmas on the issue of detention. It pointed out the destructive effect of secret examinations based on the evidence of informers on the morale of communities, the effects of inevitable reprisals like kneecapping – shooting through the knee. It understood the influence of detention on the unconvicted prisoner and the disastrous effect on his family and his future.

It was, however, unable to recommend the end of detention. In some respects the Committee was controlled by another aspect of Government activity. As a result of informal and indirect negotiation with the Provisional IRA the Government had come to an 'understanding' which implied that in return for an ending of terrorist activities the Government would limit 'harrassment' of Roman Catholics by the Army and in due course as the level of violence decreased detainees would be released. This policy has been followed; few persons have been detained in 1975, many have been released and the level of violence has declined. The detainees have thus become hostages against further terrorist activity. Part of the decline in detention is a reflection of the greater powers of the courts.

The Committee recommended reforms in the control of detention, especially that it be put under the control of a Detention Advisory Board consisting of full-time holders of judicial office in *England*, and *Wales*, and *Scotland*.

The final recommendations concern the release of detainees and here the proposals are on the lines of the Civil Resettlement Units established for returning prisoners of war. The Committee recommended the establishment of a small pre-release center and the mounting of a major long-term scheme of assistance to ex-detainees and their families, to meet their needs and offset the embitterment upon which terrorism thrives.

In spite of the generally liberal tendency of the Gardner Report, reaction to events in 1974 when the Provisional IRA extended its operations to England as a response to direct rule show how opposing influences are present below the surface. The Prevention of Terrorism (Temporary Provisions) Act 1974 revives some of the features of the Special Powers Act, applies them to Great Britain or the United Kingdom but in practice only to persons born in the Republic of Ireland or Northern Ireland with the exception of those resident in the United Kingdom for more than 20 years. It is thus specifically directed at Irishmen.

The Act proscribed the IRA in very general terms, making it an offense either to belong to or to support it or to assist in its organization; it made it an offense to wear any item of dress or to wear or carry or display any article which might 'arouse reasonable apprehension' that the person was a member or supporter of the IRA.

The Act gives the Secretary of State the power to exclude citizens of the Irish Republic from the United Kingdom and citizens of Northern Ireland from Great Britain if they have been concerned in acts of terrorism or have entered Great Britain 'with a view' to being concerned with terrorism. These provisions raise issues: if a person has been concerned with terrorism then there should be abundant provision in the law under which he might be charged; it follows therefore that only those whose alleged acts could not be proved in court would be included. The category of those whose intentions were suspect would be those who had been informed against or had been induced to confess. It also follows that since membership of the IRA is an offense carrying with it the penalty of imprisonment or a fine or both, those likely to be excluded would be those whose membership in the IRA could not be proved.

The greatest volume of criticism of the Act has been directed against the provisions giving the police wide powers of arrest and search and detention.

The police are given the power to arrest without warrant persons who may 'reasonably be suspected of an offense under the Act.' A person may be detained for up to 48 hours without being charged and for a further five days, seven in all, if the Home Secretary authorizes this. A suspect can be stopped and searched without warrant and any person found on premises being searched with a warrant may be searched. Search warrants are normally issued only by a justice of the peace on application from the police, a procedure which is carefully watched by organizations concerned with civil liberties. The Act gives a police officer above the rank of superintendent the power to sign a search warrant if he considers that there is a great emergency and immediate action is needed.

Although in the past the police have behaved as though they had these powers, and although the Dangerous Drugs Act 1967 gave them stop and search powers, this Act reduced the civil liberties of a large number of residents of the United Kingdom who could be identified as soon as they spoke, by their distinctive accent. This adds a third category to the stereotypes determining police behavior. The others are color and long hair as stigmas of criminality or drug use.

When the Act was renewed on May the 19th for a second 6 month period, the Home Secretary gave details of its implementation. Some 265 persons had been detained for less than 48 hours, 11 had been subject to further detention, 51 exclusion orders had been made, of which 39 had been executed, only one person had been convicted of belonging to a proscribed organization.

The NCCL has collected evidence which suggests that the police have used their new powers to harrass Irish families and have presented the appeals procedure against exclusion to detainees in such a form as to make it unlikely that the accused would attempt to use it, implying that the subject would be held in custody for a period of weeks.[17]

On the same day as the Act was renewed the Fair Employment (Northern Ireland) Bill, which outlaws all discrimination in employment on political or religious grounds *except in education*, received its second reading in the House of Lords. A few days earlier it had been announced that the Northern Ireland Standing Advisory Commission on Human Rights was making a study of the need for a Bill of Rights to be provided for Northern Ireland and even perhaps extended to the whole of Britain.

CONCLUSION

It is impossible to write any account of the recent history of the Northern Ireland crisis even in many thousands of pages which would adequately and accurately present the whole picture. The population involved is small, a million and a half, and the underlying political situation is almost unknown to the majority of the citizens of Great Britain. The roots of the conflict go back into Irish history and are intimately involved with culture and religion. The developments of the last fifty years have, however, distinct characteristics which do not fit into the accepted view of the class structure of society and the role of the penal system. Ireland was Great Britain's first and oldest colony and all the horrors and exploitation of colonial wars and alien administration were rehearsed there. Northern Ireland is a colony in which the 'settlers' outnumber the 'natives' by two to one. In the rest of Ireland the 'natives' have established an independent republic. Although there are marginal cultural differences between the 'settlers' and the 'natives' the real differences are social and economic maintained by separate religion and education which limit social interaction and intermarriage. The political structure is not divided along working class, middle class lines, but along religious lines, Socialist equals Roman Catholic and Republican, Unionist equals Protestant and Loyalist. The trade union movement is Loyalist and frustrated the British Government's attempt at political change by a general strike in 1974.

For fifty years an alliance of the working class and particularly the skilled urban working class with the business, industrial and aristocratic sections of the community maintained a monopoly of political powers reinforced by the control of the penal system through the Special Powers Acts and the control of employment and housing. In this situation the Roman Catholic minority was passive until under the influence of improvements in education and social services provided by the British Parliament, of increasing property and an international movement for civil rights the Roman Catholic population began to protest against individual discrimination and general disadvantage.

Resistance to this movement began a progression toward civil war in which the Royal Ulster Constabulary and its auxiliary arm, the B Specials, were compromised. In this situation the IRA which had up to that point pursued objectives by political means split and the Provisional IRA emerged as a guerrilla force defending the Roman Catholic ghettos. The replacement of the Royal Ulster Constabulary by the British Army (whose regiments are still raised on a local basis) transformed the situation into one in which a colonial revolt was contained by the army of the colonial power and the methodology of earlier colonial conflicts was introduced into Northern Ireland with its use of informers and interrogation and armed intervention.

In attempting to assess the outcome of this complex interaction process it must be said that there is no single trend.

The role of the British Government is no longer ambivalent; as a Labour Government with considerable Roman Catholic support, it has greater freedom of action than its predecessor, although on most major aspects of policy the two Parties are in accord. Direct rule has been accompanied by legislation which in the long run will reduce the disadvantages of the Roman Catholic population. At the informal level the Government has in effect negotiated with the guerrillas for a phased reduction of the conflict. This simultaneously raises the status of the Provisional IRA but reduces its influence in Ireland and Great Britain.

This policy arises out of an appreciation of the contents of many detailed studies of different events and social problems containing much evidence and often confusion, inevitable when persons with rigid frames of reference, judges for example, examine complex issues.

The recognition of the nature of the underlying conflict has been mentioned already and the remedies proposed described. The sociological and psychological analyses which are directing the attempts to reduce tension have developed from the debate on capital punishment where the role of the hero martyr was discussed and where Parliament rejected the demand for the death penalty. In other reports the role of the IRA, the effect of civil disturbance on youth and their participation in conflict, the behavior of the crowd, the influence of the demagogue and the function of rumor are all examined. The Gardner Report explicitly discussed the legitimization of the IRA by granting political status to detainees and prisoners. The destructive effects of intimidation and informing on a community were well understood. All this has a positive form.

There is then much which is contradictory. The employment of the army as a civil power has had an exponential effect and this in spite of the fact that it is not *involved* emotionally or ideologically in the conflict. The techniques of armed intervention and intelligence confirm the predictions of and increase the support for the guerrillas. The reorganization of the Royal Ulster Constabulary and the disbanding of the B Specials together with the recommendations for an independent procedure to investigate complaints against the police and military and for a Bill of Rights are major positive developments. In contrast there is the continuation of emergency legislation, detention and the introduction of legislation restricting freedom and civil liberties to Great Britain.

A traditional approach to history attributes change to heroes, an alternative view is that events and circumstances select individuals who may then initiate change. A more balanced view is perhaps that which states 'there is a tide in the affairs of men which taken at its flood leads on.' Two men are playing an important role in the events of Northern Ireland and in the wider developments of these events. Lord Gardner in his minority report to the Parker Committee on interrogation and his subsequent analysis of the future of the penal system in Northern Ireland has redirected thinking with an emphasis on civil rights. Sir Robert Mark in his contribution to the Hunt Committee's report on the police in Northern Ireland and in his many statements on the role of the police in society and his reforms in the Metropolitan Police Force is giving effect to a philosophy of law enforcement which argues that it can only operate with the confidence, consent and cooperation of the citizen. It remains to be seen whether his influence will control some of the now traditional extralegal, and under emergency legislation legal, behavior of officers at the operational level and whether the influence of Lord Gardner will sustain the overall approach of the United Kingdom Government which is to end the colonial status of Northern Ireland. If this happens it will be because in parliamentary debate or implicit in the many reports on the crisis a sociological and psychological analysis has pointed to the underlying changes which must precede a political and administrative solution.

REFERENCES

1. 'Mr Justice Melford at the Trial of Eight Provisional IRA Men,' *The Guardian*. Manchester, March 19th, 1975.
2. *Police Review*, Vol. 83, No. 4294 (1975), p. 559.
3. *Report of the Advisory Committee on the Police in Northern Ireland*. Cmd. 535, Belfast, 1969.
4. William Belson, *The Public and the Police*. London, 1975.
5. T. Hadden and P. Millyard, *Justice in Northern Ireland*. London, 1973.
6. Law Officers' Department, *Prosecutions in Northern Ireland, a Study of the Facts*. London, 1974.

7. *Report of a Commission to Examine the Purpose and Effect of the Civil Authorities (Special Powers) Acts (Northern Ireland) 1922 and 1933.* London, 1936 and 1972.
8. The *Sunday Times* Insight Team, *Ulster.* London, 1972.
9. See P. Chippindale and P. Cole, 'Anatomy of a Bomb Squad,' *The Guardian.* Manchester March 19th, 1975.
10. *Disturbances in Northern Ireland.* Cmd. 532, Belfast, 1969.
11. *Violence and Civil Disturbances in Northern Ireland.* 2 vols. Cmd. 566, Belfast, 1972.
12. Declaration of August 19th, 1969.
13. *Report of the Enquiry Into Allegations Against the Security Forces of Physical Brutality in Northern Ireland Arising Out of Events on the 9th of August 1971.* Cmnd. 4823, London, 1971.
14. *Report of the Committee of Privy Councillors to Consider Authorised Procedures for the Interrogation of Persons Suspected of Terrorism.* Cmnd. 4901, London, 1972.
15. *Report of the Commission to Consider Legal Procedures to Deal With Terrorist Activities in Northern Ireland.* Cmnd. 5185, London, 1972.
16. *Report of a Committee to Consider in the Context of Civil Liberties and Human Rights Measures to Deal With Terrorism in Northern Ireland.* Cmnd. 5847, London, 1975.
17. National Council for Civil Liberties, *Prevention of Terrorism (Temporary Provisions) Act 1975. A Report on the First 4 Months Operation of the Act.* London, 1975.

A. L. Melai

INTELLECTUAL LIBERTY AND TOTALITARIANISM

> *What did he fear?*
> *The committal of homicide or suicide during sleep by an aberration of the light of reason, the incommensurable categorical intelligence in the cerebral convolutions.*
>
> James Joyce

In our age the concept of intellectual liberty is under attack from two directions. On one side from its theoretical enemies: the apologists of totalitarianism. On the other side from its immediate practical enemies: monopoly and bureaucracy.

In our part of the world – in the democratic countries of Western Europe – any scientist or writer who attempts to retain his integrity finds himself thwarted by the general drift of society rather than by active persecution. The kind of things that work against him are the ever-growing bureaucracy and the encroachment of official bodies, the increasing concentration of the press in the hands of a few individuals, the grip of political and cultural monopoly on radio and television, and the continuous threat of war in several areas on earth whose distorting pressure no one has been able to escape. At the same time, the most characteristic rebels against the existing order are – under the flag of solidarity – in fact revolting against the idea of individual integrity. To stand alone is seen as ideologically criminal and dangerous, despite the 'protection' afforded by prison walls.

For the members of the Baader Meinhof group in West Germany, scattered over a dozen top-security jails, life in prison presented new opportunities and new dangers. The system of communication they set up to keep in touch cell to cell is no doubt the most cunning and extraordinary in the history of modern penitentiaries. It was possible because the group took advantage of the liberal German prison regulations. Their greatest success was achieved in the effective exploitation of the guilt-ridden German liberal conscience. Even thirty years after the end of the Third Reich, the new West German democracy is still extremely sensitive to the shadows of the Nazi past. In these shadows Ulrike Meinhof continued in prison to write her manifestoes which were regularly dispatched to the other incarcerated comrades as well as to the remnants of the illegal network on the outside. Andreas Baader, who (before the legal adoption of limitations this year) had a staff of no less than twenty-two lawyers on call, went on giving instructions on how to intensify the revolutionary struggle as well as composing detailed memoranda and having them distributed. Their strategies were all coordinated: when to begin a hunger strike, how far to carry it, when to end it, and how to put pressure on back-sliding comrades. For months one of the girls was regularly put – falsely – on the official medical 'critical' list for fear of the 'consequences' should it become known to the others that she had stopped fasting without official 'Red Army' approval.

The revolutionary moral and psychological weapons are 'solidarity' and 'betrayal' and their emotional counterparts 'faith' and 'fear.' This state of affairs implies the use of the device of terror in prison and on the outside. When an 'execution order' was issued for one of their young comrades who had talked to the police – Ulrich Schmücker's corpse was found in Berlin's Grunewald, disposed of by the June 2nd Movement – purloined copies of the incriminating transcripts of the police interrogation were found circulating among the Baader-Meinhof cells.

Freedom of thought and of the press are usually attacked by arguments that are not worth bothering about. We are not trying to deal here with the claim that freedom is an illusion or that there is more freedom in totalitarian than in democratic countries, but with the much more tenable and dangerous proposition that freedom is undesirable and that intellectual honesty is a form of antisocial selfishness.

Although other aspects of the question usually occupy the foreground, the controversy concerns in essence the desirability of reporting contemporary events truthfully or as truthfully as is consistent with the ignorance, bias, and self-deception from which any observer unavoidably suffers. All history is contemporary history: not in the ordinary sense of the word, where contemporary history means the history of the comparatively recent past, but in the strict sense: the consciousness of one's own activity as one actually performs it. History is thus the self-knowledge of the living mind. For even when the events which the historian studies are events that happened in the distant past, the condition for their being historically known is that they must vibrate in the historian's mind. 'To ask whether the human individual is best understood as a multiplicity or as a unity is unprofitable, not because the answer is impossible but because the answer is obvious. The humanity of the individual implies a plurality of functions and the individuality of the man implies a focus of movement and of utterance.'[1]

Having acknowledged this fundamental state of human affairs, straightforward 'reportage' is the only branch of literature that matters here, but at every literary level the same issue arises in more or less subtilized forms. It is precisely from the viewpoint of our loyalty that it is regrettable to see so many leftist cliches whose survival in speech and print is due to three mechanisms. First, the refusal to analyze words and the use of verbal hybrids purposely designed to confound the issues. Second, the use of double standards of evaluation: the use of moral or sentimental standards in some cases and of political (opportunistic) or historical standards in other but similar cases. Third, the refusal to accept historical facts as they are. We must not be fervent moralists in some cases and cool rationalists or philosophers of world history in others, depending on political circumstances. Leszek Kolakowski quotes a conversation with a Latin American revolutionary who told him about torture in Brazil.[2] Kolakowski asked, 'What is wrong with torture?' The revolutionary replied, 'What do you mean? Do you suggest it is all right? Are you justifying torture?' And Kolakowski said, 'On the contrary, I simply ask if you think that torture is a morally inadmissible monstrosity.' 'Of course,' the revolutionary replied. 'And so is torture in Cuba?' Kolakowski asked. 'Well,' the revolutionary answered, 'that's different. Cuba is a small country under the constant threat of American imperialists. They have to use all means of self-defence, however regrettable.' Then Kolakowski said, 'Look, you can't have it both ways. If you believe, as I do, that torture is abominable and inadmissible on moral grounds, it is such, by definition, in all circumstances. If, however, there are circumstances where it can be tolerated, you can condemn no regime for applying torture, since you assume that there is nothing essentially wrong with torture itself. Either you condemn torture in Cuba in exactly the same way you do in Brazil, or you prevent yourself from condemning the Brazilian police for torturing people.' In fact, one cannot condemn torture on political grounds, because in most cases it is perfectly efficient and the torturers get what they want. One can condemn it only on *moral* grounds and then – necessarily to the same extent – in Batista's Cuba and in Castro's Cuba, in North Vietnam and in South Vietnam, in Sukarno's and in Suharto's Indonesia, in Cambodia and in Israel.

To keep the matter in perspective: in the democratic countries of Western Europe the immediate enemies of truthfulness – and hence of freedom of thought – are the press and the bureaucrats, but in the long run the weakening of the desire for liberty among the intellectuals themselves is the most serious symptom of all. The point is that the relative freedom we enjoy depends on public opinion. Governments make laws, but whether they are carried out, and how the police behave, depends on the general temper of the country. If large numbers of people are interested in freedom of speech, there will be freedom of speech, even if the law restricts or forbids it; if public opinion is sluggish and inconvenient minorities persecuted, there will be no freedom, even if laws exist to secure it.

The notion that certain opinions cannot safely be allowed a hearing is growing. It is given currency by intellectuals who confuse the issue by not distinguishing between democratic opposition and open rebellion or private war. And even those who declare themselves to be in favor of freedom of opinion generally drop this claim when it is their own adversaries who are being persecuted.

The enemies of intellectual liberty always try to present their case as a plea for (ideological and political) discipline versus individualism. The issue of truth-versus-truth is kept as far as possible in the background. Although the point of emphasis may vary, the writer who refuses to sell his opinions is accused either of wanting to exploit the 'wealth' of his individuality and to save his own soul at the expense of ignoring the community, or of making an exhibitionistic display of his own personality and of resisting the inevitable current of history in an attempt to cling to unjustified privileges. Those who hold absolute (totalitarian) political or religious ideas are alike in assuming that an opponent cannot be both honest and intelligent. Each of them tacitly claims that 'the truth' has already been revealed, and that the heretic – if he is not simply a fool – is secretly aware of 'the truth' and merely resists it out of selfish motives.

In Communist literature the attack on intellectual liberty is masked by oratory about 'petty bourgeois individualism,' 'the illusions of nineteenth-century liberalism,' 'escapism,' or 'true individuality attained only through identification with the community,' usually backed up by such abusive terms as 'romantic' or 'sentimental.' In this way the controversy is maneuvered away from its real issue.

One can respect the communist thesis: that freedom will only exist in a classless society and that one is most nearly free when one is working to bring such a society about. But slipped in with this is the quite unfounded claim that the Communist Party is itself aiming at the establishment of the classless society, and that – for instance in the U.S.S.R. or China – this aim is actually on the way to being realized. If the first claim is allowed to entail the second, there is almost no assault on common sense and common decency that cannot be justified. Before elaborating on this point we wish – not without the moral and intellectual impetus of George Orwell's inspired and inspiring essayistic work – to offer some critical notes on the idea of a classless society in connection with two historically interesting books, one by Oscar Wilde and the other by T. S. Eliot.[3]

Oscar Wilde's *The Soul of Man under Socialism* was published almost ninety years ago. Its author was not a socialist himself, but he was an intelligent observer; although his prophecies have not been fulfilled, they have not been made simply irrelevant by the passage of time. Wilde's vision of a (classless) socialism – which was then probably shared by many people less articulate than himself – is utopian and anarchistic. The abolition of private property, he says, will make possible the full development of the individual and set us free from 'the sordid necessity of living for others.' In the socialist future there will not only be no want and no insecurity, there will also be no drudgery, no disease, no ugliness, no wastage of the human spirit in futile enmities and rivalries.

Pain will cease to be important: for the first time in his history, man will be able to realize his personality through joy instead of through suffering. Crime will disappear, since there will be no economic reason for it. The state will cease to govern and will survive merely as an agency for the distribution of necessary commodities. All the disagreeable jobs will be done by machinery and everyone will be completely free to choose his own work and his own manner of life in a classless society. In effect, the world will be populated by artists, each striving for perfection in the way that seems best to him. The artist Wilde of course realized that there were authoritarian tendencies in the socialist movement, but he did not believe they would prevail, and with a sort of prophetic irony he wrote: 'I hardly think that any socialist nowadays would seriously propose that an inspector should call every morning to each house to see that each citizen rose up and did manual labour for eight hours.'

Something has evidently gone wrong. Socialism, in the sense of economic collectivism, is spreading across the earth at a speed that would hardly have seemed possible a hundred years ago, and yet Utopia – at any rate Wilde's Utopia – is no nearer. If one looks more closely one sees that Wilde makes at least one unjustified assumption. He presumes that it is a simple matter to arrange to have all the unpleasant kinds of work be done by machinery. The machines, he says, are our new race of slaves: a tempting metaphor, but a misleading one, since there is a vast range of jobs – roughly speaking, any job needing great flexibility – that no machine is capable of doing. In practice, even in the most highly mechanized countries, an enormous amount of dull and exhausting work has to be done by unwilling human muscles. This explains why millions of impoverished foreign workers have been recruited by or have traveled to Western Europe to do these jobs. This state of affairs implies not only the opposite of a classless society, but also the planning, organization, and supervision of labor, fixed working hours, differential wage rates, and all the regimentation that Wilde abhors. The abolition of private property does not of itself put food into anyone's mouth. It is merely the first step in a transitional period that is bound to be laborious, uncomfortable, and long.

But this is not to say that Wilde is altogether wrong. The trouble with transitional periods is that the harsh outlook they generate tends to become permanent. To all appearances this is what has happened in Soviet Russia. A dictatorship supposedly established for a limited purpose has dug itself in, and socialism has come to be thought of as meaning secret police forces, concentration camps, and psychiatric clinics. Wilde's pamphlet and other kindred writing – *News from Nowhere*, for instance – consequently have their value. They may demand the impossible, and they may – since a Utopia necessarily reflects the esthetic ideals of its own period – sometimes seem 'dated' and ridiculous, but they do at least look beyond the era of food queues and party squabbles and remind the socialist movement of its original impetus.

The no-man's-land between political philosophy and law is alluring and fertile but it is also heavily mined: especially where one leaves the shores of abstraction and approaches the realm of legal precision. The conflict between individualism and communal morality is as old as recorded history. The successful balancing by the legislative process of individual interests against the impinging demands of communal morality is an essential condition of civilization. All experience with new alternative societies leads us back to the very idea of socialism and the discovery of even more incompatible demands hidden within it.

Socialism does not mean a state of perfection but rather a *movement* trying to satisfy demands for equality, freedom, and efficiency: a movement that is worth the effort to the extent that it is aware not only of the complexity of problems hidden in each of these three values separately but also in the fact that they limit each other and can only be implemented by compromise. All institutional changes have to be treated as means in the service of these values and not as ends in themselves, and be judged correspondingly taking into account the price we pay in one value when we reinforce one of the others. Attempts to consider any one of these three values as absolute and to implement it at all costs are not only bound to destroy the other two but are self-defeating. This was discovered long ago, but these old truisms seem to go unnoticed in totalitarian utopian thinking.

Socialism used to be defined as 'common ownership of the means of production' ('The abolition of private property,' says Wilde, 'will make possible the full development of the individual.'), but it is now seen that if common ownership means no more than centralized control, it only paves the way for a new form of oligarchy. Throughout history, one revolution after another – although usually producing temporary relief – has simply led to a change of masters, because no serious effort has been made to control the power instinct. Or if there has been such an effort it has been made only by the saint, the yogi, the man who saves his own soul at the expense of the community. In the minds of active revolutionaries – at any rate the ones who have achieved their goal – the longing for a just and classless society has always been fatally infected by the urge to secure power for themselves. The true revolutionary always loses. Defeated, he is shot by his enemies; victorious, by his friends.

In his book, *Notes Towards the Definition of Culture*, (1948), T. S. Eliot arrives at the conclusion that a truly civilized society needs a class system as part of its basis. He only speaks negatively and he does not claim that there is any method by which a highly developed civilization can be created. Eliot maintains merely that such a civilization is not likely to flourish in the absence of certain conditions, one of which is class distinctions.

The essence of his argument is that the highest levels of culture have been attained only by small groups of people – either social groups or regional groups – who have been able to perfect their traditions over long periods of time. The most important of all cultural influences is the family, and today the family is strongest when the majority of people take it for granted that they will go through life on the social level at which they were born. Having no precedents to go on, we do not know what a classless society would be like. We know only that, since functions would still have to be diversified, classes would have to be replaced by 'élites,' a term Eliot borrows from Karl Mannheim. The élites will plan, organize, and administer: whether they can become the guardians and transmitters of culture, as certain social classes have been in the past, Eliot doubts, perhaps justifiably.

Tradition does not mean worship of the past – says Eliot. On the contrary: a tradition is alive only while it is growing. A class can preserve a culture because it is itself an organic and changing thing. For this reason a classless society directed by 'élites' may ossify very rapidly, simply because its rulers are able to choose their successors and will always tend to choose people resembling themselves. Hereditary institutions have the virtue of being unstable. They must be so because power is constantly devolving on individuals who are either incapable of holding it or who use it for purposes not intended by their forefathers. It is impossible to imagine any hereditary body lasting so long – and with so little change – as an adoptive organization like the Catholic Church. And it is at least conceivable that another adoptive and authoritarian organization – the Russian Communist Party – is fated to have a similar history. If the Party hardens into a class, as some observers believe it is already doing, then it will change and develop as classes always do. But if it continues to co-opt its members from all strata of society and then train them into the desired mental attitude, it might keep its shape almost unaltered from generation to generation. In aristocratic societies the eccentric aristocrat is a familiar figure, but the eccentric commissar – as George Orwell has said – is almost a contradiction in terms.

Eliot argues that even the antagonism between classes can have fruitful results for society as a whole. This is probably true. Yet one continues to have the feeling that there is something wrong here and that Eliot is aware of it. The fact is that class privilege has somehow ceased to be defensible. It conflicts with certain moral assumptions that Eliot appears to share, although he may disagree with them intellectually.

When class distinctions were believed in vigorously, it was not thought necessary to reconcile them with either social justice or efficiency. The superiority of the ruling class was held to be self-evident, and in any case the existing order was what God had ordained. This is by no means what Eliot is saying. He would like, he says, to see both classes *and* élites in existence. It should be normal for the average human being to go through life at his predestined social level but at the same time the right man must be able to find his way into the right job. In saying this Eliot seems almost to be giving away his whole case. For if class distinctions are desirable in themselves, then wastage of talent or inefficiency in high places should be comparatively unimportant. Eliot does not say this: indeed, very few people in our time would say it. It would seem morally offensive. His approval is purely negative. That is to say, he cannot see how any civilization worth having can survive in a society where the differences arising from social background or geographical origin have been abolished.

To all appearances the old social distinctions are disappearing everywhere because their economic basis is being destroyed. 'We can assert with some confidence,' says Eliot, 'that our own period is one of decline; that the standards of culture are lower than they were fifty years ago; and that the evidence of this decline is visible in every department of human activity.' Cultures are not manufactured, they grow of their own accord; and it is worth remembering that Swift, Shakespeare, Spengler, and Huizinga – to carry the story back over three centuries – were all equally certain that they lived in a period of decline.

To what extent can we speak of 'rise' and 'decline' or of 'progress' in connection with the social or cultural life of man as Eliot does?

To justify some action conflicting with the sense of decency of the average human being it is said that nothing is ever achieved without bloodshed, lies, tyranny, and injustice; however no considerable change for the better is to be expected as the result of even the greatest upheaval. History necessarily proceeds by calamities, and each succeeding age will be as bad, or nearly as bad, as the last. One must not – it is said – protest against purges, deportations, secret police, and so forth, because these are the price that has to be paid for progress: that does not, however, alter the fact that 'human nature' will always see to it that progress is slow or even imperceptible. The British scholar, historian and Marxist E. P. Thompson has said that 'to a historian fifty years is too short a time in which to judge a new social system, if such a system is arising.' His own Utopia – *two hundred years ahead* – would be a world (as D. H. Lawrence would have it) where 'money values' give way to 'life values' or (as Blake would have it) 'corporal' is replaced by 'mental' war.

These arguments are most often used to justify Stalin's regime in the U.S.S.R., but obviously could be – and, given appropriate circumstances, would be – used to justify other forms of totalitarianism. They have gained ground as a result of the failure of the Russian Revolution in the sense that this Revolution has not fulfilled the hopes it aroused fifty years ago.

In the name of socialism the Russian regime has taken almost every ruthless measure or action that can be imagined, but at the same time its evolution is *away* from socialism, unless one redefines that word in terms that no socialist of 1917 would have accepted. To those who admit these facts, only two courses are open. One of these is simply to repudiate the whole theory of totalitarianism, which we should have the courage to do. The other is to fall back on the formula usually employed: 'You can't make an omelette without breaking eggs.' And if one replies (as George Orwell does): 'Yes, but where is the omelette?' the answer will be: 'Oh well, you can't expect everything to happen all at once.' Thompson asked people to have patience for two hundred years.

This argument is pushed backward into history to show that every advance has been achieved at the cost of atrocious crimes and could not have been achieved otherwise. The example generally chosen is the overthrow of feudalism by the bourgeoisie, which is said to foreshadow the overthrow of capitalism by socialism in our own age. Capitalism – it is argued – was once a progressive force, and therefore its crimes were justified. Stalin did terrible things, but on balance he served the cause of 'progress.' It is logical to condone tyranny and massacre if one assumes that progress is inevitable. If each epoch is as a matter of course better than the last, then any crime or any folly that advances the historical process can be justified. Crime follows crime, one ruling class replaces another, but one must not resist the process – indeed, one must be ready to applaud any villainous act – because in some mystical way, in the sight of God and perhaps in the sight of Marx, this is Progress.

The experiences of the new alternative societies have shown convincingly not only that state ownership of the means of production is perfectly comparable with all disasters of the capitalist world – with exploitation and imperialism (the 'collectivization' of the Baltic countries and the armed invasion of seven non-Russian countries that had formed independent governments, some socialist, some not: Georgia, Armenia, Azerbaijan, Ukraine, Lithuania, Latvia, and Estonia) as well as with pollution, misery, economic waste, national hatred, national oppression – but also that it adds a series of disasters of its own: inefficiency, lack of economic incentives, and above all the unrestricted role of an omnipotent bureaucracy, a concentration of power never known before in human history. This power implies the suppression by violence of all political parties (including democratic socialist ones), the abolition of free speech and free expression, and the replacement of law with the absolute power of 'the Party' as the receptacle of the 'truth.'

Modern individualism is dogged by a fear of this kind of power (authority). Since there is no way for autonomous, rational beings to discover rules that are indisputably desirable, civil peace can be preserved only by submitting to an authorized 'ruler.' A sharp distinction is made between the 'authority' and 'desirability' of any law. It is obvious that this distinction introduces an ineradicable element of arbitrariness into government. For an 'authorized' law must be accepted even when it is not approved of. Governmental arbitrariness is an inescapable consequence of the recognition of the individuality of human beings. This state of affairs makes it imperative to consider democratic ways of constituting authority as well as the criteria for judging the desirability of a law. The crucial problem here is the gap between the authority and the desirability of a law. Modern political thought has therefore concentrated on finding some way of securing perfect consensus. Two patterns have dominated modern discussions, those suggested by Rousseau and Bentham.

In his concept of the *contrat social* Rousseau destroyed the 'gap' by denying the individuality of the subjects: since the sovereign becomes identical with all the individual members of the community, there can be no disparity between the authority and the desirability of law. According to Rousseau:

> La Souverainité ne peut être représentée, par la même raison qu'elle ne peut être aliénée; elle consiste essentiellement dans la volonté générale & la volonté ne se représente point; elle est la même, ou elle est autre; il n'y a point de milieu. Les députés du peuple ne sont donc ni ne peuvent être ses représentants, ils ne sont que ses commissaires; ils ne peuvent rien conclure définitivement. Toute loi que le Peuple en personne n'a pas ratifiée est nulle; ce n'est point une loi. Le peuple Anglais pense être libre; il se trompe fort, il ne l'est que durant l'élection des membres du Parlement; sitôt qu'ils sont élus, il est esclave, il n'est rien. Dans les courts moments de sa liberté l'usage qu'il en fait mérite bien qu'il la perde.[4]

Whether or not they find it in Rousseau, this is the dream that inspires the contemporary advocates of 'participatory democracy' and the members of 'communes.'

The solution proposed by Bentham respects the separateness of individuals but at the cost of reducing right to might. Although Bentham emphasized the disagreeable connection between coercion and government, he supposed that he had discovered a formula for making certain that this coercion was exercised justly. His 'calculus of pleasures' could, he thought, make it certain that every exercise of authority would receive the consent (as to its desirability as well as its validity) of every rational man. But Bentham's formula ignored the problem of judging the value of what autonomous beings choose to want, of deciding which man's desires (or indeed which of any man's desires) should take precedence. As a result Bentham's formula instead of maximizing consent, awards the power to decide to those who can best claim attention to their demands. Bentham's proposal for a moral consensus purged of moral judgments produces – as Shirley Robin Letwin has said

– 'what is euphemistically described today as government by pressure groups, which is really no government at all, but the rule of might disguised by sophistry.'[5]

In any case, we have to be on guard so that no form of (undivided and uncontrolled) power concentrated in a few individuals will take advantage of the 'gap' between the authority and the desirability of law. The three preconditions for a civil (democratic) society are the free organization of political parties, the free expression of political thought, and fair (parliamentary) representation of existing political opinions as the critical basis (authority) of government. For the last of these purposes the people must be consulted in free direct elections after periods of no longer than four years. The most vital democratic principle implies that even a majority has to maintain the integrity of the democratic system. It is true that parliamentary democracy is a bad political system, but of all the tested forms of government in history and in the present this form of government is from the human point of view the least bad (Churchill). Therefore we must protect it (if necessary hard-handedly) against the subversive and destructive actions of the apologists of totalitarianism.

Since the revolts in Paris and in Berkeley around 1968, most radical students have used sentences written by Marx or Lenin as verbal weapons, in particular the misleading sentence: 'The philosophers have only interpreted the world in various ways: the point, however, is to change it.' As though we could change the world – or exchange the 'present' for an unknown 'future' – without a whole range of speculative and instrumentally applied 'interpretations.' It is just these very 'interpretations' which cannot be ignored, on the contrary, they must form the subject matter of free democratic political discussion *par excellence*. The disturbance of this discussion by violence should be averted by adequate means.

Today there can be no doubt about the poisonous effect of the (polarized) concentration of power and the totalitarian mythos on intellectual life. Because of this effect, known facts are suppressed and distorted to such an extent as to make it doubtful whether a true history of our times can ever be written. Consider the completely incompatible attitudes a Communist has to adopt toward the Second World War. For several years before September 1939 he was expected to be in continuous stew about 'the horrors of Nazism' and to twist everything he wrote into a denunciation of Hitler. After the Machiavellian Russo-German Pact was signed in September 1939, he had to believe for twenty months that Germany was more sinned against than sinning, and he had to drop the word 'Nazi' from his vocabulary. Immediately after the news of 22 June 1941, he had to start believing once again that Nazism was the most hideous evil the world had ever seen.

Obviously, in the world in which we live important or disastrous political events or decisions in one country are usually to be accredited to events in other countries. It certainly cannot be denied that, tragically, part of the responsibility for German Nazism – the most criminal enterprise in human history and in its creative ideas inferior in every way to the impetus of the Russian Revolution – must be borne by the Soviet Union.

When Germany collapsed, it was found that very large numbers of Soviet Russians had changed sides and were fighting for the Germans. Also, a small but not negligible proportion of the Russian prisoners and displaced persons refused to go back to the U.S.S.R., and at least some of them were repatriated against their will. These facts went almost unmentioned, while at the same time Russophile publicists cynically continued to justify the purges and deportations of 1936–1938 by claiming that the U.S.S.R. 'had no Quislings.'

A totalitarian state is in effect a theocracy, and its ruling caste has to be thought infallible if it is to keep its position. But since in practice no one is infallible, it is frequently necessary to rearrange past events to indicate that some mistake was not made or that some imaginary triumph actually happened. Then, again, every major change in policy demands a corresponding change of doctrine and (opportunistic) revaluation of prominent historical figures. This kind of thing happens everywhere – consider the political and military expeditions of the USA in China and in Southeast Asia after the Second World War – but it is clearly more subject to outright falsification in societies where the means of communication have been muzzled and only one opinion is permissible at any given moment. Totalitarianism in fact demands the continuous alteration of the past, and in the long run probably demands disbelief in the very existence of the truth. It is not remarkable, as a phenomenon, that the demonstration of the moral bankruptcy of the Nixon Administration (and with it the discrediting of so many in the liberal-conservative Establishment) proved to be of so little profit to the left. The liquidation of the Nixon Administration in itself demonstrated the inestimable merit of the freedom of press and the relative lack of corruption of the democratic institutions in the USA.

A society can also become totalitarian when its structure becomes flagrantly artificial. This can happen when its ruling class has lost its function but succeeds in clinging to power by force or fraud. Such a society, no matter how long it persists, can never afford to become either tolerant or intellectually stable. It can never permit the truthful recording of facts or the emotional sincerity that literary creation demands: think for example of the conditions of life under the military regimes of Greece and Chile. But to be corrupted by totalitarianism an individual does not have to live in a totalitarian country. The mere prevalence of certain ideas can spread a kind of poison that makes one subject after another impossible for decent purposes. Wherever there is an enforced orthodoxy – or even two orthodoxies, as often happens – good writing stops. This is well illustrated by the Spanish Civil War. 'To many intellectuals,' as George Orwell has said, 'that war was a deeply moving experience, but not one about which they could write sincerely. There were only two things you were allowed to say and both of them were palpable lies; as a result, the war produced acres of print but almost nothing worth reading.'[6]

A totalitarian society that succeeded in perpetuating itself would probably set up a system of thought in which the laws of common sense held good in everyday life and in certain exact sciences but could be disregarded by the politician, the historian, and the sociologist. It is at the point where literature and politics meet that totalitarianism exerts its greatest pressure on the intellectual. The exact sciences are not menaced to anywhere the same extent. The totalitarian state tolerates the scientist because it needs him.

Many scientists have been among the uncritical admirers of fascism, of Nazism, and of the U.S.S.R. Scientists seem to think the destruction of liberty is of no importance as long as their own line of work is for the time being unaffected. Since the Second World War the U.S.S.R. has been a large, rapidly developing country with an acute need for a variety of scientific workers and which consequently treats them generously. Provided they steer clear of dangerous subjects, such as psychology, scientists are privileged persons. Writers, on the other hand, are viciously persecuted for the slightest deviation from orthodoxy. Even in Nazi Germany, scientists – other than Jews – were relatively well treated, and the German scientific community, as a whole, offered no resistance to Hitler. At this stage of history, even the most autocratic ruler is forced to take account of physical reality, partly because of lingering liberal habits of thought, partly because of the need to prepare for war. As long as physical reality cannot be altogether ignored the scientist has his function and can even be allowed a measure of liberty.

All the same it is his responsibility to develop some kind of solidarity with his literary colleagues and not to regard it as a matter of indifference when writers are silenced or driven to suicide and newspapers systematically falsified.

When one sees highly educated men looking on passively while oppression and persecution occur, one wonders which to despise more, their cynicism or their shortsightedness. One remembers the pro-fascist bias of British Tories and corresponding strata in the USA in the years before 1939. When one heard about British Conservative M.P.s cheering the news that British ships had been bombed by Italian airplanes in the service of Franco, there was an inclination to believe that these people were actually treacherous to the democratic institutions of their own country. But when the pinch came, it was found that they were subjectively quite as 'democratic' as anyone else. They had simply based their opinions on a syllogism that lacked a middle term: Fascism is opposed to communism; therefore it is on our side. In leftwing circles there was the corresponding syllogism: communism is opposed to capitalism; therefore it is progressive and democratic.

There is no such thing as genuinely non-political literature and least of all in an age like our own, when fears, hatreds, and loyalties of a directly political kind are close to the surface of everyone's consciousness. It follows that the atmosphere of totalitarianism is deadly to any kind of writer. What impresses us in these societies is the mental and intellectual degradation. After 1920 when Trieste became Italian and the Fascists had forbidden the Slovenian language to be used in any public situation, an Italian doctor was asked: 'But how can the peasants explain their symptoms to you if they don't know Italian?' The doctor replied: 'Does a cow have to explain its symptoms to a veterinary surgeon?'

It is true that in its creative ideas fascism is inferior to the impetus of the Russian Revolution and there are certainly very few people working in the human sciences who would not acknowledge their intellectual debt to Marx. Without Marx our thinking about history would be different and in many respects poorer than it is. Nevertheless we have to accept that many important tenets of Marx's doctrine are either false or meaningless or else true only in a very restricted sense. The labor theory of value is a normative device without any explanatory power and none of the abstract (general) formulas of the historical materialism to be found in Marx's writings is admissible, because this doctrine is valid only in a strongly qualified sense. Finally, we think that Marx's fundamental theory of class consciousness is based on false presuppositions. Sartre has said: to keep alive one must, in spite of all mistakes, horrors, and crimes, recognize the obvious superiority of the socialist camp. But to keep alive we cannot have confidence in a man, who is disposed to submit his emotional and intellectual reflections to the rigid and imperative catechism of Marx and whose moral attitude is in fact a form of captivity under the psychological and tactical weapons of 'solidarity' and 'betrayal.' As James Burnham points out in *The Struggle for the World*, the true Communist is a 'dedicated man.' He has no life apart from his organization and his rigidly systematic set of ideas. Everything he does, everything he has – family, job, money, belief, friends, talents, life – everything is subordinated to his Communism. He eats, reads, makes love, thinks, goes to parties, changes residence, laughs, insults always as a Communist. For him, the world is divided into just two classes of human beings: the Communists and the others. As the unavoidable result of self-censorship, among these people writing consists almost entirely of prefabricated phrases bolted together like the pieces of a child's building set. The Communist loves mankind in the abstract but cares for nobody in particular. A writer cannot narrow the range of his thoughts in this way without killing his inventiveness.

Whatever may hold for the physical sciences, or for music, painting, and architecture, it is certain that literature is doomed if liberty of thought and free expression perish. Not only is it doomed in any country which retains a totalitarian structure, but any writer who adopts the totalitarian outlook, who finds excuses for persecution and the falsification of reality, thereby destroys himself as a writer. No tirades against 'individualism' and 'antisocial selfishness,' no pious platitudes to the effect that 'true individuality is only attained through identification with the community,' can surmount the fact that a bought mind is a spoiled mind. Unless spontaneity enters in at some point or other, literary creation is impossible and language itself becomes ossified.

At present, we know that the imagination will not breed in imprisonment or in the shadow of the omnipotent bureaucracy in the new alternative societies. German literature almost disappeared during the poisonous and ruinous epoch of the Third Reich. In his memoirs Albert Speer concludes that as a *Menschenkenner* Hitler had no equal. He knew men's secret vices and desires, he knew what they thought to be their virtues, he knew their hidden ambitions and the motives which lay behind their loves and their hates, he knew where they could be flattered, where they were gullible, where they were strong and where they were weak. He knew all this, not by study or sympathy, for his knowledge engendered in him a supreme contempt for his fellow creatures. He knew it by instinct, an intuition and unerring sense of his enemy's inner weakness. This knowledge of men explains the influence of one of his strongest weapons: his oratory. It was of the kind that speaks neither to the mind nor to the heart of his audience, but plays upon its nerves until they are strung to such a pitch of intensity that they shriek for release in disastrous actions.

The situation was not much better in Italy, and Russian literature started to deteriorate in the early days of the Revolution. In Western Europe and America large sections of the intelligentsia have either been members of the Communist Party at some time or been warmly sympathetic to it, but this whole leftward movement has produced extraordinarily few books of any literary importance. Certain themes cannot be celebrated in words – tyranny is one of them – and no one has ever written a good book in praise of the Inquisition.

We call to mind Lescek Kolakowski's attempt to fight 'doublethink' in political-totalitarian reasoning and offer in conclusion a specimen of the double standard in the political response to Dubcek's role in the Czechoslovak reform movement. According to Radoslav Selucky: 'Was Dubcek, in fact, in control of the situation? If we mean 'control' in a democratic sense, he was. If we mean 'control' in Soviet terms, he was not. In the July 29-August 1 meeting at Cierna-nad-Tissou, Brezhnev expressed doubts whether Dubcek was still in control of the Czechoslovak reform movement; Dubcek was quite sure that he was, and he pointed out that he had received a resolution supporting his policies signed by four million people. Brezhnev argued that this was no evidence, that he knew how resolutions could be produced. Dubcek assured the Soviet leader that *this* resolution was different, having been initiated directly by the people. Brezhnev rejoined: 'How can you claim that you are in control of the situation if the people sign a resolution without your prior knowledge?'. . .'[7]

NOTES AND REFERENCES

1. Justus Buchler, *Toward a General Theory of Human Judgment.* New York, 1951, p. 1.
2. *Encounter*, Vol. XLIV, No. 6, p. 90. Leszek Kolakowski was dismissed from his Chair of Philosophy at Warsaw University in 1968 during a wave of cultural and academic repression. He is now a Fellow of All Souls College, Oxford. His *Marxism and Beyond* was published by Pall Mall Press in 1969 and *The Devil and Scripture* by Oxford University Press in 1973.
3. *The Collected Essays, Journalism and Letters of George Orwell.* Penguin Books, Vol. IV, especially pp. 118 ff. and 129 ff.
4. Rousseau, *Du contrat social ou droit politique*, 1762, Liv. III, ch. 5.
5. *Encounter*, Vol. XLIV, No. 5, p. 37.
6. *The Collected Essays, Journalism and Letters of George Orwell.* p. 90.
7. Radoslav Selucky, 'The Dubcek Era Revisited,' *Problems of Communism*, Jan-Feb. 1975, p. 41.

Jac. van Weringh

THE DUTCH RAILWAY STRIKES OF 1903: SOME REMARKS ON LEGISLATION AND VICTIMIZATION

INTRODUCTION

During the last 10 years criminology has seen a special emphasis placed on the definitions of criminal behavior. How do they originate? Why are certain acts defined as criminal by a political authority and other acts not? Are there groups whose interests are served by particular criminal laws? Is the law an instrument of the ruling class?

These questions are of course not new.[1] The difference is that now a primary problem of criminology is seen to be that of definitions. As long as it exclusively concerns itself with the criminal, his motives and background, criminology will remain a study that allows its area of concern to be determined in large measure by the existing state of the law.

However, in the last few years Chambliss, Quinney and Carson, to name but three, have begun to pay attention not only to the definitions of criminal behavior, but have also attempted to use this as a starting point for a novel theoretical approach. In his study of the vagrancy laws of England and America Chambliss has demonstrated 'the importance of "vested interest" groups in the emergence and/or alteration of laws.'[2] Quinney is yet more emphatic when he argues that 'criminal definitions describe behaviors that conflict with the interests of the segments of society that have the power to shape public policy.' The interests – based on desires, values and norms – which are ultimately incorporated into the criminal law are those which are treasured by the dominant interest groups in society. By formulating criminal law some segments of society protect and perpetuate their own interests. These segments are able to control the behavior of persons in other segments. 'It follows that the greater the conflict in interests between the segments of a society, the greater the probability that the power segments will formulate criminal definitions.'[3]

According to Quinney's theory, law is the result of conflict rather than consensus among the parties involved. Although the theory has a certain attractiveness from the point of view of a (particular) political standpoint, the present author doubts its explanatory power with regard to the genesis of definitions of criminal behavior, or at least not all such definitions. The theory can perhaps explain certain definitions of criminality, though there can also be a general societal consensus that specific behavior ought be punishable. In this connection Carson advocates 'a conceptual scheme which permits the location of laws on a continuum running between the extremes of consensus and conflict.'[4] This approach would appear to be more fruitful. If we hope to gain any understanding of the criminalization of behavior in particular societies then this necessarily has to come about through research; and it might be that laws, originating in a conflict situation might later, as a result of changes in values, norms or the power structure, come to be generally accepted.

This contribution sketches the origin of a number of punitive measures taken against the railway workers' strikes in the Netherlands. It asks who were involved? What were the motives behind the legislation? And who were the victims?

THE RAILWAY STRIKES OF 1903 – A BRIEF SUMMARY OF THE EVENTS

At the end of January 1903, Holland was shaken by a strike that took place mainly in and around Amsterdam. As a result of a series of conflicts and small strikes over unionization in the docks and warehouses, railway workers, who provided the transportation, refused to work for the Hollandsche IJzeren Spoorwegmaatschappij (Dutch Iron Railway Co.). This strike grew rapidly in size and scale and a strike which threatened to cut off Amsterdam completely from all railway traffic was called for January 30. Partly out of solidarity and partly to better their own working conditions, municipal workers, other transport workers and bakers also threatened strike action and only by completely capitulating on January 31 was the railway management able to avoid a general strike.

The reactions to this complete surrender were varied. Socialist workers exulted at the demonstrated strength of the solidarity of the proletariat. 'We can stop the wheels of industry with our strength,' they shouted in the streets and in the heady atmosphere of triumph the very end of oppression seemed close at hand.

The Government of the day, led by Abraham Kuyper of the Anti-Revolutionary Party, was heavily criticized by various groups who blamed it for taking no action.

The tension did not diminish however. As a result of the railway workers' success other groups of workers began to agitate for the betterment of their own conditions. The Christian and liberal press declared that a situation of anarchy and terrorism threatened and that the Government ought to take action to prevent repetition. In fact the Government did mobilize detachments of troops 'to protect or restore the state of law and order' and the socialists saw this as confirmation of the implacable nature of capitalism. The representatives of 40 socialist and anarchist workers' organizations set up a Committee of Defense as they suspected that the Government was preparing to take repressive legislative action against strikes on the part of railway workers. The Christian Trade Union Movement established a League of Order to promote, among other aims, that the Dutch Iron Railway Company 'at all times and under all circumstances might count on the loyal cooperation of its employees.'

On February 25 Kuyper, the Premier, appeared before Parliament to make an official policy statement. The Government had not intervened, he said, because in the absence of appropriate measures vigorous action was impractical. The strike was moreover completely unexpected and its undesirable outcome had also meant that there was no relaxation of the tension. The enthusiasm of the workers had turned into 'social and political threats' and that was why the military had been called in to ensure order. As a result of the strike, he continued, lacunas in the law had come to light which had to be rectified. He announced three proposed measures: additions and amendments to the Penal Code, the establishment of a 'railway brigade,' and the institution of a commission of inquiry to investigate the working conditions and legal status of the railway workers.

The announcement of the proposed legislation brought immense and hitherto unknown disturbances in its wake. The newspapers minutely discussed the implications of every detail of the proposals. Not unexpectedly the socialist sector of the press was 100% opposed, the Christian press completely in favor, while some liberal papers were somewhat critical of the proposed legislation and suggested that the results of the commission of inquiry might better be awaited first. Throughout the country there was great discussion. Groups of (non-socialist) citizens petitioned Parliament to reject (or at least postpone) the proposed legislation. Other groups pressured Parliament to accept the legislation immediately. In a pamphlet of the time the Committee of Defense stated: 'The Government has yielded to the pressure of anxious capitalists and has proposed legislation that constitutes a frontal attack on the minimal legal protection that the Dutch worker has hitherto enjoyed.' The socialists referred to the anti-strike laws as bluntly coercive and the renowned political cartoonist Albert Hahn in a famous cartoon entitled 'Under the Repressive Laws' depicted a policeman on horseback dragging a striker along through a deserted Amsterdam street.

The daily newspaper associated with the Premier's Anti-Revolutionary Party *De Standaard* wrote critically of the opposition to the proposed legislation: 'It is not the socialists and anarchists who must bow to authority but it is the Government which has to yield to the noisy revolutionary rabble.' It was in such an emotional atmosphere that on March 10, 1903 Parliament assembled to discuss two interpellations concerning the events, one of which had been initiated by Pieter Jelles Troelstra, the leader of the Social Democratic Workers' Party. Neither these debates nor the Government's explanations managed to subdue the agitation however and throughout the country widely attended meetings were held both by supporters as well as opponents of the Government.

In the meantime the Second Chamber of Parliament had begun work on the proposed legislation and by the time the so-called Provisional Report came to be discussed on April 2, several amendments had been proposed. Many further petitions had been sent to Parliament both supporting and opposing the proposed amended legislation. A Professor of Constitutional Law among others from the University of Groningen argued in a petition, that no good would come of a law originating in such emotional circumstances that was hastily drawn up to redress a wrong. Though they also wished to await the results of the commission of inquiry,

ZONDAGSBLAD. 15 MAART 1903.

HET VOLK

ONDER DE DWANGWETTEN.

'Under the Repressive Laws' – a cartoon by Albert Hahn (1877-1918), published in the Sunday newspaper of *Het Volk* (The People) on March 15, 1903.

nevertheless the debates took place as planned. After three days of debate, during which feelings throughout the country rose to fever pitch, the Committee of Defense called a new strike. Their manifesto stated: 'This is the path to slavery. This is the way in which all our rights in our struggle for a better life will be eroded. This so-called Christian Government will ensure that our lives will have to be led under the most "unchristian" conditions – hunger and misery will be our lot while the capitalists proceed to fill their pockets with the fruits of our labor. The laws which are about to be passed will throw workers completely at the mercy of the boss-class.'

Within a half-hour of the strike proclamation, troops arrived in Amsterdam to guard railway lines and stations. Up and down the country demonstrations and actions of various forms were the response to this. On April 9 Parliament (the Second Chamber) voted in favor of the new laws by a large majority and two days later the legislation was ratified by the First Chamber which had been specially convened for the purpose. It is seldom if ever in Dutch Parliamentary history that legislation of such radical character has been passed through Parliament with such haste. Immediately after ratification by the First Chamber, the Queen set her signature to the new laws and that very same evening they were published in a special issue of the *Staatscourant* (Official Gazette).

This short summary has attempted to give but a general sketch of the events without going into details,[5] the purpose being mainly to show the extent of the disturbances of the time.

MOTIVES AND BACKGROUND OF THE REPRESSIVE MEASURES

The question as to whether particular behavior ought be rendered punishable would in general come to the fore if that behavior was seen as damaging or dangerous to individual or to society. Further, the more general the perception of danger the less resistance to the criminalization of that behavior is likely. Of great significance is the question of who sees the behavior as threatening or damaging to their interests and who or what might be the victim.

Kuyper's Government had not until then concerned itself with the question as to whether or not railway workers could strike. It was completely outside their purview. Unions and workers had complained for years about their miserable social and economic conditions but little or nothing had happened to make the Government concerned or attempt to redress these grievances, and although the situation of the workers had not changed, the Government continued its 'laissez-faire' policy.

When suddenly a strike between workers and management in private industry occurred the Government still saw little reason to intervene, though by the time Kuyper made his official statement to Parliament on February 25 it was obvious that in the meantime the Government had taken a very clear standpoint. The Premier spoke of 'social and political threats.' He had discovered lacunas in the law to be filled and further declared that this was not merely an economic struggle between workers and their employers but 'a bold attack on the main element of the very life force of society,' an unacceptable thwarting of the Government and an attack on the welfare of all for the benefit of one class. For these reasons steps had to be taken, and he added '*what is criminal must also be recognized as such in the eyes of the law.*'

Thus, in a very short period the Government had come to the opinion that a 'crime' could be referred to. Without awaiting the results of the investigation by the commission of inquiry into the legal position and working conditions of the railway workers a definition of criminal behavior had been introduced. How did that arise?

An important part of that definition might be traced back to the reactions to the spontaneous strikes of the last days of January. Apart from the understandable feelings of elation and triumph of the socialists, a feeling of panic and bewilderment had spread to other social groups. *De Standaard*, the daily newspaper of Kuyper's Anti-Revolutionary Party, referred to a 'coup d'état': 'In the last week a new state of order has established itself among us. A strong well-organized attempt *to transfer power* (italics mine – v.W.) has been made, and it has completely succeeded.' (Feb. 2) In other Christian circles the mood was the same. A state of anarchy had begun. The well-oiled machinery of the state was in danger and if nothing was done about it a small daring group would soon have the whole of the Netherlands in its power. Right had changed into might.

The Government received heavy criticism especially from the groups which usually supported it. It is to be recalled that this Government which was elected in 1901 on a 'law and order' platform had further promised to reestablish Christian statesmanship in the Netherlands. The action of the strikers could obviously not be tolerated. It was criminal some newspapers said.

During this period the image of the strikers and those who supported them was presented in an ever less favorable light. The pretense that they were in a position to take over power within a very short time was maintained, as was the idea that this was a group that set itself apart from Christian society. They preached class conflict and wished to overthrow the God-given power of the authorities. 'A Christian worker would never join a railway strike in order to bring the whole country to a standstill to pursue his own private gain. He knows, as a child of the Lord, that such deeds are criminal, and he would never again be able to kneel and pray to his Father in Heaven if he were ever to let himself be tempted to commit such atrocities.'[6]

These anti-socialist sentiments became more vehement as the socialists and their allies, united in the Committee of Defense, attacked the legislation proposed by the Government. Their resistance was especially directed against the additions and amendments to the Penal Code. The Government wanted to render strike action by civil servants and railway workers liable to punishment. A railway employee who refused to perform his usual duties could be sentenced to 6 months imprisonment or a 300-guilder fine. If two or more committed that offense as the result of conspiracy the conspirators could be punished by a maximum of 4 years imprisonment, and in addition the culprits could be deprived of certain rights (to hold certain offices, to serve in the armed forces, to vote or to run for public office). And as a finishing touch, it would also be punishable to unlawfully force a worker to join a strike or to compel an employer either to hire or to dismiss certain persons. The socialists feared that by means of these regulations any attempt to form an adequate trade union movement would be made impossible. From the scale of the discussions about the proposed legislation inside and outside Parliament it is clear that much more than the conflict in the railway industry was involved. The position of the incipient workers' movement itself was at stake – especially in relation to those groups which wielded power at the time. The sudden success and especially the demonstrated solidarity were perceived as real threats to the status quo.

In the beginning of April, the Association of Dutch Employers confidentially circularized its members with a proposal to establish a popular weekly magazine, aimed especially at the working population. 'This plan originated in our Board of Directors,' it was admitted, and 'it is absolutely necessary to create a counterbalance to the influence of the socialist magazines and newspapers by means of a regular and systematic press action. The new magazine should be supported by people of all religious and political persuasions who agree with employers that the tendency of the current popular leaders is harmful for industry and thus for the workers.' The letter concluded with the words 'It is desirable to *avoid even the suspicion* that this magazine has been established by our Association.'[7]

A number of prominent Catholics, including a Member of Parliament, distributed a confidential circular letter containing a request for money to support a large campaign of lectures, pamphlets and propaganda against the socialists and anarchists. It was stated: 'We have to meet action with action, rabblerousing with order, lies with truth,' and in addition the circular referred to the agitation and the destructive influence of terrorism. Unless vigorous action was taken immediately, the danger that lies might prevail over truth could not be excluded. 'Therefore we appeal to you. We ask you *in the name of Commerce and Industry* as well as Labor whose interests are also threatened and on behalf of our Christian workers whose souls we have to snatch from the claws of the godless deceivers of the people – we ask you in the name of our Fatherland whose future is at stake to send us a generous contribution, so that we will be able to mount a powerful campaign in the coming weeks.'[8]

In an article in the *Nieuwe Rotterdamse Courant* published during the Parliamentary debates, it was suggested that the strike was not the manifestation of long-bottled-up dissatisfaction but rather the commencement of the effects of widespread anti-State doctrines. The article further went on to suggest the existence of an abnormal group living outside the structure of society and in irreconcilable conflict with existing ideas of justice and reasonableness which hitherto had prevailed in the neutral trade union movement – a group which sets the general interest aside in favor of the desires of the few.[9]

When a second strike broke out during the Parliamentary debates the anti-socialist tone became shriller. The Christian daily paper *De Nederlander* published a workers' song in which the socialists are referred to as 'devil's spawn' and a gang which mocks all that is Holy and denies 'the Lord of our fathers.'[10]

Several times during the debates it may be seen that the proposed laws go further than merely the regulation of strikes. The Anti-Revolutionary Talma was strongly of the opinion that 'the purpose of these penal laws has a definite connection with the behavior of the anarchist elements.'[11] A Catholic member of Parliament expressed the wish that the laws would be passed and thus 'free us of the terrorism of the socialistic workers.'[12]

In the middle of this verbal violence in the Second Chamber in which supporters and opponents were attacking each other, the Free Democrats, a moderately progressive group, were attempting to make reasonableness and common sense prevail. Their spokesman, Drucker, pointed out that the Government had not made the slightest criticism of the actions of the managements of the railway companies 'to which a great deal of the blame for what has happened may be ascribed.' No word of excuse for the workers was uttered, nor extenuating circumstances claimed. The proposed legislation delayed the return to normality among the agitated. The insinuation by the Government that those who were against the proposed laws were also against law and order was not just. A Government may not enlarge the Penal Code with new provisions 'just because it thinks it desirable or expedient to do so.' If the circumstances are really as critical as has been suggested, are these legal amendments likely to be adequate measures?[13]

But the voice of common sense which was to be heard both inside as well as outside Parliament was ignored and the Government maintained its view of the situation as a threat to law and order. In its Memorandum of Reply to the Provisional Report of the Second Chamber the response to the request of a number of members to temporarily abandon the initiation of the new penal laws was as follows: 'In the opinion of the Government the signs of the times are not sufficiently understood if it is assumed that under the current circumstances the postponement of the proposed legislation will allow the settlement of the social conflicts which have arisen, in a manner which is acceptable to the Government and of long-term peaceful validity. Postponement would only promote the already initiated process of public moral decline. No State can maintain its authority if its citizens are not fully aware of their obligations to the community.'

The Government reply continued by referring to the 'immorality of the strikes' and 'this treachery committed against the common good.' Withdrawal of the proposed legislation would be seen by the offenders as weakness on the part of the State authority and recognition of their own strength. 'Above all, at the present time, *the supremacy of the authority of the State above all social unrest* has to be legally demonstrated and thus the first condition realized for the real and prompt improvement of the grievances of the workers, the promotion of national prosperity and the guarantee of our internal and external security.'[14] The proposed legislation was passed with the socialists and Free Democrats voting against it.

THE REPRESSIVE MEASURES: A CLOSER ANALYSIS

In the foregoing the motives for and background of the repressive measures relating to the railway workers' strikes were discussed. A conflict of limited extent in the Amsterdam harbor suddenly spread, work stopped completely and the employers' side capitulated unconditionally. How these events were perceived is most significant for what followed. The powerful groupings in the country felt threatened by the socialists and anarchists. In the most shrill of voices it was suggested that society was at the very edge of the precipice. Positions were taken up as a result of an exaggerated paranoid perspective and one might fairly speak of a 'witchhunt.' Although the socialists rose to the occasion and saw the imminent approach of the just society they had to change their view of the structure of power in the country. Police and military were both in the service of and completely loyal to the Government of the day, as were the groups which supported and elected it. That the socialists used revolutionary language is fully understandable; they had scarcely any other means at their disposal. Universal suffrage had not yet been achieved in the Netherlands – that came only in 1917 and even then was restricted to male citizens. Only those who paid more than a specific sum in taxes were eligible to vote. A large sector of the population was thus systematically excluded from the process of political decision making. Their voice was represented in Parliament by a small number who had been able to get elected in a limited number of districts but any real influence was out of the question and they had to struggle against heavy odds. The Premier, in fact, considered them as second-class citizens because they professed no belief in the God of whom he considered himself such a doughty champion.[15]

The power against which the socialists came into conflict, was however not executed by a homogeneous group. Different groupings were allied whose common interests were supposed to be protected by means of criminal legislation. For some it was a traditional belief in the values of religion and authority, for others it was purely economic interest. The Free Democrats who socially and economically might be ascribed to the power elite saw themselves, however, as defenders of other values which might be described as those of reasonableness and common sense. In their view it was unsound to make something punishable and only later investigate the conditions that led to the conflict from which the very criminal behavior stemmed. That was putting the cart before the horse. They also realized the impossibility of making reasonable decisions in an atmosphere of tumultuous emotions. They considered the consequences of the proposed legislation within that specific emotional context and came to the dissenting opinion that it was opportunistic legislation which would not solve the problems involved.

In the criminalization of behavior, in general the relationship will not be quite as simple as suggested by Quinney's theory. The powerful do not inevitably form a homogeneous front to protect their interests in every situation. Much will depend on the particular issue at stake. A few years later in the Netherlands an alliance of liberals and socialists came into being for the purpose of opposing legislation in the sphere of morality, which had been proposed by a Christian Government. The interest that alliance defended at that time against the paternalism of the Government was concerned with the freedom of expression that was perceived as a right by both liberals and socialists. In 1903 the socialists were, however, still counted among the outsiders and have-nots and the liberals were their opponents.

THE VICTIM OF THE RAILWAY STRIKES

In its Memorandum of Reply the Government stated that it was concerned to 'devise measures necessary to protect State and Society against the repetition of such criminal acts.'[16]

In this view the victims of the crime are the State and Society. During the Parliamentary debates it was suggested that the criterion for punishment should be a threat to 'the common interest.' The common interest is thus threatened by a small group of strikers and becomes the victim; but what does this mean in this context? The various groups concerned in this conflict saw 'the common interest' quite differently. To the strikers the common interest was the interest of those with power, and from which they were excluded. To the others the common interest was seen as equivalent to the status quo, whether or not based on a religious viewpoint, but which in any case ought not be tampered with. We might call this view of the common interest as potential victim the legalistic view – that of the legislators and those who support them. What Quinney in a general sense considers as 'the victim' applies in any case here – it is a social construction[17] which is comprised of different elements such as the feeling of being threatened, selective perception, and discriminatory tendencies.

If we look at the relationship between victim and offender from the legalistic point of view we have to conclude that the victim, that is 'the common interest,' has provoked the criminal behavior. For years, workers' grievances over their miserable conditions had been ignored. The common interest had nothing to offer them and they were simply excluded from the opportunity to help shape this common interest. However, beside this constructed victim were the *real* victims: the striking workers. No heed was paid to them when they shouted louder and louder – instead they were regarded as criminals and a danger. Some thousands were dismissed and many of them remained without work for a very long time because of their stigmatization as ringleaders. A Union of those dismissed in 1903 was inaugurated which might be regarded as an alliance of victims. Public opinion, in this case the mouthpiece of the common interest did not entertain much compassion, however. *De Standaard*, the Premier's mouthpiece, argued that the railway managements would have handled it wrongly if almost all strikers had been rehired: 'This would have been perceived as weakness and would lead to renewed agitation in the unions with the slogan 'You'll be rehired in the end anyway.' (May 5, 1903) The same newspaper also proposed to send the dismissed strikers to the Dutch colonies. As late as the 1920's it was necessary to establish a fund for the financial support of needy ex-strikers.

SOME CONCLUDING REMARKS

The railway strikes of 1903 had a traumatic aftereffect in the Netherlands. For years afterward there was a distinct feeling of distrust between the socialists and other political groups and inside the socialist movement itself heated discussions continued about the appropriateness of the tactics used in 1903 which culminated in some groups even separating from the movement as a consequence of these differences. The assimilation of the socialists into Dutch society, through universal suffrage among other factors, gradually created a climate of opinion more favorable to discussion than outright antagonism and as a result the trade union movement gained recognition for itself. In fact, the socialists who in 1903 were regarded as terrorists and godless atheists provided a number of Premiers from their ranks after World War II.

The railways themselves became a state-run operation in which the legal rights and working conditions of the workers were improved. The punitive laws were never repealed and civil servants and railway employees are still not allowed to strike. In the last few years, however, the right of civil servants to strike has come more to the forefront of public discussion. When that right is secured it will again be demonstrated that the law is not eternal and immutable but liable to change as a result of social, cultural and economic influences. What is tragic is that the path to that insight is littered with victims, who with the advantage of hindsight are often seen to be innocent.[18]

NOTES AND REFERENCES

1. For example by Clara Meyer-Wichman in her book *Misdaad, Straf en Maatschappij* (Crime, Punishment and Society). Utrecht, 1930.
2. William Chambliss, 'Vagrancy Law in England and America,' in Donald Black and Maureen Milesky (eds.), *The Social Organization of Law*. New York and London, 1973, pp. 132–146. Compare also his article 'The State, the Law, and the Definition of Behavior as Criminal or Delinquent,' in Daniel Glaser (ed.), *Handbook of Criminology*. Chicago, 1974, pp. 7–44.
3. Richard Quinney, *The Social Reality of Crime*. Boston, 1970, pp. 16–17.
4. W. G. Carson, 'The Sociology of Crime and the Emergence of Criminal Law: A Review of Some Excursions Into the Sociology of Law,' in Paul Rock and Mary McIntosh (eds.) *Deviance and Social Control*. London, 1974, p. 78.
5. These events are discussed in detail in A. J. C. Rüter's standard work *De Spoorwegstakingen van 1903 – Een Spiegel der Arbeidersbeweging in Nederland* (The Railway Strikes of 1903 – A Mirror of the Workers' Movement in the Netherlands). Leiden, 1935. Another very important source is *Actestukken der Samenzwering, Gedenkboek der Werkstakingen van 1903* (Reports of the Conspiracy – Memorial Volume of the 1903 Workers' Strikes). 2 vols., Wageningen, 1903 and 1904.
6. From an article in *De Standaard*, quoted in *Actestukken der Samenzwering*. vol. I, p. 199.
7. *Actestukken der Samenzwering*. vol. II, pp. 428–429.
8. *Ibid.*, pp. 430–431.
9. *Ibid.*, p. 533.
10. *Ibid.*, pp. 581–582.
11. *Handelingen der Staten-Generaal, Tweede Kamer* (Proceedings of the Second Chamber of the

States-General [Dutch Parliament]). 1902/1903, p. 1055.
12. *Ibid.*, p. 1069.
13. *Ibid.*, p. 1057.
14. *Actestukken der Samenzwering*. vol. II, pp. 435–436.
15. On Abraham Kuyper's social, political and religious views, see: Jac. van Weringh, *Het Maatschappijbeeld van Abraham Kuyper* (The Social Views of Abraham Kuyper). Assen, 1967.
16. *Actestukken der Samenzwering*. vol. II, p. 435.
17. Richard Quinney, 'Who is the Victim?' in Israel Drapkin and Emilio Viano (eds.), *Victimology*. Lexington, Mass., 1974, p. 107.
18. I am much indebted to Rijnhard Haentjens for his comment and to Gerry Paster for his translation.

Karl O. Christiansen

THE INTERACTION OF CRIMINAL POLICY AND THE STATE OF CRIME

INTRODUCTION

In this article 'criminal policy' refers to current criminal political *practice*, not to the *planning* of criminal policy. It should not be denied, however, that the discussion of reforms implying changes in existing laws or practices may at least indirectly already have some impact on the state of crime. In all other respects 'criminal policy' is taken in the widest sense of the word, including legislation as well as the administration of criminal justice at various levels, such as the decisions of the court, prosecution activity, and police practice, areas where the power of discretion may exert a considerable influence.

The 'state of crime' may be described in a number of different ways. Here we will focus on the numerical description of various forms of offenses, particularly against the criminal code but also to some extent offenses against special laws which apply sanctions defined in the criminal code.

The problem this article will deal with may then be formulated in the following simple way: Is there any connection between changes in criminal policy and changes in the state of crime? The method will mainly be the study of changes over time, the implications of geographical variations being more difficult to assess. The article will be based largely on Scandinavian, and particularly Danish, experiences.

The relationship between politics and criminal policy is a very close one because the criminal justice system is to a large extent a product of political decisions. This aspect of the problem will not be treated in any detail here.

LEGISLATION

The legal *definition of punishable behavior* determines to a substantial extent the incidence of crime.

In Denmark, a decriminalization of punishable forms of intoxication in 1959 might have reduced the number of arrests by about 15,000, i.e. over 33%. Correspondingly, an abolition of penal sentences for less serious thefts in 1965 would presumably have led to a reduction in the number of reported violations of the Criminal Code from slightly over 155,000 to just over 60,000 and the number of judical decisions involving sentences heavier than fines from about 7,000 to around 1,000, the precise figure depending upon where the boundary between 'serious' and 'less serious' was drawn.

It is, however, possible under special circumstances to discover less hypothetical examples of the importance of political conditions for criminal legislation and criminal policy.

In Denmark after World War II, 13,521 persons were punished for various forms of collaboration with the occupying power. Most of these acts were not defined as criminal until the amendment to the Criminal Code of 20 May 1945. If this *retroactive* law had not been adopted, prosecution could only have been instituted against acts covered by the Criminal Code then in force, and the number of persons sentenced would have been reduced to less than 2,000. If, on the other hand, membership in the Nazi Party had been criminalized, as it was in Norway, the number would have risen to about 50,000, and if civilian employment by the Germans had also been included, it would probably have approached 150,000.[1] Finally, let those whose imagination is vivid enough imagine the purge after a German victory. The above numbers would then have approached zero, while other groups of undesirables might have been weeded out.

This is a drastic example, but the increase in special laws and ordinances in wartime demonstrates the same fact: more regulations means more transgressions. Unfortunately Danish statistics on such minor offenses are scarce and for the war period almost nonexistent; but it is known that the government and the ministries issued close to 140 laws, instructions, orders and circulars during the German occupation. The country was occupied on the 9th of April 1940 and liberated on the 5th of May 1945. The first regulation was a circular sent out by the Ministry of Justice on April 12, 1940 forbidding all public meetings except in churches and the last one, near the end of the war, was an order from the Ministry of the Interior about the treatment of German refugees.[2] Some of these provisions were clearly in the interests of the occupying power, others were meant to protect Danish citizens or interests. As a rule proceedings were only initiated at the request of the Germans or in certain cases as an attempt to handle the trial under Danish jurisdiction. The number of such cases was very large; in the period April 1, 1941-April 1, 1942 alone, about 1,000 Danes received a sentence or agreed to pay a fine in cases where German interests had been infringed. In the following year, in Copenhagen alone, 1,296 persons were charged; for 205 the charge was withdrawn, mostly because the Germans forgot the case.[3]

The most important change was Law No. 219 of 1 May 1940 which stated that both minimum and maximum punishments would be doubled and that no suspended sentences would be imposed in cases of violation of the Criminal Code, if the offense was carried out under, or made more serious because of, blackout restrictions, or occurred during an air raid or threat of air raid. The part dealing with crimes committed during a blackout was of great practical importance. Although it can hardly be proved, this may have influenced the frequency of crime. It is at any rate certain that the customary court practice changed, among other things, because of this law. Suspended sentences for men declined from 35% of the total number of sentences for men in 1937 to 21% in 1943. For women the decline was much smaller, from 65% in 1937 to 60% in 1943. At the same time there was an increase in sentences of more than three months imprisonment for both sexes, the increase for men being larger.[4]

In Norway, the number of violations of price and rationing regulations rose from 41 in 1939 to almost 24,000 in 1944, whereas violations of the already existing police ordinances fell from 54,000 in 1939 to just over 31,000 in 1944. In Sweden, the number of violations of emergency legislation increased threefold from 1940 to 1943.[5]

The Criminal Code, however, is not the only factor influencing the extent of criminality. *Other laws* may also indirectly bring about changes in the pattern of crime. For example, the prohibition of alcohol in Finland 1920-1929 led not only to a large number of violations of prohibition, but was also accompanied by an increase in crimes of violence.

In the nine year period 1905-1913, which in Finland began with a general strike, crimes against life, i.e. the number of persons killed, increased from 3.14 per 100,000 inhabitants in 1899-1904 to 5.04. The years 1914-1916 brought with them an equally sharp decrease to 3.57. For 1917-1919 comparable rates are not available, but in the following 13 years 1920-1932, which is the period of *total prohibition*, the number of crimes against life 'exceeds all limits and attains a formidable height, one that exceeds considerably the level of the general strike period and its succeeding stormy years,' the average rate being 8.43 per 100,000 inhabitants 'or 16 times as high as the corresponding ratio in Sweden.' Let it finally be added that the rate decreased immediately after the abolition of the prohibition laws, to 5.75 in 1933-1935 and 4.16 in 1936-1940. The picture is with few exceptions the same in all the Finnish counties.[6]

It was, however, not only the number of crimes against life which changed in Finland during these years. The rate of intoxicated violent offenders and the rate of intoxicated victims also changed. In the two periods 1904-1913 and 1920-1929, the rate of victims of homicide who were under the influence of alcohol was 3.3% and 4.8%, respectively, for victims of assault with serious bodily injury, it was 44.8% and 52.3%, respectively.[7]

A similar situation occurred in the USA during the prohibition period of 1919-1933, where the effects were even more violent and longlasting. A major part of the present-day organized crime in the USA can be traced back to Chicago in the twenties.

Legislative changes, however, may also be the result of the development of crime. This is obvious of alterations in the narcotic laws in many countries. Without an initial increase in the abuse of certain new drugs (methadone and amphetamines) and probably without an even more well-founded fear of an increase in the use of drugs among the younger age groups, Law No. 169 of 24 May 1955 would probably not have been introduced in Denmark. The later development has overwhelmingly confirmed that the anxiety was not exaggerated.[8]

The interaction between legislation and the state of crime is clear, but the influence of the development of crime upon criminal policy becomes even more obvious when we look at the decisions and practice of the legal authorities.

THE ADMINISTRATION OF THE CRIMINAL JUSTICE SYSTEM

Legislation partly determines and largely influences the administration of justice.

The association between *law enforcement* and political conditions *may* become greater if the rule of compulsory prosecution is replaced by the rule of discretionary nonprosecution. The latter would give the prosecuting authorities discretion to decide whether a charge would be brought or not. There is, however, reason to believe that political circumstances are indirectly of even greater influence through appropriations made for police training and technical equipment, and through decisions as to the size and salaries of the police force. In the (utopian) event that a police force were built up to such a size and level of efficiency that practically all reported crimes were solved, the number of convicted offenders in Denmark would be increased three- to fourfold.

The relationship is especially obvious in countries in which the police, other law-enforcing authorities, national and local civil servants, and politicians are corrupt and where the population more or less cynically accepts these circumstances and leaves it up to the individual to defend his rights, to acquiesce or perhaps to attempt to derive as much as possible out of a corrupt social situation. It is tempting to quote an American.

Adlai E. Stevenson pointed out that in the campaign against illegal gambling in Illinois it was necessary in some places to withdraw the authority of the local police and of the local government in order to gain control over this activity. It was a 'break-down of local law-enforcement, the break-down of decency in government ... the triumph of greed, corruption and, perhaps worst of all, cynicism.' He blamed the political appointment of civil servants, the low standards of education, inadequate salaries of the police, and the policy of wholesale replacement of civil servants when the post of governor changed hands as major contributors to the corruption. These conditions are necessary prerequisites for organized crime. Profits from illegal gambling are estimated to be between 7,000 and 50,000 million dollars and those from the sale of heroin around 30 million dollars. Usury, which often must be paid for loans to pay gambling debts, is said to range between 1% and 150% per week, most often 20%.[9] In addition, prostitution and the illegal production and sale of alcohol are thought to be on the increase. Without a certain degree of political corruption such forms of criminality could probably not exist in the USA. It is thus no coincidence that questions of politics and crime are often treated in American textbooks together with questions of organized crime–a better example of the connection is hardly to be found.

This, however, should not be looked upon as a statement which attempts to hide the importance of the connection between criminal policy and the state of crime in countries where corruption is a minor consideration. In Denmark the development of four different indexes of crime against the Criminal Code from 1937 to 1948 once more throws light on the interaction process.

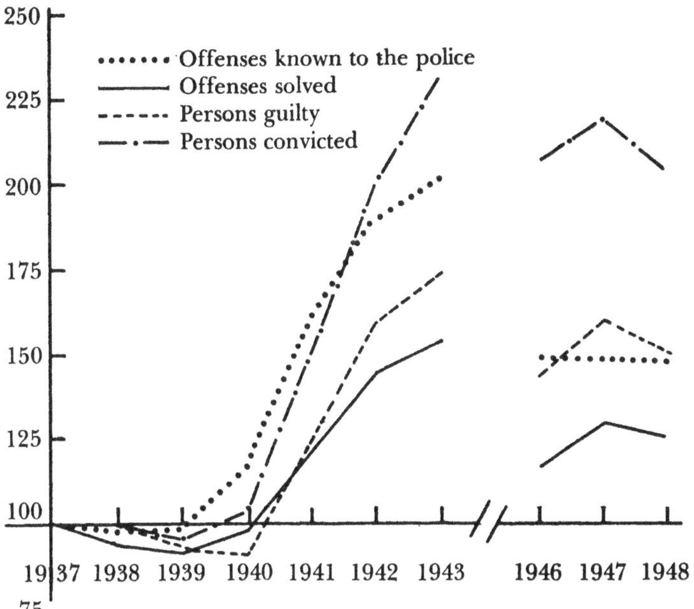

The Trend of Crime in Denmark from 1937 to 1943 and from 1946 to 1948

The trend of crimes known to the police, crimes solved, convictions together with cases where the charge was withdrawn, and convictions alone shows, as can be seen in Graph 1, that the war and immediate postwar years were generally accompanied by a major increase in crime. It might be expected that the curve for convictions would follow the curve for solved crimes, since solved crimes determine that part of criminality with which the prosecution and court must work. But this did not happen. The figure shows that the risk of conviction in the period 1937 to 1943 rose substantially more (130%) than the number of solved cases (50%). This was true for all offenses except for crimes of violence. For the latter, the increase in the number of solved cases was 70%, whereas the number of convictions increased by only 50%, which probably implies that a considerable number of the solved crimes of violence could not be brought to trial given the conditions of occupation and the more or less political nature of the crimes. More remarkable, however, is the fact that sexual offenses, in spite of a minimal increase in the number of reported and solved cases (5–8%), had a considerable increase in the rate of conviction (17%).

Conditions of war, which bring about a general increase in crime, often lead to changes in the criminal justice system which reinforce the general impression of a dangerous situation. These changes may be rationally planned in the sense that, from knowledge of past experience, sentences are chosen which are deemed suitable for counteracting the increase in crime. But irrational factors also come into play. This observation is supported by the fact that in Denmark during World War II there were a number of actual intensifications of the severity of law: (1) an increased tendency for initiation of prosecution, (2) a reduced percentage of suspended sentences, (3) a more frequent use of longer prison sentences, and (4) a more indiscriminate application of these intensified measures. Various types of offenses which showed quite different changes in their incidence were met with equally strict reactions. This may be seen in the identical treatment of sexual offenses, for which the incidence of reported cases increased only slightly, and crimes of violence, which doubled; of swindling and embezzlement, which remained relatively stable, and theft, which increased sharply. A reverse tendency can also be noted, in that the greater strictness chiefly affected men even though female criminality increased almost twice as much.[10]

It should also be emphasized that it was not merely the attitudes of the law enforcement authorities that changed. The attitude of the population on the question of crime and punishment also changed. The conditions during the occupation were marked by insecurity, the occupying power exerting a constant pressure that did not allow opportunity for open resistance. From a social-psychological point of view it is not surprising that at this time more than during normal conditions the increase in crime was felt as a hostile attack and that the ordinary offenders who were available for punishment were punished more severely. The Danish experience during World War II thus indirectly supports the hypothesis that our present-day criminal policy is also a product of society's emotional attitude toward crime and not simply the result of a rational consideration of the best methods to combat crime.

An even more drastic illustration of how the influence of wartime conditions in an occupied country can affect ordinary criminal policies may be taken from the war period during which there were no police in Denmark.[11] It should first be mentioned, however, that the seven and a half months without police, from 19 September 1944 until liberation on 5 May 1945, should not be taken simply as an example of how criminality is affected when criminals are not prosecuted or subject to punishment. One month after the ordinary police were removed by the Germans a 'Community Guard' was organized and authorized with certain police powers and at the same time the prosecution authorities expanded their functions and the courts meted out much stricter punishments for those who were brought to trial and convicted. On the whole, however, law enforcement was weakened to a very large extent and the available information from this period leaves no doubt as to the disastrous consequences in the form of a sharp and marked increase in crime. It has been denied, however, that it is possible to conclude anything about the influence of the law enforcement authorities in isolation from all other special conditions and the necessity of comparing the figures for crime during this period with the preceding period has been emphasized.

The number of robberies in Copenhagen from 19 September 1944 to the end of that year has been estimated to be at least 300, and for the period 1 January 1945 to the capitulation (5 May) to be about 500. At the same time robberies became more violent and more dangerous. The significance of this development may be illuminated by a comparison with the figures for reported robberies in the preceding years: 11 in 1939, 21 in 1940, 46 in 1941, 59 in 1942, and 127 in 1943. According to a report made by the Copenhagen police immediately after liberation, there were 167 persons killed and 79 injured in Copenhagen between 19 September 1944 and the end of the year. From 1 January 1945 until liberation, the corresponding figures were 405 killed and 143 injured. In comparison, the reported figures for murder in the preceding years were: 4 in 1939, 5 in 1940, 4 in 1941, 20 in 1942, and 22 in 1943. It should be noted that a majority of the killings registered during the final months of the occupation were committed for political reasons. This is not true, however, of the above number of robberies in which the cases assumed to be connected with the Resistance Movement are excluded. There is no reason to believe that the number of sexual offenses increased. During this period, however, blackmail was a flourishing crime.

The number of reported thefts rose in the period just after 19 September 1944 to three times the figures for 1943, then in the course of three to four weeks fell to less than twice the number in 1943; the value involved in the thefts rose still more. The Community Guard in Copenhagen during the final months before the liberation received more than three thousand reports monthly. In April 1945 the number of reported crimes rose to five thousand.

THE PUNISHMENT

Considerations of this complex of problems lead naturally to the question of the significance of the politically determined societal system of reactions toward offenders. It has mainly been discussed under two headings, each covering a vast and on the whole uncharted field, which in short may be called rehabilitation and general prevention or general deterrence.

The influence of the punishment on the individual offender has its own positive or negative value. It has, on the other hand, also had far-reaching consequences for the development of criminal policy in general. It is one of the indicators of the functioning of our penal system. A great part of the reforms which have taken place toward the end of the last century and in this century up to World War II have been explicitly aimed at reducing recidivism, but it is questionable whether our reactions to the individual criminal have succeeded in these efforts.

Most penalties imply by definition an element of suffering which also manifests itself in the overwhelming majority of sentences pronounced by the courts. This, of course, is not a decisive objection to the application of punishment as a reaction to criminals. It is not possible to bring children up without causing them some pain either. A surgical intervention can entail heavy suffering, and it may be extremely painful to pay a visit to the dentist. For the criminal the punishment involves something which is worse: its stigmatizing effect, the brand of disgrace at being labeled as a criminal, the degradation. This holds true even for young offenders who have their charges withdrawn or are given some kind of a probation sentence. The typical example, however, is the prison sentence where the harmful influences are obvious. First the deprivation of liberty is in itself damaging, although the most harm results not so much from the physical confinement as from the psychological influence of a narrow, degrading milieu. Second, the deprivation of a normal sexual life has a negative effect, and probably it is not as much the deprivation of sexual intercourse with persons of the opposite sex which is harmful as the fact that male prisoners are forced to live in a purely masculine society, which is bad, and female prisoners in a purely female society, which may be worse. And thirdly, the prisoner is deprived of his independence or rather his self-reliance and originality in a more thoroughgoing way than in any other place in the world apart from the worst of concentration camps. The high rates of recidivism should not surprise anybody.

A great interest in the study of the prison community has manifested itself in the last three or four decades, but no attempt has been made, as far as the present author knows, to assess empirically the general harmful effects of a prison stay. In recent years a number of cost-benefit analyses in terms of money have been made. This is obviously more easy than to assess the amount of human suffering and its harmful consequences in an average prison population.

The *severity of the sanction* has often been considered the most important factor of deterrence and a great portion of the discussion on general prevention has concentrated on this aspect of the problem. This is a rather dubious assumption. Although it is possible that the length of prison sentences and the possibility of using capital punishment are of somewhat greater value for general prevention than they are for the resocialization of convicted offenders, severe sentences are far from having the status of top deterrent.

THE POLITICAL SYSTEM

If Sutherland and Cressey's definition of crime is accepted there is no reason to question its dependence on politics. Crime involves three elements: a value which is appreciated by a group or a part of a group which is politically important; isolation of or cultural conflict in another part of this group so that its members do not appreciate the value or appreciate it less highly and consequently tend to endanger it; and a pugnacious resort to coercion decently applied by those who appreciate the value to those who disregard the value.[12]

The politically important group that can decently apply coercion is of course the one that has the political power at the moment. So far, the criminal political practice as defined above must almost by definition be a policy which aims at the preservation of the existing order. Only very infrequently will the politician use criminal policy as a tool for the establishment of a new social order. He usually has a more direct means at his disposal. The *planning* of a criminal policy, however, is often made to further more general political ideas.

The question of *the general influence of an authoritarian or a democratic form of government* on criminality is more difficult to answer. These terms are so broad and so vague that the topic is hardly suitable for scientific investigation. In those societies which are termed dictatorships or democracies, the limits of variation of the social and cultural circumstances are so great that the more obvious and direct crime factors may become predominant. If connections exist, they can at most be of an indirect nature. This is an area, however, where it is not even possible to formulate general hypotheses or to predict what the results of empirical investigations might be.

MORE GENERAL THEORIES

The interaction of criminal policy and the state of crime has been described by Radzinowicz in the following way: In times of dire economic depression, striking changes occur in the structure and extent of criminality. The most prominent characteristic is an increase in juvenile delinquency and the number of first offenders and first recidivists. This influences law enforcement in that it leads to a more extensive use of short-term imprisonment, which produces overcrowding in prisons and fewer employment opportunities for discharged prisoners. 'Economic crisis leads to penal crises.'

The State, although not able to stop these trends, attempts to solve the crime problem by shortsighted changes in legislation and criminal policy. Interest in the person of the offender fades into the background and punishments are made stricter. Radzinowicz characterizes this change in the administration of criminal justice as *reactionary*. Conversely, improvements in economic conditions, when crime is reduced and social tensions relaxed, allow the opportunity for long-term planning of criminal policy and the imposition of milder punishments and individual treatment of offenders.[13]

An example of the interrelationship described by Radzinowicz can be found in Denmark during World War II, when the above mentioned changes in criminal policy were instigated in the face of an increasing crime rate. Here it was not the actual increase, however, but the legislators' and the law enforcing authorities' view of that increase that decided the changes in criminal policy.

The development described by Radzinowicz more or less presupposes that the decision-makers act in a way which they themselves consider rational. This is not always the case. The theory on the function of punishment of Durkheim and Fauconnet may throw further light on the problem.

In his book, *De la Division du Travail Social*, Durkheim maintained that the function of division of labor was to strengthen the solidarity of the members of society. Solidarity was most clearly expressed through the legal rules. Crime was formally defined as every act which brings about that reaction called punishment. He attempted, however, to supplement the formal definition with a material description. Crime consists with few exceptions of acts that arouse general disgust among the members of society. 'In other words, it cannot be said that an action wounds the collective consciousness because it is criminal; it is criminal because it wounds the collective consciousness. We do not disapprove of it because it is a crime; it is a crime because we disapprove of it.'[14]

The 'collective consciousness' in Durkheim's terminology is more or less equivalent to values held in common by the members of society.

The function of punishment is to create a possibility for the release of emotions that are aroused by the crime. Punishment is not explained by deterrence, retribution, expiation, reformation or utility. This is shown by the fact that it need not be the guilty party that is punished; the important thing is that punishment occurs! Closer analysis, however, shows that just and expiating punishments best fulfill the penal system's useful and necessary function. Through punishment society proves to its members that it is still strong enough to protect honest citizens from the criminal.

Fauconnet's conception of the function of punishment was not very different from Durkheim's, but he gave a more detailed description of 'society as the cause of crime.' The cause was not to be found in the criminal because the criminal did not create the moral evil. The individual was only an occasional cause. It is, however, decisive that Fauconnet supported the theory with a series of observations concerning collective, indirect and passive responsibility. He explained certain characteristics of responsibility among primitive peoples from the hypothesis that punishment is directed toward the crime.

Fauconnet illustrates this idea by comparing punishment with the bullets from a badly sighted gun. Although they do not hit the same mark it will eventually be seen that they gather more and more around the bull's-eye, i.e., they have been aimed at a target. This target is the crime, not the criminal.

This somewhat paradoxical theory is also expressed in the following way: First comes the *crime*; then, because the crime has alarmed the honest people, *punishment* to reestablish society's trust in itself; and finally, to permit the application of punishment which cannot annihilate the crime, *something*, probably a human being, perhaps the culprit, *to be held responsible* for the deed.

Thus a punishment which hits the criminal is not far from being the sacrifice of an individual for the welfare of society. The criminal is not so different from other deviation scapegoats, and the conviction and the execution of the sentence is 'essentially a ceremonial reaffirmation of the societal values that are violated and challenged by the crime.'[15]

Related views on the function of punishment have later been advanced by a number of leading sociologists and psychologists. G. H. Mead, who in 'The Psychology of Punitive Justice' approaches the problem partly from another angle, stresses that the attitude of hostility against the criminal unites all members of society in an emotional solidarity of aggression. The cry of thief or murderer is attuned to profound complexes, and the citizens stand together against the common enemy. 'The criminal does not seriously endanger the structure of society by his destructive activities, and he is in fact responsible for a sense of solidarity, aroused among those whose attention would otherwise be centered upon interests quite divergent from those of each other.'[16]

Ranulf has through studies of Greek literature found many pieces of evidence which support the views of Durkheim and Fauconnet. In his book, *The Jealousy of the Gods and Criminal Law at Athens*, he goes one step further and attributes the expansion of criminal law to moral indignation which is basically a kind of disguised envy. Although somewhat exaggerated and much oversimplified, this conception might be expressed in the well-known wording: moral indignation is a description of our observations of others doing what we would not venture to do ourselves.[17]

Reiwald, on the basis of psychoanalytical observations and considerations, makes the sociological description somewhat more detailed, but he accepts the theory on the emotional function of punishment. Not to take into consideration the mutual interdependence of social and asocial persons would be a falsification of facts.[18] Punishment is a method by which society fights for its continued existence. Whereever there is some form of social life, there must be punishment. In its origin it is a sacrifice to the gods. The asocial and the criminal is a safety valve or a lightning conductor for social aggressions. He is the object which society needs for the relief of aggressive tensions, and he establishes by his example a standard of comparison which may make the socially well-adjusted citizens feel good and just because they can see him as their glaring contrast. 'Society appears to fight him with all its strength, but in practice it does everything to retain him.'[19]

The educational function of punishment is underlined by Aubert. The administration of justice is well suited for painting a picture of society in black and white. It makes it possible to identify with the law-abiding majority because the contrast is so evident, and this identification may strengthen social solidarity.[20]

Christie agrees on this point and adds that the criminal satisfies the societal needs best when he is most deviating; he ought to be an extreme phenomenon, the opposite of a saint. If we know him too well he will lose his useful function.[21]

Cohen expresses a similar view. In a community of saints goodness is natural and indifferent; nobody has any special claim to respect. 'The deviants provide the contrast effect that makes conformity something "special" and a source of gratification.' In limited quantities it contributes to the vitality and efficiency of organized social life.[22]

There is no more reason to underestimate the roundabout, irrational, functions of the criminal justice system than there would be to deny the existence and influence of general prevention. 'Quantitatively, these (irrational) effects may well be much more important in the long run than individual prevention.'[23]

Those who are not satisfied with the evidence based on observations in primitive societies and from ancient times may have a look at a few cases of lynching in the USA. The post-war purge against the collaborators with the Germans during World War II in some European countries led to a number of comparable instances. In Denmark, people eagerly were looking forward to, and earnestly discussed 'the night of the long knives' and 'the fourteen lawless days' where the just should take revenge on the traitors.

A CONCLUDING REMARK

Just one concluding remark would seem to be called for. The interaction between the function of legislators and administrators of justice on the one hand, and the state of crime, established by the lawbreakers, on the other, is even more complicated than indicated above.

One intervening variable is the attitude of the general population. The voice of the common man should not be ignored. It cannot be substituted by judicial arguments. Sooner or later the legislators, judges, prosecutors and police will allow themselves to be influenced by his demands. This, of course, will generally appear as a result of profound legalistic thinking far beyond the primitive call for justice from ordinary citizens.

NOTES AND REFERENCES

1. Karl O. Christiansen, *Landssvigerkriminaliteten i sociologisk belysning*. Copenhagen, 1955, pp. 23–24.
2. Based on information in Niels Alkil (ed.), *Besættelsestidens fakta*. Vol. I, sec. A. Copenhagen, 1945.
3. *Ibid.*, sec. D.
4. Karl O. Christiansen, 'Crime in Denmark from 1937 to 1948,' in Thorsten Sellin (ed.), *The Effects of the War on Criminality. Select Papers on Penal and Penitentiary Affairs*. Berne, 1951, pp. 562 ff.
5. See articles by Andreas Aulie and Sven Rengby in Sellin (ed.), *op.cit.*, pp. 644 and 673 ff., respectively.
6. Veli Verkko, *Homicides and Suicides in Finland and their Dependence on National Character*. Copenhagen, 1951, ch. VII.
7. *Ibid.*, pp. 79 ff.
8. H. H. Brydensholt, *Narkotika og Straf.* Copenhagen, 1971, chs. II and III.
9. Adlai E. Stevenson in *The Challenge of Crime in a Free Society: A Report by the President's Commission on Law Enforcement and Administration of Justice*. Washington, 1967, ch. 7.
10. See Christiansen, 'Crime in Denmark from 1937 to 1948,' *op.cit.*, pp. 566 ff.
11. Most of the data for 1944–45 cited in the following are from Jørgen Trolle, *Syv Maaneder uden Politi*. Copenhagen, 1945.
12. Edwin H. Sutherland and Donald R. Cressey, *Principles of Criminology*. 6th ed., Philadelphia-New York, 1960, p. 15.
13. Leon Radzinowicz, 'The Influence of Economic Conditions on Crime,' *The Sociological Revue*, 33 (1941), pp. 1–36 and 139–153.
14. E. Durkheim, *De la Division du Travail Social*. Paris, 1937, p. 48.
15. Paul Fauconnet, *La résponsabilité*. Paris, 1920. See also A. R. Lindesmith, 'Punishment,' *International Encyclopedia of the Social Sciences*, 13 (1968), pp. 217 ff.
16. G. H. Mead, 'The Psychology of Punitive Justice,' in L. A. Coser and B. Rosenberg (eds.), *Sociological Theory*. New York, 1964.
17. S. Ranulf, *The Jealousy of the Gods and Criminal Law at Athens*. 1–2, Copenhagen, 1933–1934.
18. P. Reiwald, *Society and Its Criminals*. Timperly, Altrincham, 1949, p. VIII.

19. *Ibid.*, p. 34.
20. V. Aubert, *Om straffens sociale funksjon.* Oslo, 1954. See also A. K. Cohen, *Deviance and Control.* Englewood Cliffs, N. J., 1966, p. 8.
21. N. Christie, *Kriminalsosiologi.* Oslo, 1965, p. 9. Similar ideas have been advanced by Cohen, *op.cit.*
22. Cohen, *op.cit.*, pp. 10–11.
23. R. Hood and R. Sparks, *Key Issues in Criminology.* London, 1970, p. 175.

Kees Schuyt

THE SELF-CREATED CONFLICT: CIVIL DISOBEDIENCE IN THE UNITED STATES AND THE NETHERLANDS COMPARED

The present-day problems in law and the legal order have been influenced for a part at least by the fact that practicing lawyers and legal scientists were not prepared to react to the deep political and social changes of our time. Many premises on law and order, on law enforcement and punishment, on hierarchical structures of authority, on the State as *the* central agency in society, on the right to resistance against the lawful governors, on the consent of the governed, have been heavily attacked and criticized. A reassessment of all these premises is going on now. The citizen's duty to obedience is another such problem.

The problem of obedience to the law raises the question: obedience by whom? Unfortunately in our rich world today the main political leaders do not show much respect for the law. Their unbound cynicism in the political struggle and their refusal simply to obey national and international rules put the question of the citizen's obedience to the law in quite a peculiar perspective. Disobedience of the citizen as a reaction against departures from the law and irregularities of the authorities has to be distinguished from disobedience in situations in which the authorities carry out their tasks and duties within the boundaries of the law. This is the important difference between civil disobedience in the USA[1] and civil disobedience in the Netherlands. Different aspects must be considered in the Dutch situation. The problem is not whether we have to choose between absolute obedience on the one hand and disobedience on the other. After 1945 an absolute duty to obedience is simply impossible and unacceptable, at least for the 'war-children' generation. The heart of the matter in this moral problem lies in the drawing of the line: where, when and why can disobedience be justified, or even stronger: when do we have the duty to disobey.[2] The problem becomes even more complicated if we add: *in a democracy*. Civil disobedience is specifically the problem of minorities, time and again overruled by an apathetic or intransigent majority. Hence the minorities believe they are absolved from the duty to obedience. It is not the problem of a permanently and persistently oppressed minority, such as is the case in a dictatorial state. Civil disobedience is the problem of the permanent losers: their voices *are* counted, but they never become a majority; they are free to organize but they will find social obstacles and hindrances in their way, they are free to enter a contract, to become owners, but they are powerless because of their socioeconomic conditions to make their liberties count in an effective way.

They are bound to play the game and to keep the rules. But for the one who loses time and again, the play loses its attractiveness. The play analogy, used so many times in democratic theory, is rather interesting here. The problem of the eternal loser has been solved in plays and games: the rules are changed, the winners are handicapped so the chances of winning are open again. In democratic theory the problem has not yet been solved.

In other words we can call minorities those people living in moral and political ghettos, in a society which for the rest has all characteristics of a democracy. To what extent are these people bound to obey the law? Civil disobedience has taken place in history[3] against imperialistic warfare (Thoreau's resistance against the Mexican War), against racial discrimination in South Africa (1908–1910), against colonial rule in India (Gandhi 1930–1933), against fascist rule in Norway, Denmark and Holland (1940–1945), against racial discrimination in South Africa (Luthuli in 1952), against racial discrimination and poverty (SNCC, CORE, SCLC and Martin Luther King 1958–1968), against discrimination and oppression of Chicanos and Indians, against the war in Southeast Asia, against corruption in government, against exploitation and powerlessness, against ecocide, against paternalistic bureaucracy and the double standards of political leaders and university administrators, all in the United States; against legal and political discrimination of Catholics in Northern Ireland in 1968 (the civil rights march organized by B. Devlin in Londonderry). Put briefly: it has mainly been a struggle on behalf of black, brown, red and yellow people against white supremacy.

In looking at civil disobedience in the Netherlands the author cannot suppress a feeling of smallness and parochialism – and not only in a geographical sense.

In America everything happens on a heavier scale: the president has more power, his weapons are more cruel, crime is more criminal, radical students are more radical, corruption is more corrupt, the rich are richer, the poor are poorer, violence is more violent, and so on. All those aspects place the problem of obedience to the law in its particular setting. More concretely, the inevitable conclusion, in this author's opinion at least, is that in the Dutch situation it is more difficult to justify disobedience for moral and political reasons.

But the problem of civil disobedience in the Netherlands cannot be solved and abandoned so quickly. Many sparks have been produced by the question how to govern or how not to govern people. Political protest started in Amsterdam with the provos, soon after the Berkeley revolt in 1964. We have to find answers to our own situation. This has been marked the last few years by student sit-ins in university buildings, occupation of consulates, occupation of the Enka factory, of churches nominated to be razed, by the boycott of the so-called f 1,000 Tuition Act, which raised the tuition fee from the pre-war level of f 200 to the level of today. We have had a soldiers' strike, roadblockades set up by protesting farmers and fruit and vegetable growers, the disobedience of gas station owners, of truckdrivers and recently of the small shipowners.

There has been a rise in direct action in our indirect democracy. Open disobedience suddenly has become 'normal' and with the exception of severely deprived social groups, e.g. the elderly and young unskilled laborers, nearly every interest group in the Netherlands has had its share of the fruit of the tree of knowledge of good and evil. The question is how much political trouble a political system can bear?

Many acts of protest in the Netherlands in recent years have been referred to as acts of 'civil disobedience' whereby the concept was used in a very loose manner. The labeling came primarily from journalists and politicians. But labeling is not the main problem (although sociolinguistical analysis would not underrate the influence of qualifying words). As the author sees it, the protests of the last few years raise the question of interpretation: are they indicators of a short-term governmental crisis or a long-term crisis in legitimacy of the Western liberal democracy. In addition there is the fact that some protests are quite unclear themselves. Sometimes a group protests against an unwelcome measure. Other acts of protest, e.g. the boycott against the environment tax, are supported both by people who resist incidentally and by people who do not accept the structure of capitalist society at all.

There is a mixture of short-term resistance and a permanent and well-organized denial of the legitimacy of our system. The ambiguity is quite obvious in the special nuclear energy tax (Kalkar *heffing*). Resistance to a very specific legal rule is often combined with more or less far-reaching ideas and ideals on a new society, new ways of governing and new decisionmaking processes. Roel van Duyn, the former provo leader and presently member of the city council of Amsterdam shows this ambiguity in his behavior. He joined the ranks of those who govern and in so doing accepted a great part of the political structure, but he refuses to cooperate in specific cases. This ambiguity offends many people, perhaps mostly the zealous ones. It is seen as a rejection of the system as a whole. Those people ask for complete loyalty, such as we have seen recently with Nixon and his staff.[4] All protests raise the following question: Is it a short *conflict* between a government whose legitimacy is beyond question or must it be seen as a wholesale rejection of the government, or even a rejection of government as such?

The first can be called a policy problem, the second a problem of legitimacy. Of course there is a relationship between the two. A bad solution to the conflict can lead to a crisis in legitimacy. There can be an escalation or a spreading of the conflict, or a cumulation of conflicts with one powerful group, although here much depends on what kind of group coalitions occur. The farmers were against the student protests, the students were against the truckdrivers and the truckdrivers were against the farmers' roadblockades.

In the author's opinion, the protests during the last two years in the Netherlands have been mostly policy problems and on a much more minor scale crises in legitimacy.

A further interesting question is the fact that a political interpretation of direct acts of protest reflects a social science measurement problem: what are the valid indicators for legitimacy?

Or to put it another way: if we see a parent tugging at a reluctant child, must we conclude that the child is a discontented child whose request for a new toy has been refused *or* a child that has decided to leave the parents' house and is now waiting for a good opportunity to run away. Do *discontented* children run away more often or more quickly than *neglected* children. How discontent do we have to be to leave home?

Can we interpret the Dutch protests as discontentment under the tacit assumption that we want to remain in the home or can we speak of neglect of our fundamental rights and interests and of the rights and interests of future generations (take the ecological problem)? We can measure legitimacy with attitude scales, e.g. a constructed compliance-scale. This type of measurement is inadequate and will give false results, because no distinction is made between 'compliance' and 'legitimacy,' between norm conformity and the meaning of obedience, between authority as such and legitimacy as the assignment of meaning to authority.

The other way to approach the problem of legitimacy in an empirical way is to use the concepts 'exit, voice and loyalty' coined by Hirschmann.[5]

There is a relationship between rejection of legitimacy and the willingness to use violence. By maintaining the empirical referents it becomes possible to focus on social action instead of social behavior and to overcome a reductionist approach to the problem of legitimacy. It always remains uncertain how the attitudinal willingness to obey, measured outside the situational context, will correspond to action within the context. Gerrit van der Veen would have had a high score on the compliance scale, but his social action happened to follow other patterns in February 1941, and so he became an important member of the Resistance movement.

The concept of legitimacy has, much more than the concept of obedience, a normative, deontological character. Legitimacy refers to an appeal to a principle,[6] a higher rule, an elaborated reasoning, to values or an ideology.

Exit of one or of a number of group members brings such justifying principles into question. Voiced criticism is expressed with words and paper, pen and pencil. Here we as social scientists will find our empirical data, although we cannot measure them. Loyalty consists of words and actions: the word is critical, the action is still supportive. Criticism is a form of loyalty. In a situation where exit is impossible, or nearly impossible, such as is the case in a nation-state, the use of political violence is an indicator that one wishes to cut the ties with society. Terrorist groups will find in their socializing processes a point of no return beyond which they cannot go back to the society they came from. Use of violence against fellow citizens and directed at the State is an indicator that the legitimacy has been rejected. The *right* to exist or the right of that type of political structure has been rejected. Legitimacy has to do with something that *ought* to be in the relations between men. It refers not to a factual existence, but to a right, to a claim to existence.

This kind of approach, which centers on meaningful social action, leads to a different qualification of our present-day problem of disobedience. The political effect of this approach means that we are not in panic so quickly because of some disobedient acts. The legitimacy of our democracy is not fundamentally threatened by many of the acts of protest in the Netherlands. Compared with, for example, the

United States in the late sixties and early seventies we cannot speak of a crisis of legitimacy in Holland. The discontentment of many Dutch social groups has led to direct action and large-scale disobedience. If one goes back to the ideological roots of all those groups then only a few protests where legitimacy has been rejected remain. Many of the protests recall an old Dutch tradition: resistance to payments to the (Spanish) ruler. The f 1,000 tuition boycott, the gasoline distribution, the environment tax ('the industry pays first'), the protests of the farmers, the retailers and the truckdrivers, all have more to do with the problem of distribution of scarce resources. Integration and distribution are two main problems any society has to solve. The first is a Hobbesian problem, the second a Marxian problem. They are not independent of each other but integration, thus legitimacy, becomes a problem only if the mode of production and distribution (e.g. by market or by plan) is rejected. This is not the case for most acts of protest in Holland: they are policy problems and problems of inadequate legislation, not a crisis in legitimacy as such. The most striking difference between civil disobedience in the United States and in the Netherlands lies in the political power of the groups who acted disobedient willfully and in their value-orientation. Both the protests abroad and the literature which describes and comments on them, view civil disobedience as political protest and resistance against norm-departures or rule-violations of authorities. They appeal to universal (legal) principles, e.g. the Constitution, the Nuremberg principles, the Declaration of Human Rights, the Constitution of the Soviet Union. Theirs is a fight for *universal values.*

When these values are under attack – and that happens most of the time slowly and gradually – there is a call for resistance. If we compare Dutch protests, the most striking thing is the fight for *particularistic interests.* None of the Dutch protests – with the exception perhaps of the boycott of the nuclear energy tax – have appealed in fact to general interests. The best illustration here is the protest organized by truckdrivers and their employers. They decided to massively demonstrate their unwillingness to accept a new Act, which required all trucks to be outfitted with a tachograph, making it possible to monitor driving time, etc. The Act was intended to increase public safety, by reducing the long driving hours made by many truckdrivers. But it would be difficult to bring such protest activity within a universal value-orientation.

The author has referred to civil disobedience as the weapon of the consistent loser. But in Holland the disobedient groups are relatively powerful pressure groups (students, farmers, retailers). Physicians were listened to as soon as they threatened to resort to so-called 'civil disobedience.' Those who are used to winning most of the time see their first or new loss as a disastrous threat to their social position. On these grounds they claim a justification of disobedience, but the critical question is whether those powerful men do not perhaps end their reasoning a bit prematurely. The reasoning of these groups themselves forms an indicator that no connection can be found with the philosophy of civil disobedience abroad, as developed by Thoreau, Gandhi, King, Rawls, Walzer, Chomsky, Zinn, and others.

The Dutch protests mentioned aimed at policy options, which happened to burden various groups. But the policymakers did not *exceed* the authority given to them – as in many American cases – nor did they violate general interests. The main cause of the trouble between authorities and citizens is to be found in the complexity of public administration in the modern industrial state rather than in the evident violations of the fundamental rules of society's game. It becomes more and more difficult to localize responsibility for decisions. We cannot localize it at all or we can only localize it too late. Direct action and mass disobedience then become a way of fabricating an opportunity to see the responsible authorities for once, to hear or even feel them concretely, with the possibility that they will make mistakes so we can catch them immediately. Hanna Arendt argues that the anonymity and invisibility of authority is one of the main causes of the widespread unrest and disorders. 'In a fully developed bureaucracy there is nobody left with whom one can argue, to whom one can present grievances, on whom the pressures of power can be asserted. Bureaucracy is the form of government in which everybody is deprived of political freedom of the power to act; for the rule by Nobody is not no-rule and where all are equally powerless we have a tyranny without a tyrant.'[7]

The non-responsiveness, hardness of hearing and slackness of structures of authority speeded up the problem of obedience to the law and brought it to our attention on so wide a scale. One could speak here of a 'decline of authority,' but the author prefers to call it a 'decline of autonomy' or a 'decline of citizenship.' Authority bears on an autonomous acceptance of rules and decisions. Authority is not a one-way street. And hence a rise of technocracy without modes of participation and without a more precise and clear structure of responsibility and public liability will lead us further on the way of transformed rule of law toward the almighty 'power-state,' in which power can no longer be fought.

If this is true, civil disobedience in the Netherlands can be interpreted against the background of our structure of authority. To summarize: civil disobedience can be seen as a protest against three forms of governmental action:

(1) as a protest against *illegal* activities of a government (civil rights in USA, warfare in Southeast Asia, against governmental 'disobedience');

(2) as a protest against an *immoral* government, where the activities are formally within the rules and boundaries of the law but violate principles of human dignity (South Africa);

(3) as a protest against a *non-responsive* government.

Acts of civil disobedience in the Netherlands fall primarily into the last category in contrast to most cases abroad. In Holland it is not fundamentally a struggle against gross injustice, but rather a struggle against powerlessness of well-to-do citizens and against the 'minor injustices.' When trying to reach governmental agencies a busy-signal or a disconnected number are often the sole result of our efforts. No answer is given to grievances, complaints, needs, requests.

Although it is a difficult task to compare directly the seriousness of the Dutch acts of civil disobedience and those in the United States, we can put the question whether or not the growing powerlessness, frustration, lack of self-respect, and identity in our small society can be articulated in the same way as Martin Luther King and his followers did: nonviolent action. But those protests do not have to be illegal per se. On the contrary. By many forms of social action one can draw attention to a cause, to special need, or to the growing insecurity about present and future life. Such protest probably will cause conflict with authorities. The way in which authorities react to those self-created conflicts can be decisive for the course the so far legal action will take. An arbitrary, irresponsive and one-sided solution to the conflict will be experienced as unjust by those who created it and this sense of injustice will engender protest.

Abroad (Northern Ireland, USA and South Africa, for example) gross injustice breeds conflict, violence and mass disobedience; in Holland it is just the intemperate reaction to conflict that breeds injustice and hence mass disobedience (e.g. the provo cases).

From this perspective the nonviolent two-sided solution to the occupation of the Enka factory gives some hope. An initially one-sided decision to fire 800 workers, made without notice or participation of the workers, was transformed into conflict resolution by mediation and bargaining. Pressure from below prevented an authoritarian decision from above. Perhaps the Enka factory case shows us how to solve conflict with each other in the complex welfare state. To overcome a permanent inflation of civil disobedience we need more nonviolent conflict strategies and some 'rules of domestic warfare.'

In this essay on civil disobedience in the Netherlands the author has expressed his opinion in only one concrete case. He has refrained from saying 'this was a very strong case and that one was not,' for if the aim of civil disobedience lies in recapturing moral autonomy and personal responsibility for every citizen, then the citizen has to decide him- or herself, where he or she draws the line between obedience and disobedience.

A moral censor – whether or not in the guise of a scientific essay – conflicts with the philosophy of civil disobedience: every citizen is his own expert in civil disobedience and in the moral evaluation of his rights and duties, even when this brings him into conflict with the law.

NOTES AND REFERENCES

1. C. J. M. Schuyt, *Law, Social Order and Civil Disobedience*. Rotterdam University Press, 1975, which gives a description of many American cases.
2. Cf. M. Walzer, 'The obligation to disobey,' in *Obligations*. Harvard University Press, 1972.
3. To go further back in history, see D. Daube, *Civil Disobedience in Antiquity*. Edinburgh University Press, 1972.
4. On the relationship between loyalty and liberty and on the differences between authoritarian and democratic loyalty, see C. Bay, *The Structure of Freedom*.
5. O. Hirschmann, *Exit, Voice and Loyalty*. Harvard University Press, 1972.
6. Cf. P. Selznick, *Law, Society and Industrial Justice*. Russell Sage, 1969, ch. 1.
7. H. Arendt, 'On violence,' in *Crises of the Republic*. Harvest Book p. 178.

Katja Vodopivec

CRIMINOLOGY: ITS MEANING AND CONTENTS - AN ESSAY

WHAT IS CRIMINOLOGY?

Numerous definitions have been given for criminology, however, we shall confine ourselves in the present paper to enumerating the fields criminology has engaged in. Willem H. Nagel emphasizes that the number of these fields has expanded since World War II and includes not merely the etiology of crime, but victimology and the sociology of criminal law as well. ('L'avocat du diable en ce qui concerne "le terrorisme," ' p. 15). Still other subjects could be added to these. Perhaps we could say that originally criminology was concerned with criminality and has long been trying to deal with it without adequate knowledge regarding the fate and feelings of socially stigmatized offenders. Until now we acted on the basis of our perception of people outside ourselves, a reflection of others in us.

It is only since World War II that we have begun to think about ourselves in the role of those responsible for social control, in the role of lawmakers and in the role of possible victims of crime. Is it that we became aware of our own insufficiency in the first field? Probably not.

There is danger in thinking that we know more about others if we know more about ourselves. It is simply easier to understand processes of which we are a part than those that happen outside our own sphere of living and working. Up to now the perceptions of writers from capitalist countries with reference to processes in socialist countries and vice versa (especially insofar as sketchy generalizations about social processes in different capitalist countries are concerned) seem to prove how ungratifying it is to try to understand social processes of which we are not a part.

But in fact is it any easier to understand ourselves and the processes in which we live from a moderate distance? 'If we spoke merely of things we could really understand we would not have much to say. And that would be a pity.' (Gottschalch, quoting Alfred Grosser, p. 137). The conclusion 'I know that I know nothing' is inevitable after having followed the professional path for some time.

CRIMINOLOGY'S AIM

Criminology is theory: it deals with research and generalizations. The criminologist's medium is communication, verbal or written. Usually the communication lacks feedback from the addressee. When the addressee is a socially stigmatized offender, there is one partner less in the game.

So apparently we communicate, mold and teach. On the Continent criminologists teach jurists in particular and perhaps some policemen and institutional employees, i.e. guards and educational staff. Jurists become district attorneys, judges, civil servants, business lawyers, they work in lawmaking bodies, in politics or they become advocates.

Except in the last two cases, therefore, we seem to shape future bureaucrats in the widest sence of the word.* This, no doubt, is a special stratum of social structure with a specific role to play. Law is an instrument of power, and the function of bureaucratic administration in this context is managing and controlling people. These, then, are the addressees of our educative communication.

Bureaucracy works within the framework of the 'mandate as expressed by the members of the social community to their representatives and decides merely about its realization.' (Bučar, p. 555). According to Marx this is 'a closed corporation.' (Marx, p. 82). 'The essential features of the bureaucratic spirit, then, are the adoration of authority and the understanding of the world as an object of manipulation, according to Marx.' (Jacoby, p. 238). As Mitscherlich emphasizes, 'The culturally induced ideologies that people have made for themselves can be divided into those originating from wisdom and those originating from wishes. According to the first Man is loving or destructive while the second postulates his goodness. The first as a principle of organization has not succeeded anywhere in the world, while the second demands obedience and passive adjustment.' (Mitscherlich, pp. 113–114).

Within the bureaucratic system, however, Bučar still expects creativity, especially since ideas concerning social order tend to be general and necessitate many other ideas concerning realization. But the ideas generated by bureaucracy are such as to serve 'direct and mostly short-term needs . . . That is why ideas generated by public administration (administration in general, K.V.'s note) tend to have very relative value.' (Bučar, pp. 555–556).

There is one more quality characteristic of bureaucracy. 'Its specific, and to capitalism welcome, characteristic makes it more welcome the more it dehumanizes itself and the more it succeeds in eliminating all irrational feelings while solving the official problems which it is supposed to solve.' (Jacoby, quoting Max Weber, p. 231).

The more the bureaucratic net spreads out, the less clear it becomes for the ordinary man who should help him. In spite of the fact that bureaucracy would like to do everything for people and instead of them, people nevertheless have the feeling that bureaucracy does nothing and that 'every bureaucrat wants to declare that he is not the competent person.' (Jacoby, p. 242).

By enumerating these characteristics of modern bureaucracy we have tried to present *the first dilemma:* in the future should we try to keep bureaucracy as it is, i.e.

* According to Bučar administration includes the judicial branch, the differentiation between lawmaking, judicial and administrative branches being mainly of historic importance. (Bučar, pp. 236–237).

dependent on the mandate and legal authorizations, or should we try to open its field of work to more creativity and thus risk more discretional power in its hands?

Policy decision making has ever more problems to solve because of: economic growth and the growing power of the State; greater demands for education and higher qualification of people; intervention necessary because of technological innovations (e.g., how to change the qualifications of manpower); greater international economic and political cooperation; increasing social welfare tasks and the necessary coordination of internal controls and leadership. (Jacoby, pp. 290–293). It is probable then, that the increase of bureaucracy is not due entirely to Parkinson's Law, although it also plays a part in the increase.

Can the system of self-management reduce the need for administration? Up to now this has not happened. Decentralization and self-management cause the growth of many more centers of policy decision making. But good policy decision making is possible only on the basis of good and specified information, which has to be prepared by someone. The increased number of decisions (that might be basically similar) results in a greater amount of information and makes it more difficult to oversee the situation. Despite the hope that the system of self-management will have more chance in the future than the system of central planning, it has not been proved up to now that the role of administration would be substantially reduced because of it. It does, of course, free the creative participation of the people, but the problem with which we are concerned is different. It will be possible, perhaps, for the system of self-management to change the nature of administration in the future, since it will be forced to reflect the interest of the people more directly. This, however, is a long-term process and 'it demands long-term changes not merely in social and political relations, but in the culture, knowledge and consciousness of the people as well. A new attitude is necessary toward human nature and society; new relations among people freed from selfishness, isolation and the struggle for existence; freed from exploitation of man or community.' (Džordžević, p. 374).

And so we arrive at *the second dilemma:* while general interests are becoming individual interests bureaucracy should eliminate itself (Marx, p. 83), since the less need there is for bureaucratic intervention the better it is for the rights of an individual. (Bučar, p. 559). But, is it realistic to expect that bureaucracy will eliminate itself, and will the future complicated social and economic relations allow that at all?

Finally, if the bureaucratic machinery provides what the masses want, the danger arises that it will make decisions that will please the masses but will readily turn out to be damaging. On the other hand, there is the danger of opposing people in what they want and doing things really believed to be appropriate.

Therefore, we face a *third dilemma:* should bureaucracy always reflect the wishes of the people (which seems to be especially difficult in the field of the treatment of criminals) or should it lead the people and thus unavoidably 'become paternalistic? From paternalism to dictatorship is only one step.' (Bučar, p. 565).

THE CRIMINOLOGIST IN THE ROLE OF TEACHER

Consciously and unconsciously the criminologist makes his decisions within the framework of these dilemmas. With his work he may resolve them, diminish them, or open and deepen them.

To emphasize the mandate and legal authorizations of bureaucracy means to emphasize rigidity and to defend the *status quo*. To try to diminish their importance may induce higher creativity on the one hand but greater abuse of power on the other hand. In particular, jurists educated in Europe and those who have already experienced the consequences of this abuse and illegality, know very well that the principle of legality is the result of a difficult struggle that went on through most of cultural history. We do not want to lose it.

What rate of success we can expect by telling our addressees to eliminate their own *raison d'être* is impossible to say. But in our field especially, to fight for justice in the administration of justice and for meaningful reaction to deviance means protecting deviants from the half-conscious and primitive vindictiveness of the people, i.e., it is not merely an apology to the existing social system. This, after all, is the origin of the modern administration of justice. We cannot mold the future with measures belonging to the past. (Ancel, p. 10).

If anywhere, then certainly in our field, it is hard to always take public opinion into account. It is possible that we do not know public opinion very well and that we do not differentiate it sufficiently (Jürgen-Malow-Pfuhlman), but research of public opinion in Ljubljana has shown that people expect more convictions than in fact are obtained.

To what are we going to orientate our addressees: to registering and taking into account public opinion or to mandarins' attitudes? The third possibility, perhaps, is communication with public opinion. In this case too, however, the one with the most information, can manipulate others.

While we have shown these dilemmas in their extremes, they are always present in our work. Whatever stand we take, we are always moving between two extremes.

Jacoby follows Pollock and Presthouse in describing three types of people who work within the bureaucratic system. They are: irresponsible, apathetic, incompetent and uninvolved bureaucrats on the one hand; authoritative arrivistes and pragmatic people of position on the other hand. Between these two extremes there is the introvert, sensitive loner with intellectual habits who tends to stand out of line. According to the author this type represents the core of the democratic process, the core that even in autocratic regimes represents an element of democratic rebellion. This type of person partly materializes within the structure, but in part he remains latent as long as the given structure persists, or else he dies off as a frustrated person. (Jacoby, pp. 321–323). Even such a type does not exist at the outset – the teacher helps to form him and is partly responsible for his fate.

As many authors emphasize, the relations within bureaucracy and bureaucracy's attitude toward the rest of society depend on the general social climate. (Jacoby, p. 306; Fromm, p. 267). Some think that basic social changes can be achieved only by radical means, while others believe in the evolutionary change of social consciousness. It seems that most criminologists act on the basis of the latter approach, but not without the participation of others *(supra)*. This is their great responsibility.

REFERENCES

Ancel, M., 'Le jurist devant le criminologue,' *Annales Internationales de Criminologie,* No. 1–2 (1973), pp. 7–11.

Bučar, France, *Uvod v javno upravo.* Ljubljana: Uradni list SRS, 1969.

Džordževič, J., *Pojam, pojavni oblici i suština birokratije i birokratizma i mogućnost njihovog savladanja- Birokratija i tehnokratija.* Vol. II. Belgrade: Sedma sila, 1966, pp. 357–385.

Fromm, Erich, *Anatomie der menschlichen Destruktivität.* Stuttgart: Deutsche Verlags-Anstalt GmbH, 1974.

Gottschalch, Wilfried, *Soziologie der politischen Bildung.* Frankfurt/M: Europäische Verlagsanstalt, 1971.

Herbst, Jürgen, Ursula Malow, Klaus Pfuhlmann, Renate Pfuhlmann and Wolfgang Pook, 'Argumente zu Zielen des Strafvollzugs und zum Model eines Behandlungsvollzuges,' *Monatschrift für Kriminologie und Strafrechtsreform,* 1975, pp. 25–40.

Jacoby, Henry, *Die Bürokratisierung der Welt.* Neuwied and Berlin: Luchterhand Verlag, 1969.

Marx, Karl, *Kritika Heglovega državnega prava – Marx-Engels Izbrana dela.* Vol. I. Ljubljana: Cankarjeva založba, 1969, pp. 57–134.

Mitscherlich, Alexander, 'Aggression und Anpassung in Marcuse,' in Rapoport et al. (eds.), *Aggression und Anpassung in der Industriegesellschaft.* Frankfurt/M.: Suhrkamp Verlag, 1968, pp. 80–127.

Nagel, Willem H., 'L'avocat du diable en ce qui concerne le "terrorisme," ' *Etudes Internationales de Psycho-Sociologie Criminelle,* No. 20–23 (1971), pp. 15–17.

Parkinson, Northcote C., *Parkinsonov zakon ali prizadevanje za napredek.* Mladinska knjiga, 1973.

Selih, Alenka, 'Dojemanje odklonskih projavov,' *Revija za Kriminalistiko in Kriminologijo,* 4 (1974), pp. 302–313.

C. I. Dessaur

TOWARD A MACROSOCIAL CONFLICT MODEL IN CRIMINOLOGY

I. INTRODUCTION

Criminology's predicament in the early seventies shows a striking similarity with that of psychiatry at the turn of the century. At that juncture, psychiatrists in England, France and Germany were seriously attempting to humanize conditions in mental hospitals. This was consistent with their view that hospitalization was the only possible method of treating ailments for whose causes and stages they had little more than labels. Since that time there have been two major developments. Firstly, the two pioneers in the field of psychodynamics, Freud and Jung, sought to develop a terminology covering the domain of psychic reality and to detect, explain and predict the processes occurring in it. Regardless of the differences between their findings and one's own assessment of both, their methods distinguished themselves by the attempt to establish psychological 'laws' for psychological realities. Secondly, the sciences of biochemistry and pharmacology have manifested an explosive development and helped us to control many of the symptoms of mental illness that afflicted our ancestors. In our time, hysterics are subdued, schizophrenics often return to work and anxieties and depressions are not seldom alleviated by drugs.

Criminals, i.e., both those persevering in minor offenses over long periods of time and those guilty of major crimes, find themselves in a situation today very much resembling that of psychiatric patients some seventy years ago. There is a powerful movement all over the world advocating the humanization of prisons or, more generally, the humanization of what is increasingly coming to be known as 'penal treatment.' Nonetheless, penal authorities can do little beyond sending as few individuals as possible for the shortest terms possible to penal institutions that are being run as humanely as possible. They do not really know what made those particular individuals end up there or what is essentially the matter with them (discounting the tautological knowledge that they are 'deviant'). They do not know what good any penal treatment could conceivably do them – in fact they know it generally harms people regardless of whether the treatment in question is 'humanized' or not. They do not know what effect the penal sytem of laws and sanctions and treatments as such has on society as a whole. To put it straightforwardly, their efforts to bring about a reduction of social tension, conflict and disruption are inevitably blind no matter how 'humane.'

Once again, the situation meets with a twofold response. Once again, there are the 'symptom fighters' (the criminological equivalent of psychiatrists working with electroshock therapy and drugs) who look for a behavior therapy that will change the overt behavior of individuals who disturb society's sense of good citizenship. In societies not known for a high degree of ethical sophistication, such as the United States, it may be the behavior of adult male homosexuals that is considered in need of change. In ethically more promising countries, such as the Netherlands or Scandinavia, the only type of behavior that is regarded as calling for reconditioning may be the aggressive or the economically disturbing variety. However this may be, more and more techniques of behavioral and drug therapy seem to be coming our way and these may help the penal establishment accomplish its goals – provided, of course, that it is seriously interested in accomplishing them.

Once again, on the other side of the fence there are those searching for social 'laws' to describe and explain what goes on in social reality when criminality occurs (or when some behavior or other is so labeled and subsequently detected, subjected to prosecution and treated). Their objective is a social description and explanation of social phenomena (or more precisely, a set of interrelated social phenomena). In this category, sociologists of deviance have for a few decades dominated the field. They tend now to be superseded by sociologists who for philosophical, methodological, empirical or practical reasons are becoming impatient with what the 'deviologists' have had to say, despite their appreciation of the humanizing effect that 'deviologist' insights have had on jurists and the general public alike.

The aim of this article is to indicate what is wrong with the use of the sociology of deviance as a basic tool in explaining criminality, what alternative tool or tools might be tried and what kind of research will be called for by the novel approach proposed here, referred to as the macrosocial 'sociology of conflict' approach to criminological phenomena.

II. CRIME AS DEVIANT BEHAVIOR: COMMENTS AND CRITICISM

In a recent attempt at a critical appraisal of the sociology of deviance in the United States Van Zeyl,[1] quoting A. K. Cohen, states that the only truly sociological question that can be asked about deviance is, 'What is it about the structure of social systems that determines the kinds of criminal acts that occur in these systems and the way in which such acts are distributed in the systems?'

His 'critical appraisal' leads to the conclusion that, by and large, theories of deviant behavior have not answered this question.

Manning[2] in a survey essay on five recent books in the field of the sociology of deviance writes (summarizing Lemert) that 'since the early sixties there has been a declining degree of originality and precision in the conceptualization of the central problems of deviance. A political and moral tone suffuses the work which tends to cast us "good guys" in defense of politically weak groups against the "bad guys" . . . sinisterly wielding the establishment's power.'

He also writes that there has been 'an increasing emphasis upon the arbitrary nature of social control processes and definitional and phenomenological matters at the expense of careful investigation of the complexity of the operations of social control, of human interaction, and the constraints upon human action. . . . In sum the central drift has been towards the vulgarization and politicization of ideas, a failure to develop conceptual precision and to construct detailed analyses of the conditions . . . under which a given tenet of labeling theory might hold.'

In the same essay Manning even speaks of 'the exhaustion of the labeling perspective' and concludes that 'the quasi-paradigmatic setting work of Lemert is now in the process of disintegration.'

New frontiers are now to be found, according to this author, in 'Marxism, historical research, policy considerations, phenomenological-existential sociology and sociolinguistics as conceptual preoccupations.'

Similar critical comments (and similar overall indications of what might be the right medicine(s) for the ailments afflicting the sociology of deviance, that all-pervasive and eminently prevailing conceptual model in criminology) are to be found in Taylor, Walton and Young.[3]

Our question here is: what exactly is it that at present leaves some criminologists and sociologists of deviance (the two categories greatly overlap) so dissatisfied with the traditional deviance approach?

This question may be broached in analytic fashion by distinguishing separate levels of criticism and by leaving aside for the moment the relative merits and non-merits of the proposed alternatives.

The three levels of criticism we wish to consider here (with full acknowledgment of their non-existence within clear-cut boundaries in the literature itself) are: (a) criticism at the strictly theoretical level, (b) criticism at the methodological level and (c) criticism at the empirical level.

(a) Theoretical criticism of the conception of criminal behavior in terms of deviant behavior

Like any theoretical model, the 'deviance perspective' is meant to produce a description that both clarifies and simplifies its subject matter, an explanation of it that is hopefully causal and, lastly, the tools for prediction.

There are two principal ways of using the deviance perspective as a descriptive tool. In the words of Van Zeyl,[4] either 'deviance is looked on as an intrinsic characteristic of the deviant, and so it is assumed that the causes of deviance must be located in his (*sic*) own personal background,' or 'it is not the form of deviant acts or the characteristics of deviant individuals which sociologically differentiate deviants from non-deviants. . . . it is the structure and effectiveness of the concrete processes of social control which serve to define social actions as deviant.'

In both instances, as well as in attempts at eclectic combinations of them certain philosophical (anthropological) suppositions are implied.

Invisibly underlying what we shall here term the static 'attribute' conception of deviance (cherished by older, biologically oriented criminologists as well as by psychologists and psychopathologists, by the adepts of sociological 'learning' theories such as the differential association theory and its offshoots, and by adherents of classic anomie theory and the notions that stem from it) is a conception of humans as determined by their biological and/or psychological constitution(s), their social experiences and, occasionally, the interaction of these. The hidden assumption is that if we knew which factors (be it at the biological, the psychological or the social level) determine which behavior, we might be able to manipulate (the impact of) such factors and where necessary control behavior.

'Attribute' thinking within the deviance perspective purports to offer a causal explanation at the ontological level in terms of concrete factors from genes and enzymes to social influences. Whether its practitioners know it or not, the underlying philosophy is a naturalistic, more or less mechanistic, deterministic conception of humans who are seen in every instance as a network of 'factors.' The critical question then becomes: who or what is being influenced by these factors or, conversely, if a human is no more than their sum total, who or what 'combination of ontological factors' produces this insight?

The dynamic 'interaction' conception of deviance tells us that the significance of deviant acts or the manner in which a person interprets her- or himself and her/his acts is determined by social processes. However, the causal explanation here is not at the ontological but at the psychological level. It is not persons or acts but their interpretation, the 'significance' given to them (first by others and then, by dint of internalization, by ourselves), that causes behavior to turn deviant.

It is easy to see how, in this perspective, the sociology of deviance may be combined with the still more basic concepts of symbolic interactionism, of the role-self 'theory' and of phenomenology or its American counterpart, ethnomethodology.

Here, the underlying philosophical assumptions are harder to unravel. They amount perhaps to a 'model' of humans that stresses their creativity in constructing reality. But that is not all. Equally hidden from view, but equally present in my judgment, is the old-fashioned, nineteenth century philosophical idealism which negates any reality outside the human conception of it. If the majority of humankind had agreed that Hitler's behavior was both clever and good, if we had given this 'meaning' to his behavior for one reason or another, then there would be no criterion whatsoever for objecting to it.

A further problem is that we do not know at what level the really important 'meanings' are doled out: is it that of our statements, that of the majority or of the power establishment or, again, is it the level of our deepest convictions? Is Mao's China very good because all the people of China are compelled, by means physical or psychological or both, to profess that it is very good and to behave accordingly?

Neither underlying model of humans and of reality in the sociology of deviance is a very satisfying or convincing one. Perhaps much of the present general dissatisfaction and search for alternatives stems from a vague and only partly conscious inkling that this is so.

(b) Methodological criticism of the conception of criminal behavior in terms of deviant behavior

The basic concept in the sociology of deviance may be interpreted as either an attribute or a process in the relevant literature, as was mentioned above. However, if deviance is conceived as an attribute, either of a person or of an act, operational procedures are needed for deciding whether or not this concept can be applied in a given empirical situation. It is at this point precisely that tautological reasoning in nearly all theoretical criminological literature takes over. People, or acts, are deviant because they are designated by law and/or morals as contravening dominant values for a given setting. And we decide that the behavior of people who commit such acts is explained by their being deviant.

This propensity for tautological reasoning (which may occur in any science) was noted as early as 1959 by Wootton[5]: 'For to say that a persistently anti-social person behaves as he does because he is a psychopath, when psychopathy is defined as persistently anti-social behavior, is indeed on the same level as saying that what puts people to sleep puts people to sleep, or that the room is cold because the temperature is low.'[6]

One has only to substitute the currently fashionable concept of 'deviance' for the then fashionable concept of 'psychopathy' to see that analogous criticism holds.

It may have been from a more or less instinctive horror of this uncanny way of reasoning that the labeling theorists within the sociology of deviance stressed the nature of deviance as a process instead of an attribute. The label of deviance, when succesfully imposed, is internalized by the person whose acts are so labeled. This internalization then leads to behavioral consequences and further societal reactions. This interaction process is what most of modern theoretical criminology is about.

However, the basic question remains: 'What makes Sammy run?' What is the starting point, the initial stimulus for this complex and cumulative interaction process? And what makes it stop if it does stop, and under what boundary conditions?

If we cannot answer these questions (and we cannot), we find ourselves driven to the kind of answers that biologists tend to give about evolution. It is all a matter of chance that things come into being and once they are there the very fact of their existence proves that the haphazard combination of 'factors' they happen to embody has had the highest survival value.

Even if we accept this kind of reasoning, it remains to be seen what should be taken as the social equivalent for the biological concept of survival of the species. One encounters all sorts of contradictions when one thinks of the labeling of acts and/or people as deviant and the internalization of this labeling in terms of 'social survival.'

Further methodological criticism concerns the fact that if one uses a concept like deviance it should lead to the possibility of somehow or other scaling behavior on a deviance scale, in order to make empirical investigation meaningful. How much deviance from what leads to how much or what kind of societal reaction? These questions are never answered, except by very general (and again tautological) notions like Lemert's 'tolerance quotient.' People or acts are seriously and persistently labeled as deviant because the 'tolerance quotient' (the term 'threshold' or even 'limit' would have been less mathematically revolting here) of society has been exceeded. And acts or people are deviant because they are beyond the critical value of this 'quotient.'

In short, from a methodological point of view the concept of deviance is either senseless (inasmuch as it lacks any and all explanatory power) or unfounded. And in either case it is unfit for meaningful empirical research.

(c) Empirical criticism of the conception of criminal behavior in terms of deviant behavior

From a practical point of view one might defend the notion that concepts and theories which cannot stand the test of theoretical and methodological analysis but which happen to 'work' are useful in the absence of superior options. But even from this pragmatic point of view – all right, so there's a crime problem and we're paid to solve it – little can be said in favor of the sociology of deviance.

A recent publication by Springer[7] contains a secondary analysis of empirical tests applied to current criminological theories. (These are, for all practical purposes, identical with deviance theories.) Springer's analysis concerns reports of hypothesis-testing research material published in the *American Sociological Review* from 1948 through 1969. The results he obtained are distressing. With the possible exception of Merton's 'innovation' hypothesis, attempts at empirical corroboration of common criminological theorizing have not, in the main, yielded any promising results.

Neither Sutherland's theory (even when conceptually refined), nor Cloward and Ohlin's hypothesis, nor A. K. Cohen's or W. B. Miller's suggestions concerning the relationship between subculture and criminal behavior has so far proven capable of satisfactory operationalization and corroboration in the research samples studied. The same goes for the hypotheses derivable from the concepts of 'neutralization techniques' (Sykes and Matza), of Yablonsky's 'near-group' and Becker's 'definition of the situation.' This is not the place to go deeply into technical details about the methods used (both by Springer and those research workers whose results he sampled and analyzed). Suffice it to say that both Springer's remarkable secondary analysis and incidental attempts at testing some part or other of our dominant 'theories' give little cause for optimism about the applicability and usefulness of our current way of thinking about criminal behavior.

III. IS CRIME AND ITS PROCESSING A MACROSOCIAL CONFLICT?

Since the beginning of the twentieth century criminologists, and in their footsteps members of the penal system and laymen, have learned to think of the explanation of criminal behavior and its processing in terms of various attributes of the people labeled criminals.

The explanatory answer given by an older and more speculative generation by evaluating the moral consciousness of the criminal, was changed by Lombroso and his followers to an evolutionary biological one.

Then came the era dominated (at least on the Continent) by Freud and the other psychopathologists, explaining our object of study by means of the attributes of the criminal's (subconscious) psyche.

After World War II, a development that had long been going on in the United States swept over to European criminology. Explanatory variables now were sought no longer 'inside' the criminal, but primarily in her or his surroundings. Influences from the criminal's social and cultural environment or her/his interaction with significant others were considered of primary importance in explaining the genesis and epidemiology of crime, its persistence and its cure.

Regardless of conceptual, theoretical or methodological weaknesses of any of the explanatory models indicated so far, it is evident that in principle one may expect more or less interesting answers from any of them. Or maybe one should turn this statement around.

In scientific enterprise, the heuristic reality is that answers (be it tentative answers) must be present before any attempt at data collection for the construction and testing of hypotheses can start. The 'narrow inductivist conception' of scientific inquiry (by which it is supposed that an unbiased collection of data as such can lead to meaningful insights) has been convincingly proved to be fallacious by Hempel and others.[8]

In the words of Hempel: '... what particular sorts of data it is reasonable to collect is not determined by the problem under study, but by a tentative answer to it that the investigator entertains in the form of a conjecture...'[9]

Thus, the very search for biological, psychological or social attributes of a certain type among persons labeled criminals, implies that one entertains a tentative answer to the 'riddle of crime,' which directs the research (be it clinical or social, empirical or logical) and restricts the range of possible outcomes.

From methodological considerations it also follows that it is hard to claim on behalf of any conceptual scheme for approaching the crime phenomenon that it is nearer to 'the truth' than some other approach.

Modern empirico-theoretical science is essentially 'instrumental' and pragmatic: the most powerful model, giving the most useful explanations and (hopefully) predictions, is to be preferred, according to our scientific ethos. 'Truth' assumptions, however, are seldom made, at least not in scientifically sophisticated quarters. (Whether we should or shall always be content with modern instrumentalism – a reaction toward older essentialism – is another matter, not to be discussed here).

Just as there can be no fundamental objections to considering crime to be a biologically or psychologically or microsociologically explainable phenomenon (regardless of the severe criticism that one may have of some of the concrete applications of these general approaches), there can also be no sound objection against an attempt at describing and explaining crime and its processing in macrosocial terms and specifically in terms of macrosocial conflict.

The right question in present-day science is not: *is* crime a macrosocial conflict, but is it 'worthwhile' (in terms of theory-formation, of operationability, of applicability) to define our object of study in this way?

This leads us to the next question: what are definitions and in what way are we going to define crime and its processing as a macrosocial conflict?

IV. ON DEFINITIONS

The overall aim of empirico-theoretical science is the demonstration of logical relationships between statements. For these statements we have to make use of terms which may not have empirical indicators (e.g. logical terms have no empirical indicators).

In order to achieve an unambiguous, constant and clear use of terms, it is usual to define them. Definitions are generally of the type in which one term (the *definiendum*) is described with the help of other (supposedly already well-known) terms (the *definiens*). One may again try to define the latter, but in the end there will be a final set of so-called 'primitive terms' which cannot be defined, unless one admits still another set of primitives.

Definitions are usually classified as either verbal or nonverbal (and then further subdivided) and, of course, as admissible or inadmissible. (Among the latter are persuasive definitions, which try to put the *definiendum* in an advantageous or disreputable light.)

For our purpose it is important to realize that whereas there exist definitions which are truth-functional (of which it may meaningfully be said that they are either true or not true), there are also definitions about which no truth-statement can meaningfully be made.

A very simple example of the non truth-functional type of definition is the kind of definition in which a kind of name is stipulated, e.g.:

$$\text{'a} \times \text{a'} = \text{'the square of a' (def.)}$$

More complex examples of stipulative definitions are those which define the *definiendum* (say 'conflict') by means of a set of logically interrelated statements, for instance a set of statements describing a mathematical model. It is in this latter way that a definition of 'conflict' for the purpose of criminological theory-formation may be attempted by means of, say, a Markov Chain Model.[10]

From a mathematical point of view then one may say that the model is a formal, abstract representation of crime as a macrosocial process (although one might interpret the model as many other things as well). From a methodological point of view one might stipulate the model as a definition of crime as a macrosocial conflict.

This procedure, though technically legitimate and probably profitable, may be psychologically unsatisfying for many people in several respects. Therefore, in the next few paragraphs a more substantial motivation for interpreting crime as a macrosocial conflict will be given. If this substantial argumentation is convincing, the preference for one formal model or another (for one stipulative definition or another) will become a matter of mere research tactics. (The question whether and how a strictly nonverbal, operational definition might have been chosen which, in contrast to a stipulative definition, may become truth-functional, will not be discussed in the present context.)

V. ON DEFINITIONS. A TAXONOMY AND A TYPOLOGY OF CONFLICT

Crime is a macrosocial phenomenon generally involving three parties: the person(s) whose behavior has been labeled criminal (and who will be detected, prosecuted, judged and 'treated' as such); the penal establishment, as a specialized department of the government; and the general public. The last is involved in crime in three ways: as the potential victim of crime, as the delegator of power to the penal establishment, and as interactor with individuals who have once been labeled criminal.

It would be fruitless to go into any discussion concerning the genesis of crime in a historical sense. Whether the labeling of behavior as 'criminal' resulted from a need to categorize undesirable social behavior rather than a tendency to categorize social behavior as such depends on the type of crime under consideration. There possibly exist, in addition to types of behavior that normally elicit penal responses (murder, rape), types of legislation that themselves produce 'crime.' The boundary between these two categories will be drawn according to one's value system. To return to a previous example: in the opinion of the American legislator, the scandalous immorality of homosexuality between consenting adult males should be formally recognized as crime. From another point of view, an arbitrary selection from all possible statistically deviant behaviors was in this case made into crime by the legislator.

Once there is a set of behavior that has been legally designated as crime in a given spatiotemporal setting, it seems wiser just to note that a structural value conflict exists between such and such behavior and the penal reaction to it. The Dutch conflict sociologist Valkenburgh[11] recently expressed the same opinion about structural conflicts in general. It is useless to look for the genesis of conflicts that are structurally present in a given social system, he says. It is, however, meaningful to investigate their development and solution.

Partly for logical and methodological reasons, partly because of the distressing results of all former attempts at a genetic approach toward criminality, we, too, shall restrict ourselves here to an approach toward crime as a macrosocial conflict which focuses on conflict development (escalation, stabilization or de-escalation) and conflict resolution. Another aspect of criminological theorizing, viz. explanations and predictions concerning the distribution of these conflicts and of their stages of development, will also be left out of consideration at this stage. Our primary task here will be to define crime as a specific form of macrosocial conflict and to compare it with other macrosocial conflicts to see whether our model is tenable.

(a) On definitions of conflicts

Definitions of conflict may be concrete or abstract, static or dynamic, explanatory, teleological or purely descriptive and, of course, macrosociologically relevant or not. They may also be evaluative or neutral.

In the literature I found that some authors have a tendency to confuse conflict with power. The Dutch author De Moor,[12] for example, writes: 'Conflicts in a sociological sense are those acts which are aimed at forcing certain authority figures to serve alien goals or to accept alien values to a greater extent than they did before and notwithstanding their resistance.' (My English paraphrase – C.I.D.)

A similar identification of conflict and power is to be found even in Weber[13]: '*Conflict* is to be termed a form of social interaction to the extent that the action involved is geared toward the goal of making one's own will prevail against the resistance of the other party.' (My translation – C.I.D.)

Analytically, it seems more sophisticated to make a distinction between conflict and power. Conflict is often an interaction process *about* power, against power or for the purpose of gaining power (i.e., being in a position to make decisions for other individuals or groups, without regard to their consent). But it is more enlightening perhaps to distinguish conflict as such from what is often (but not necessarily always) its aim.

Dahrendorf is one of the authors who, while rejecting negative evaluations of conflict, have given a positive evaluation instead, but not a definition in the technical sense.[14]

Krysmanski,[15] citing Coser, gives a typology of conflicts plus a (positive) evaluation of them:

> 'Social conflict can be defined as a struggle for *values* or *status claims*, for *power* and *scarce resources*. In this struggle the aims of the contending parties are not only the coveted values but also the neutralization, harming or putting out of the way of their rivals.
>
> Such conflicts may occur between individuals, between groups or between individuals and groups. Inter- and intra-group conflicts are permanent hallmarks of social life.
>
> Conflict is an important element of social interaction. Far from always being a 'negative' factor that disrupts, social conflict may contribute in many ways to the perpetuation of groups as well as to the strengthening of interpersonal relationships.' (My translation–C.I.D.)

Veblen[16] gives a causal explanation of conflict in his 'definition' of it: 'Any social system implies an allocation of power, as well as wealth and status position among individual actors and component subgroups. Conflict ensues in the effort of various frustrated groups and individuals to increase their share of gratifications. Their demand will encounter the resistance of those who previously had established a "vested interest" in a given form of distribution of honor, wealth and power.'

Bernhard[17] is one of a few authors to prepare the ground for a real definition:

'Sociologically speaking, conflict exists between groups *when there is a fundamental incompatibility in their values, goals, interests etc., so that if one group gets what it wants, the other group cannot get what it wants.*' (Italics mine – C.I.D.)

Conflict so conceived can exist independently of the subjective reactions of members of the groups. The members of the groups in conflict may and in fact often do need affection and feel affection for one another as in the case of the conflict between the sexes or generations. Nor is hostility a necessary concomitant of conflict, viewed sociologically.

Conflict in this sociological sense should be distinguished from misunderstanding: in a misunderstanding groups may feel that a conflict exists when in fact none does. Nor should conflict be confused with aggression. Aggression may occur where there is no conflict and conflict may occur without aggression.

It is not, in fact, always possible to determine whether a conflict actually exists, that is whether the goals, values, interests etc. of two groups are actually incompatible.

One of the best, be it also the most abstract, definitions of conflict has been given by Boulding[18], who claims that his definition satisfies dynamic as well as static models: 'Conflict may be defined as a situation of competition in which the parties are *aware* of the incompatibility of potential future positions and in which each party *wishes* to occupy a position that is incompatible with the wishes of the other.' (Italics mine – C.I.D.)

We note Boulding's insistence that conflicts do not exist unless the parties involved are conscious of them. We shall see below whether this view is economical and realistic.

Boulding distinguishes two general models for any system: the static and the dynamic. For both the static and the dynamic model of conflict there is the following framework of concepts:

> *The party.* A conflict is a situation that involves at least two parties. A party is a *behavior unit*, that is some aggregate or organization that is capable of assuming a number of different positions while retaining a common identity or boundary.
>
> *Behavior space.* The position of a behavior unit at a moment of time is defined by a set of values of a set of variables that defines the behavior unit; all possible future positions of the behavior unit are what we mean by its behavior space.
>
> *Competition.* Competition in the broadest sense exists when any potential positions of the two behavior units are mutually incompatible.

In my view one of the most important definitional stipulations should be that sociological conflict is not about material or social objects (say money or status-derived privileges) but about values attributed to any desirable goal, whether material or immaterial.

What happens at the sociological level when two 'parties' are in 'competition' about 'future positions' is that essentially these values are allocated in a given social setting. The allocation of values is the central point of issue.

If we admit material objects in our definition of the subject matter of conflict, it will in the long run prove hard to distinguish conflict from hostility and aggression which are, in fact, mere instrumental means in the conflict.

If we admit 'concrete' social objects (such as social privileges that go with certain social positions), we will soon find ourselves slipping back to the psychological level of explanation where ambition, desire and the like are important explanatory concepts. Only by sticking rigorously to a definition of the subject matter of sociological conflict in terms of the allocation of values can we remain at the sociocultural level of explanation which is our own.

Boulding's insistence that conflict properly so called is necessarily conscious conflict strikes the present author as an uncalled-for submission on the part of sociology to current psychology (the same goes, by the way, for a trendly, allegedly sociological concept such as 'internalization').

There may, for instance, be two or more mutually incompatible sets of values that a party adheres to without being 'conscious' of this fact and without being conscious of why and when it lets one or the other set determine its behavior. In such a case one might, by analogy, speak of a 'social neurosis' – assuming that a competent onlooker were able to decide that the party in question is thwarting its own alleged goals.

In the case of criminology, Boulding's 'parties' are the criminal(s), the penal establishment and the general public – the last in the threefold position of potential victim, delegator of power and social reactor.

The competition is about the allocation (or distribution) of values. If, for the sake of simplicity, we restrict ourselves here to the conflict between the penal establishment on the one hand and criminals on the other, it becomes clear that there are two basically different (though in practice not easily distinguishable) situations. Either both criminals and the penal establishment adhere to the same set of values but are at odds about the definition of the situation in which they should be applied, (Nearly all ordinary offenders are against robbing, stealing, murdering, rape. But banks, shops, rich people and such 'can spare the money' or 'have stolen it themselves' and this, so the argument runs, gives one the right to take it back. Attractive women are not human beings, but sexual organs plus frills created by a male god to give pleasure to those created in his image, and so forth.) or there is a real clash of values as in the case of 'political' offenses, where the value of property or of certain power distributions may be denied and completely new sets of values substituted for them.

We shall ignore these subtleties for the moment and concentrate in the most general way on the value conflict between the penal establishment and criminals as opposing parties. What lies at the basis of their conflict?

(b) A taxonomy and a typology of conflicts

Before we go deeper into the characteristics of the parties involved and the conflict aspect of their interaction, it is important to remember a taxonomy of conflicts by Rapoport[19] which, combined with his well-known conflict typology (*fights*, *games-debates*), gives some elucidating results.

Rapoport's taxonomy makes a distinction between endogenous and exogenous conflicts, symmetric and asymmetric conflicts, issue-oriented and structure-oriented conflicts: *Endogenous* conflicts are, roughly, conflicts between parties for which a larger system exists that may control or resolve the conflict between them. (*Example:* a civil law type of conflict between two citizens, with the State, and specifically its judicial system, as conflict manager.) *Exogenous* conflicts are conflicts for which such a supersystem is lacking. *Symmetric* conflicts are conflicts in which the parties are roughly similar systems. In *asymmetric* conflicts the parties may be widely disparate or perceive each other in different ways. Rapoport gives as an example of an asymmetric conflict a revolt or revolution. 'An *issue-oriented* conflict is resolved when the issue is settled.' 'A *structure-oriented* conflict is not resolved unless the structure of either system or of the supersystem changes.'

Rapoport adds, as a warning for overeager critics, that his 'taxonomy, like most, is no more than a formalization of idealized conception. In nature there are no pure types separated by sharp boundaries . . . .'

So far, we may conclude that the kind of conflicts that we have in mind here as an object of study for criminology are exogenous (penal law is a matter between the State and the citizen, both in principle, from a theoretical judicial point of view, and in practice since the feelings, wishes and interests of victims are, as a rule, hardly taken into account, except insofar as they may help to construct a formal judicial proof). We may further conclude that they are evidently asymmetric and that they are structure-oriented conflicts in Rapoport's terminology. If a person found guilty of a crime repents after the crime and tries to make amends for it, that does not necessarily end the State's interest in prosecuting, sentencing and sanctioning her or him. Given the pluriformity of stated goals of the penal system, a criminal's manifest 'resocialization' might be taken into account in administering the sanction, but it would hardly protect her or him against being sanctioned. What the State really is after is a matter still to be discussed, but it will not be a simple issue (like restitution of damage) in cases that fall under penal law.

As for the *fights-games-debates* typology, this is a trichotomy that would roughly correspond to Freud's well-known Id-Ego-Superego tripartition of the human psyche. Fights, says Rapoport, stem from irrational (or arational) impulses, of an 'instinctual' type: '. . . actions are for the most part reactions to stimuli provided by "the enemy" and are seldom, if ever, modified by learning.'

A game, on the other hand, 'is characterized by an analysis of the *situation* and of *other situations* foreseen as outcomes of *decisions*, both one's own and those of an opponent.'

A debate is 'a conflict of ideas.' The objective of this type of conflict is '*converting* the opponent to one's own way of perceiving or evaluating the enivronment.'

Again, there are no sharp boundaries in empirical reality. Yet, one may contend that regardless of some highly ritualized aspects of crime processing and regardless of gamelike elements in the interaction between the police and the criminal or the public prosecutor and the criminal (consider the American practice of 'plea bargaining' in this respect), crime and its processing by the State, if defined as a macrosocial conflict, shows mainly the characteristics of fights and/or debates.

The compulsive criminal (if she or he exists) and the compulsively sanctioning State (for all practical purposes neglecting information from empirical social scientists about (*a*) the criminogenic function of jails and prisons and (*b*) much more effective measures for crime reduction than a sanctioning system) are engaged in an irrational fight.

The political criminal, but also the common criminal in some respects, is engaged in a debate. The State, defending its stated values, norms and interests, is moreover trying to convert the apprehended criminal (and all who might be tempted to follow her or his example) into a citizen in its image and likeness.

In summary: either a fight or a debate (or aspects of both) is manifest in the exogenous, asymmetric, structure-oriented conflict under discussion in criminology.

The next question then is: what is this conflict about? A Marxist would certainly answer: class interests. This, in fact, is the answer that has also implicity been given by those criminologists who primarily stress the attribute 'membership in the lower class' as one of the main explanatory variables for crime. (Being relatively young and, above all, being *male* are such overpoweringly evident attributes of most criminals that they are seldom explicitly mentioned, much less used in theory-formation. As happens in so many fields of life, the by far most evident things are often overlooked).

Another answer to this question might be: the exogenous, asymmetric, structure-oriented fight and/or debate that is the subject matter of criminology (in its aspect of a fundamental, macrosociological science) is about *values* allocated by the parties involved. We shall define 'value' as: 'a general principle which provides people with a standard for making judgments about specific acts and goals.' This implies, in the case of criminal acts, that the actor either essentially adheres to the same set of values as those 'defended' by the penal law, but that she or he is defining the situation differently (or allocating values differently) from what is expected by penal law (*Example:* 'it is all right to steal from big corporations, who have themselves stolen money'), or – as in the case of 'political' crime – that different standards for behavior have been adapted (*Example:* some of the crimes committed by the Weathermen; by people from the hippie culture, and such).

VI. THE CONFLICT PROCESS

Much preliminary work on the development of sociological conflict approach in criminology has been done by Turk.[20] After separating the 'deviance-pathology' approach from the 'social conflict political' approach (an important enterprise in these fuzzy and eclectic times) and emphasizing once more (but never too often) that being labeled a criminal is 'a category of *status* rather than of *behavior*,' Turk goes on to formulate a set of propositions for a theory of criminalization. His theory, however, concentrates on a distinction between what he calls social norms and cultural norms, between high status parties and low status parties as participants in the conflict process (on both sides), and between, in his terms, realistic moves versus unrealistic moves in the conflict.

Our approach will have a slightly different slant, since what we are first and foremost interested in is not so much the strategies of the parties but (*a*) whether crime and its processing can be fruitfully represented by a conflict model and (*b*) if so, whether the process of the conflict approximates an optimal path (as defined by the model).

However, the conflict process is to be considered as a function of the interaction of the parties. So if, as one may expect from our present knowledge, the conflict process shows considerable deviation from this optimal path, this will be interpreted by us as inadequate behavior of one or both parties involved.

Since we are dealing here with an asymmetric conflict in which one of the parties, viz. the State, is the more important determinant of the actual process, almost all deviations from the optimum can be ascribed to this party.

In practice this will result in the hypothesis that the way in which the crime conflict is solved will not be optimal, due to 'irrational' behavior of the penal establishment.

If crime and its processing can in general be defined as a macrosocial conflict about the allocation of values, one then wonders what the distinguishing characteristics of this value conflict are. If a normal model is developed that can represent ('define') any type of macrosocial conflict (as has e.g. been attempted by Zwanenburg and Moor[21]), can one then predict where significant differences in the conflict resolution process will occur? This has to be determined empirically of course.

For both theoretical and technical reasons, it seems unfeasible to try and compare, say, 'crime' as one overall category with just any other macrosocial conflict, say from the field of labor conflicts. As all criminologists know, there does not exist any unified category of behavior which is 'crime,' nor does there exist a uniform approach toward the reduction of several types of criminalized behavior.

What we propose to do is to compare two kinds of criminal behavior, which are clearly being treated differently by the State. Therefore, two types of 'economic' crime have been chosen: tax law violations versus common theft and embezzlement. Both types of behavior have in common the fact that they score in the same way on Rapoport's taxonomy and typology. Our prediction is that the reaction of the penal establishment and the overall way the tax law conflict is being handled is closer to the rational optimum that the conflict management in the case of common theft and embezzlement.

By approaching the problem of crime and delinquency in the way just outlined, there is the methodological advantage of a truly macrosocial conflict model for criminology that: (1) is explicit about its inevitable philosophical basic assumption: this it has in common with symbolic interactionism in its more refined forms; (2) is capable of being mathematically formalized and tested: this it has in common with the applied systems approach; (3) regards crime not as an 'attribute' of one party (the individuals labeled criminals) but as a matter of (primarily macrosocial) interaction, and specifically as a matter of value conflict between several parties, among them the penal establishment, the public at large and the individuals labeled criminals: this it has in common with the Neo-Marxist approach.

It distinguishes itself from the symbolic interactionist approach by turning, after philosophical explicitness has been achieved, to mathematical models for its formalization and for the testing of its hypotheses.

It distinguishes itself from the applied systems appoach by its interest in criminology as a fundamental empirico-theoretical science, viz. a branch of general sociology.

It distinguishes itself from the Marxist approach by its elimination of any ideology dictating desirable results. Also it rejects the muddled methods (research as social action) that characterize some Neo-Marxist criminological activities.

VII. EPILOGUE: A PERSONAL COMMENT

One of the main heuristic elements, leading to the approach sketched above, has been the following consideration: The State (in the sense of the government of a macropolitical unity) has a twofold function toward its subjects. On the one hand it is 'Mother State,' protecting and taking care of her citizen children the best she can, in their own interest and often against their ill-considered, impulsive judgments. On the other, it is 'Father State,' repressing and threatening his citizen children and wanting to make decisions for them, by virtue of his metaphysical right to power. Under both aspects the State strives toward ends that are opposed to the self-realization that is the goal of autonomous human beings.

The tension between the State and its citizens essentially concerns the control of behavior. Citizens unable to cope with themselves, with each other and with their wider common interests, delegate power (the right to decide for them, if need be against their momentary wishes) to an external institution which of course soon starts to lead a life of its own and to serve its own interests. At the same time citizens may come to resent the externalized power over their behavior (they did not really delegate this power as individuals in their own right) and oppose its values and decisions.

Stripped to its psychological origins, the State is to be understood as the answer to the human need for externalized discretionary power – and it does in fact so function. If people live under a dictatorship, they may have to accept that functioning of the State. If they live under a 'democratic' male government, they may feel they have opted for this state of affairs. In either case, however, the State represents externalized discretionary power.

Once the State has come into existence and accomplished its cancerous proliferations (as it has done in both East and West) what universally characterizes it is the absence of any recognition on its part of evil as something to be perceived, conquered and transformed. We are all agreed that all of us are extremely good people (the state bureaucracy included, of course) and that the task of the State is to take care of the misfortunes that come about through lack of intelligence, unfortunate social conditions or unfavorable influences upon citizens. Instead of helping us to cope with evil (in ourselves and each other), the State helps us repress it by negating its very existence and becomes our most powerful ally in our belief that all is for the best in this best of all possible worlds – disregarding for the moment a few technological problems whose solution is a matter of time, and some non-humans in a far-off country that serve as a most welcome scapegoat image of wickedness. (In former times the scapegoat function was fulfilled by criminals and lunatics in our immediate environment. But thanks to scientific progress, nowadays everybody knows that those people, too, are beyond good and evil in that they are the victims of circumstance, biological, sociological or otherwise. It is highly characteristic of modern criminology as well that any discussion of evil is taboo except in the form of a very unspecific, hesitant projection of evil onto the power-wielding establishment.)

The State has become our ally in the repression of evil. It has thereby become an evil force in its own right, though it is seldom recognized as such except by a few scattered youth groups and political minimovements. ('Den Teufel spürt das Völkchen nie, Und wenn er sie beim Kragen hätte.' – *Faust.* English translation: People never spot the devil even when he has them by the collar.)

We see at present in Western countries as well as elsewhere, States trying to get as much grip as they can on every last detail of their citizens' lives: data banks, income taxes of up to 71%, bureaucratized rents carefully geared to one's income for standardized housing; absolute State control over schools and universities; control over artists through an elaborate system of subsidies; control over subsidized newspapers, subsidized social work, subsidized farmers and subsidized churches and even, or so one may expect in the near future, control over subsidized political parties. Once this last development has come about, the State will have become a self-feeding moloch. First it breaks all natural market mechanisms by its system of taxes and legal controls. Then it comes to the rescue as Mother State and next, in the guise of Father, it erects its ultimate barriers against individual autonomy.

Insofar as the average offender is concerned, the State is indeed confronted with individuals who for one reason or another have been unable to act autonomously. Its natural task would therefore be to restore them to an autonomous way of life in which they can fend for themselves. However, the realization of this goal – which the penal system claims as its own – is thwarted by each and every measure that same system takes (from legal proceedings to imprisonment and 'therapy' in a penal setting).

What prevents the penal system from functioning effectively (apart from insufficient scientific knowledge and ordinary common sense as well as inadequate insight into the desirability of individual autonomy) is its very insistence upon self-perpetuation as a non-vital and thus essentially superfluous segment of society.

We must, however, come to grips with what is meant by the reality of evil mentioned earlier. Our definition of it is as follows: evil is whatever, in terms of attitude or conduct, springs from a consciousness that refuses to – or claims it cannot –

accept responsibility for one's own behavior or for one's response to that of others. Stealing and robbing may be evil because the individuals committing such acts do not fully grasp the consequences of their behavior for others. The fact is that most of the acts that most of us commit most of the time are evil in the sense of being 'unconscious.' This is what Christianity originally meant by sin (a highly transmuted concept) and what spiritually inclined individuals seek to overcome by heightening their moral awareness.

The penal establishment selects a minute portion of all evil acts for 'processing' by the males in power. Since the penal establishment itself belongs to the State (that institution *par excellence* for alienating humans from themselves) it can hardly be expected to heighten the consciousness, and thus enhance the moral autonomy, of those individuals (predominantly young, lower class males) whose behavior it seeks to control. Further, if the penal establishment were conscious of what it is and does, it would strive primarily to reduce itself to minimum size and eventually to transform itself into something more conducive to the evolution of humankind. In the existing state of affairs such a transformation is unthinkable. What we witness instead is a penal establishment paying lip service to its professed goal (one among several) of restoring the autonomy of those individuals whose behavior it controls for just that purpose, but striving in fact for the perpetuation of its own alienated and alienating existence.

It is no accident, by the way, that nearly all of the members of the penal establishment as well as of the individuals whose behavior it seeks to control are of the male sex. Women in our culture are, in the dominant male image of them, the very symbol of unconsciousness (and thus of evil, with all its ambivalent magic). But neither does their behavior require control by such partial measures as the penal system can provide.

VIII. CONCLUSION

For theoretical and methodological as well as empirical reasons the sociology of deviance in either of its two main forms is a poor basis for criminology. The present tendency to combine the deviance model with conflict thinking, as in Denisoff and McCaghy,[22] does not alter this fact one bit. By being told that deviance is a consequence of (macrosocial) conflict, one's insight into what criminological conflict is about, what makes it a specific type of macrosocial conflict or what makes deviance models undesirable as a frame of reference for further research is not improved in the least. The tendency to combine a fundamentally weak deviance approach with a very unspecific conflict approach (full of political and trendy overtones) can hardly be considered a step forward in our thinking and research concerning phenomena at the sociocultural level.

As a basis for an explicit conflict model (capable of formalization and operationalization) and for specific hypotheses to be derived from them, some philosophical, metaphysical or 'phenomenological' thinking, or whatever one wishes to call it, has been done. At the roots of any 'hard' scientific model and procedure there is always some philosophical or other thinking and it is best to make this very explicit. It is at this level that the real heuristic processes take place. It is also at this level that the 'ultimate' explanations are given.

The philosophical considerations here presented concerning the State as externalized discretionary power, as our ally in the negation of evil and thus, in the last analysis, as an evil force in its own right, has in part been done before (cf. for instance, Nagel).[23] Superficially similar reasoning often amounts to no more than the observation that the members of the State establishment behave 'immorally;' this, however, is quite different from the point made here. The police are not bad because they beat people up now and then (although they should not), they are essentially evil inasmuch as they embody externalized alienation and violence. And we should not only recognize them as such but also recognize our own contribution to this state of affairs and try to transform it.

By merely pointing to the abstract State (instead of lunatics, criminals or the 'Commies') and making it into another scapegoat nothing changes for the better. Given such thinking about the State as has been developed above with regard to criminal behavior and the clash of values (the allocation of values) that constitutes crime as a macrosocial conflict, the basis for new types of empirical research is laid.

NOTES AND REFERENCES

1. C. J. Van Zeyl, 'The Sociology of Deviance in the United States: A Critical Appraisal,' English article in the Dutch periodical *Mens en Maatschappij*, 1974, pp. 374–391.
2. P. K. Manning, 'Survey Essay on Deviance,' *Contemporary Sociology*, 2 (1973), pp. 123–128
3. I. Taylor, P. Walton and J. Young, *The New Criminology: For a Social Theory of Deviance*. London, 1973.
4. Van Zeyl, *op.cit.*
5. B. Wootton, *Social Science and Sociological Pathology*. Londen, 1959.
6. One may doubt the expediency of the latter example. There is a difference between the soporific element in sleep-inducing substances and the temperature as an indicator of coldness.
7. W. Springer, *Kriminalitätstheorien und ihr Realitätsgehalt*. Stuttgart, 1973.
8. C. G. Hempel, *Philosophy of Natural Science*. Englewood Cliffs, N. J.: Prentice Hall, 1966, pp. 10–18. (On the role of induction in scientific inquiry).
9. Where I have used the ellipsis marks at the end of this quotation, Hempel adds: 'or hypothesis.' Since *this* kind of tentative, preliminary 'hypothesis' should be well distinguished from one that is based on data already collected and that is correctly formulated (according to the rules for confirmation and falsification in the neo-popperian tradition), the use of 'hypothesis' at this stage of the heuristic process is confounding. It would be better to speak of 'conjectures' or 'preliminary hypothesis.'
10. See, for example: M. A. Zwanenburg and L. G. H. Gunther Moor, *A Formalization and Operationalization of a Macrosocial Conflict Model in Criminology*. Nijmegen: Institute of Criminology, 1975.
11. P. Valkenburgh, 'Het Conflict,' article in Dutch in the Dutch periodical *Acta Politica*, Vol. 9 No. 3 (1974), pp. 253–256.
12. R. A. De Moor, *De verklaring van het conflict*. Assen, 1961.

13. M. Weber, *Wirtschaft und Gesellschaft*. Tübingen, 1921.
14. R. Dahrendorf, 'Sozialer Konflikt,' in *Wörterbuch der Soziologie*. Stuttgart, 1970.
15. H. J. Krymanski, *Soziologie des Konflikts: Materialien und Modelle*. Hamburg, 1971.
16. T. Veblen, *The Theory of the Leisure Class*. New York, 1928.
17. J. Bernhard, 'The Conceptualization of Intergroup Relations with Special Reference to Conflict,' *Social Forces*, Vol. 29 No. 3 (1951), p. 243.
18. K. E. Boulding, *Conflict and Defence: A General Theory*. New York, 1963.
19. A. Rapoport, *Conflict in Man-Made Environment*. Harmondsworth: Penguin, 1974.
20. A. T. Turk, 'Conflict and Criminality,' *American Sociological Review*, 31 (1966), pp. 338–352.
21. Zwanenburg and Moor, *op.cit.*
22. R. S. Denisoff and C. H. McCaghy, *Deviance, Conflict and Criminality*. London, 1973.
23. W. H. Nagel, 'Structural Victimisation,' *International Journal of Criminology and Penology*, Vol. 2 No. 2 (1974), pp. 99–132. 'Nearly every State and society is more or less criminogenic and makes victims. Even the new society and the brand new State wich we create in the place of the old ones will become criminogenic. That is our *condition humaine*.' (pp. 113–114). Although the present author agrees with the point made, her point about the relationship between the State and evil is a different one altogether.

Paul Moedikdo

CRIMINOLOGY AND POLITICIZATION

1.

Nagel's inaugural address *Het strafrecht en de onmens* (Penal law and the inhuman monster), as professor at Leiden University in 1956 treated implicitly the connection between political development and social reaction to crime. In bygone ages a man, when considered criminal, was put outside the law; he was dehumanized, made an inhuman monster without rights, so that he could be treated inhumanly. The first modern penal code, according to Nagel, was put into effect in France in 1791, two years after the Revolution against the absolutist ancien régime. It defended the individual by delimiting the power of the State to penalize, by mitigating the penal sanctions, and by demanding proportionality between acts and punishment. The criminal was less unprotected against arbitrariness because he was formally considered to be a party in the legal procedure and was no longer merely an object of investigation, to be tortured if need be (1956: 19).

Two years later, in a discourse on sociological criminology held for the Dutch Sociological Association, Nagel again referred to political issues. After positing that sociology of criminal law is indispensable to the proper development of criminology (1958: 89), he asserted that the legal order should be considered as a compromise between the State and individuals and so, naturally, it has no eternal validity (1958: 94). And then there is this pronouncement, remarkable for a jurist and a criminologist at that time: 'Het is goed, de zedelijke betrekkelijkheid, ja de aanvechtbaarheid van de wet telkens onder de ogen te zien' (It is good to face again and again the moral relativity, yes, even the contestability of the law.) (1958: 99).

Recently, Nagel has treated these themes of political awareness and the contestability of the legal-political order of the early years of his professorial career recurrently and in a more explicit and extensive manner in his criminological work (1971, 1972, 1974a, 1974b). In a paper presented at the VIIth Congress of the International Society of Criminology in Madrid in 1970, he parries a warning of the chairman to avoid politics in the discussions with the statement that the opinion that criminology as a science should have nothing to do with politics is a political statement in itself (1971: 1). Using the telling metaphor of socio-economic values riding the law as a donkey and the criminologist in a humble position studying the by-products of the donkey, Nagel stipulates that critical criminology will not stand aloof from politics as criminology used to do. The term 'political criminal' should not only be used to denote people in a certain victimological relationship to the authorities, but also authorities victimizing people and perhaps whole populations, like those responsible for genocide. Political State criminality comprises organizing murder of citizens, imprisonment without trial, colonialism, racism, exploitation, war, etc. He concludes that political criminality is not a subject that should be broached by incidental interventions; as one of the most important criminal phenomena it should be listed in the programs of criminological congresses (1971: 2–5).

Nagel has never theoretically elaborated his views on critical criminology, probably because to him they are self-evident, as he must have pondered over them since the time when some new criminologists were still children. Therefore he is sometimes misunderstood. One of his colleagues seems to equate Nagel's perspective with the polemological approach (Hoefnagels 1974: 75), and Taylor, Young and Walton, exponents of a criminology for a 'socialism of diversity,' unnecessarily and a bit smugly judge unjustly that Nagel's views fall outside the scope of their compilation on critical criminology (1975: 4–5).

In this essay, the author proposes to discuss succinctly the legalist view of criminology, its (political) implications and its present position in the Netherlands. Thereafter he will briefly review some alternative criminological perspectives that have been formulated in the last decade, in the hope that this will contribute to somewhat elucidating the theoretical implications of Nagel's pioneering critical stance in Dutch criminology. But before going on with criminology proper, the author will attempt to delineate the much used, but seldom clarified concept of politics.

Max Weber gives the following definitions:

> ',,Politik" würde für uns also heissen: Streben nach Machtanteil oder nach Beeinflussung der Machtverteilung, sei es zwischen Staaten, sei es innerhalb eines Staates zwischen den Menschengruppen, die er umschliesst. . . . Wenn man von einer Frage sagt: sie sei eine ,,politische" Frage, von einem Minister oder Beamten: er sei ein ,,politischer" Beamter, von einem Entschluss: er sei ,,politisch" bedingt, so ist damit immer gemeint: Machtverteilungs-, Machterhaltungs- oder Machtverschiebungsinteressen sind massgebend für die Antwort auf jene Frage oder bedingen diesen Entschluss oder bestimmen die Tätigkeitssphäre des betreffenden Beamten. Wer Politik treibt, erstrebt Macht: Macht entweder als Mittel im Dienst anderer Ziele – idealer oder egoistischer –, oder Macht ,,um ihrer selbst willen": um das Prestigegefühl, das sie gibt, zu geniessen' (1972: 822).

The political scientist Robert Dahl voices the same opinion in his definition: 'A political system is any persistent pattern of human relationships that involves, to a significant extent, power, rule or authority' (1970: 6). In both definitions the State, its organs and its functionaries are the most important participants in political action in modern societies, while at the same time they form the most important goals of the influence exerted by groups and individuals behaving politically. It is this notion of politics as the striving for and about power that has lately become an often used interpretative model or paradigm in analyzing social phenomena that are usually considered to be nonpolitical, like family relations (Laing 1971), female social emancipation (Millet 1970) and deviant behavior as recently also noticed by Broom and Selznick (1973: 586).

In an interesting analysis of political organization Schattschneider proposes '*describing politics as the socialization of conflict*. That is to say, the political process is a sequence: conflicts are initiated by highly motivated, high-tension groups so directly and immediately involved that it is difficult for them to see the justice of competing claims. As long as the conflicts of these groups remain private (carried on in terms of economic competition, reciprocal denial of goods and services, private negotiations and bargaining, struggles for corporate control or competition for membership), no political process is initiated. Conflicts become political only when an attempt is made to involve the wider public. Pressure politics might be described as a stage in the socialization of conflict' (1960: 39).

Earlier Schattschneider pointed out: 'Whether a large conflict is better than a small conflict depends on what the conflict is about and what people want to accomplish. A change of scope makes possible a new pattern of competition, a new balance of forces and a new result, but it also *makes impossible a lot of other things*.

While the language of politics is often oblique and sometimes devious, it is not difficult to show that opposing tendencies toward the pıivatization and socialization of conflict underlie all strategy' (1960: 17–18).

It is clear that he actually adheres to the earlier-mentioned conception of Weber and that the socialization of conflicts is but an often used, effective means in the social struggle for power. But it is this also in the promulgation of political awareness concerned with an articulated public good, without the actor himself seeking power. With respect to this last instance, Bay's distinction between 'politics' and 'pseudopolitics' is relevant. Bay criticizes behavioristic definitions such as Dahl's, which 'gravitate toward the most conspicuous *facts* and shy away from all reference to more norm-laden and less easily measurable aspects of social life. . . . Politics should refer to power, but the term should also refer to some conception of human welfare or the public good. . . . I would define as *political* all activity aimed at improving or protecting conditions for the satisfaction of human needs and demands in a given society or community, according to some universalistic scheme of priorities, implicit or explicit. *Pseudopolitical* . . . refers to activity that resembles political activity but is exclusively concerned with either the alleviation of personal neuroses or with promoting private or private interest-group advantage, deterred by no articulate or disinterested conception of what would be just or fair to other groups' (1967: 14–15).

In this essay, when the author uses the term 'politics' he has Weber's definition in mind, comprising Bay's two categories. When he mentions 'politicization' or 'political awareness,' he tends more to Bay's formulation, inclining to exclude the *mere* insight into power relation and social conflicts. But the author would readily admit that such an insight is necessarily part of 'political awareness' or politicization in Bay's sense.

The present author holds that criminological definitions and theories, as constructions of reality concerned with subject matter of (possible) societal conflicts, presented to a public, should be considered in their functions with regard to the privatization or socialization of conflict, as meant by Schattschneider.

2

Until recently, the prevalent view that criminology should study crimes in the sense of acts made punishable by law has been little contested. The subject matter of criminology has thus always been: product of the State, the body politic, as formulated in legal statutes, which may vary according to the national political structure. From this obvious determination by politics of the subject matter of criminological study it seems to be a small step to discerning the political features of governmental reactions toward crime and to conferring on politics an important place in criminological theory and research. However, the opposite is true: criminologists in the Western liberal tradition have generally conscientiously kept politics outside criminological scrutiny. The argument has been that criminology as a 'value-free' scientific endeavor should not mingle with politics, a value-laden enterprise. The practical aim of criminology is to provide objective, empirical data and scientific insight into criminality that will serve

(1) the administration of justice, which stands above political controversy and intrigue, and

(2) governmental policy to control and further prevent crime, which would benefit society as a whole.

Vis à vis the decisionmakers concerned with the administration of justice and public policy criminologists closely resemble forensic expert witnesses in the courtroom, who are only supposed to answer the questions about facts that are posed and refrain from prescribing anything normative to the court. This is in agreement with Robert K. Merton's carefully phrased dictum concerning the commitment of social scientists to social problems, while they ought to avoid 'the misplaced career cf trying to impose their own values upon others.' 'Through his work, the sociologist does not remain aloof from social controversy, but in his capacity as sociologist – rather than as citizen – he takes a distinctive and limited part in it. He introduces pertinent sociological truths so that the substantive morality and the social policy governing the issues at stake can take account of these truths . . . In his capacity as sociologist, emphatically not in his capacity as citizen, the student of social problems neither exhorts nor denounces, neither advocates nor rejects. It is enough that he uncovers to others the great price they sometimes pay for their settled but insufficiently examined convictions and their established but inflexible practices' (1961: 710).

Merton's prescriptions are not free from ambiguity. There is no problem in situations where the social scientist can reasonably foresee that 'the great price' he will uncover will *not* cause the others to change their moral convictions but eventually only influence adaptations of the technical means to achieve their moral goal, which the social scientist himself may acclaim or abhor. The influence of his sociological work can then readily be considered as merely technical. But if the social scientist can reasonably expect that by uncovering the costs he will persuade some others to adopt his moral or political stance, there is a moral dilemma. Willing to subscribe to Merton's views, he may refrain from surreptitiously imposing (his) values upon others and keep 'the price' covered, or, he may present 'the hard facts,' well aware that he is an advocate of his own value judgment.

But accepting the legal definition of crime and forbearing political and normative issues, criminologists have avoided such moral dilemmas by ethicizing the legal norms for themselves and others. They have taken the established sociopolitical constellation for granted and as a consequence thereof have taken the State agencies of crime control as reference groups, even if they themselves are not functionaries of such agencies. They have treated the governmental actions against crime as principally justified and primarily as dependent variables, that is, conditioned by the existence of crime. Hence in their research methodology they have tended (formerly more so than in 'modern' criminology) to rely extravagantly upon the 'hard facts' about results of governmental processing of criminals and crime (such as prison populations and official crime statistics) as sources of information about crime. Their theoretical questions, analyses and explanations have been constrained within the limitations of the practical problems of those agencies, and because service to those agencies has always been a primary goal, practical applicability for or at least basic acceptability to the agencies has been an important factor in shaping criminological theories. With the development of specialized expertise within the organizations of crime control, specific biological, psychiatric, partially sociological and lately multidisciplinary approaches to the study of crime have been constructed. These fragmentized theoretical approaches have served to obscure most effectively the political nature of crime and its control. In short, the identification of crime with acts punishable by law as the subject matter of criminological study, together with the generally accepted image of criminology as an auxiliary of State control of crime (which have often been organizationally determined), has resulted in a feigned nonpolitical criminology harnessed to the established political structures in society. Such 'nonpolitical' criminologists have undeniably exerted certain humanizing influences in the methods of crime control. In the Netherlands, the mitigation of the prison regime and the setting-up of a probation and parole service have been connected with criminological efforts. But the asylums to keep recidivists and 'psychopathic' offenders in custody practically indefinitely, and the inhuman application of brain surgery (lobotomy) or castration to criminal 'psychopaths,' as still practiced in some countries, have also been criminologically inspired. The criminological influence on jurisprudence may have tended to prevent too abstract moralistic juridical reasoning by the confrontation of jurists with concrete opportunities for protecting the individual rights of criminals, on the other hand it may also have tended to muddle juridical reasoning by inciting them to spurn individual rights in the name of social defense. Yet, because the point of departure has always been the self-evident justice of the criminal law and the injustice and the essential intolerability of crime, whatever the influence of 'nonpolitical' criminologists may have been on crime control agencies, and even if their theories have not been at all heeded, the fundamental social impact of their work has been the legitimization of the existing legal and political order. Concurrently they may unwittingly divert public attention from relevant issues of flagrant social injustice by dramatizing problems connected with criminality.

Indeed, since the politically turbulent sixties harsh criticism has been raised against those social scientists who have professed to be apolitical, i.e. scientists without political duties or consciousness. But this critique, however well-reasoned or passionate it may have been, has by no means shaped the scientific morality of the majority of social scientists. Merton, while in 1971 extensively revising his comments on deviancy in his well-known handbook on social problems (cf. Merton and Nisbet 1961: 723–731 and Merton and Nisbet 1971: 824–838), upheld the dictum cited earlier (Merton and Nisbet 1971: 808–809). And whereas Taylor, Young and Walton have recently acclaimed that the process of politicization of the human sciences has proceeded farther in the area of criminology and deviancy theory than in most previously 'nonpolitical' areas (1975: 1), 'nonpolitical' criminology, as rejected by them, is, at least in the Netherlands, still paramount. That pretended 'nonpolitical' and 'value-free' Dutch criminology is still a reality today we shall prove by calling on a leading expert, whose criminological points of departure (though with some modern modifications) are fairly in accordance with the views exposed at the outset of this section.

This expert is Buikhuisen, the most energetic Dutch criminologist to have appeared on the scene in the last decade, and who, because of his alleged position in the forefront, has been hailed as 'the Eddy Merckx of Dutch criminology' (van Weringh 1971: 5). Buikhuisen was professor of criminology in Groningen for seven years and within a few years after his appointment he set up the best-equipped and most productive (as regards publications) criminological research center in the country. Since 1973 he has been (re)organizing a full-fledged research center of the Department of Justice (now called: W.O.D.C., Scientific Research and Documentation Center) and, having recently joined the staff of the Secretary-General of the Department (van Weringh 1975), his strategic position with regard to directing the development of criminological research in the Netherlands has been strengthened considerably. For as director of W.O.D.C. he is also responsible for the allocation of departmental research funds for non-departmental projects, while as an advisor to the secretary-general his voice may be decisive with regard to the necessary permission for the external use of departmental data and facilities.

Buikhuisen elaborated his basic views on criminology in his inaugural address as professor at the University of Groningen (1966). His main conclusions can be summarized as follows: every theory that tries to explain criminality as a totality is, to put it mildly, incomplete. It does not do justice to the factors which are responsible for the shape that criminal behavior acquires. Besides that, in order to determine which factors are at the base of certain criminal acts, . . . the criminologist will have to move his field of inquiry to the period before the moment the offense was committed. The object of study is not merely criminal man, but also man in the process of *becoming criminal* (1966: 26).

The W.O.D.C. is seen by Buikhuisen as a research service institute, which in principle is engaged in matters relevant to the administration of justice. Its relation to external research includes maintaining contacts with scientific institutes because it is of great importance for a department to know in which fields other research workers are busy. The W.O.D.C. can offer help to make research problems of these research workers policy-ripe, that is to formulate them in such a way that there is the most chance for a positive reaction from the public authorities (van Weringh 1975: 129–130).

Buikhuisen's *domain-assumptions* (Gouldner 1970b: 29) are not difficult to discover. They are: the subject matter of criminology should be based on the legal definition of crime and criminology should be an auxiliary science of criminal jurisprudence and policy. Once these assumptions belonged to the 'communis opinio' of Dutch criminal jurisprudence and criminology, at a time when most of the Dutch criminologists were academically trained jurists. But the present dissenting voice about the relationship between criminal law and criminology has not been raised by the academically trained sociologists and social psychologists who since the sixties have manned the criminological institutes as research workers, presumably to professionalize criminology. Apart from their possibly being ideologically motivated, these 'research experts' seem so committed to the positivistic empirical methodology (the mastery of which distinguishes them from the older generation of 'amateurish' jurist-criminologists), that C. Wright Mills's caustic critique of empiricists (1959: 50–75) is applicable to them. 'Possessed by the methodological inhibition' (1959: 55), they stick to the established criminological domain-assumptions as a convenient manner to get their empirical researches going. For 'computerizable' data about official crimes and official criminals are either already stored up by governmental agencies, or with the willing support of governmental functionaries relatively easy to obtain 'independently.' Compared with the older generation of criminologists these professional social scientist-criminologists may tend even more to identify themselves with official public policy agencies, for as a group they lack the training given at our law schools, to respect or at least optimally protect the individual's rights, that the jurist-criminologists had. To these 'value-free' scientists the goal of smooth social control may then more readily sanctify the means of curbing individual rights.

'Nonpolitical' criminology is still thriving, perhaps not only because of ideological or organizational commitment, but also because a coherent alternative is not altogether manifest. Since the sixties alternatives in a confusing amount and variety have been ventured to oppose orthodox criminology. This proliferation of alternatives surely highlights the crisis in criminological theory and practice, but at the same time it tends to obscure the essential problem of the lack of political reflection in traditional criminology. For that matter several alternatives could be fitted, either readily or with some squeezing, into 'nonpolitical' criminology, such as the 'labeling perspective' (e.g.: Erikson 1964, Becker 1963, Schur 1965, Lemert 1967, Hoefnagels 1969, Bianchi 1971), the conflict perspective (e.g.: Turk 1969, Dessaur 1974b) and phenomenological approaches (e.g.: Cicourel 1968, Philipson and Roche 1974, Bianchi 1974b, Cohen 1971). Explicit political stances have been argued by humanistic (H. and J. Schwendinger 1970), critical (Nagel 1971), radical (Platt 1973), new (Taylor, Walton and Young 1973) and materialist (Taylor, Walton and Young 1975) criminologists.

Some efforts at explicit politicization of criminological issues seem, however, to have led outsiders to totally ideologizing the study of crime. Especially claims that criminology should fundamentally oppose capitalism and promote the (revolutionary) construction of a new socialist society, and that Marx should be the only or superior guide thereto may have deterred criminologists in the Western liberal tradition from taking serious account of the arguments presented for the necessity of political consciousness in practicing criminology as a profession. Quinney, one of the foremen in 'politicized' criminology, writes: 'Marxism is the one philosophy of our time that takes as its focus the oppression produced by a capitalist society. It is the one form of analysis that is historically specific and locates the problems of the age in the economic class relations . . . Only a Marxist critique allows us to break out of the ideology and conditions of the age. . . . The purpose here, then is to develop a critical Marxian analysis of crime control in capitalist society' (1973: 87). And the final chord of Taylor, Walton and Young's *New Criminology* sounds: 'For us, as for Marx and for other new criminologists, *deviance* is normal – in the sense that men are now consciously involved (in the prisons that are contemporary society and in the real prisons) in asserting their human diversity. The task is not merely to „penetrate" these problems, not merely to question the stereotypes, or to act as carriers of „alternative phenomenological realities." The task is to create a society in which the facts of human diversity, whether personal, organic or social, are not subject to the power to criminalize' (1973: 282).

Perhaps some acquaintance with the thoroughly politicized criminology of Eastern Europe has brought Western liberal criminologists to associate the problem of politicization with bringing criminology under unreserved political tutelage. In an East German handbook of criminology one can find among a host of unabashedly political statements a passage saying that socialist or Marxist criminological practice should start 'von den Grunderkenntnissen, den sie von den Beschlüssen der Partei und durch die Gesellschaftswissenschaften schlechthin hat' (from the fundamentals that it plainly got from the Party decisions and the social sciences) (Buchholz, Hartmann, Lekschas and Stiller 1971: 68). And in the chapter on the causes of criminality there is indeed the following quotation from the program of the 11th 'Partei-tag der S.E.D.' in 1963: 'Die Lösung der Aufgaben des umfassenden Aufbaues des Sozialismus ist der Grundlage für den systematischen Kampf um die schrittweise Verdrängung der Kriminalität aus dem Leben der Gesellschaft. In der Deutschen Demokratischen Republik wurden die kapitalistischen Ausbeutungsverhältnisse überwunden und so die sozialökonomischen Wurzeln der Verbrechen im wesentlichen beseitigt. Der Ubergang vom Kapitalismus zum Sozialismus vollzieht sich jedoch unter vielfältigen Widerspruchen und im Kampf gegen zählebige kapitalistische Lebens- und Denkgewohnheiten, die durch feindliche Einflüsse von auszen immer neu genährt werden. Dies spiegelt sich auch in der Kriminalität wider . . .' (1971: 94).

Consequently the causes of the punishable act have to be considered as relics or rudiments of the old capitalistic social order and emphatically not as expressions of the new, socialistic relations (1971: 130).

But despite all semblances there is a distinctive disparity between this kind of socialistic criminology and the emerging politically conscious criminology in Western countries. The latter, whether Marxist-oriented or not, has turned away from a criminology subservient to the institutionalized power of the State, whereas socialist criminology à la Buchholz and his colleagues, as well as nonpolitical criminology à la Buikhuisen, advocates a willingness to cooperate with the State. Les extrèmes se touchent!

Buchholz and his colleagues idealize and support the sociopolitical structure of the socialistic society celebrated in the program of the S.E.D. If Buikhuisen and other 'nonpolitical' criminologists have some image of society, and they ought to have one if they study crime as a societal phenomenon, they start from an idealized image of Western democratic society, which they further take for granted and support. Perhaps this image is like the one Lipset formulated in a once famous publication: '. . . democracy is not only or even primarily a means through which different groups can attain their ends or seek the good society; it is the good society itself in operation . . .' identifying it with the existing Western societies, where in his opinion democratic social revolutions had triumphed (Lipset 1963: 439–445).

So socialistic criminology à la Buchholz and his colleagues in Eastern Europe and 'nonpolitical' or 'value-free' criminology in Western Europe practice criminology under political acceptance of and even under political tutelage by (the difference may be in consciousness or frankness and in degree) the established official power. Ignoring the fact that power tends always to corrupt, they primarily strive to support official power and bypass the liberation and emancipation of oppressed groups. But, as already alluded to above, there still is by far no consensus among criminologists who are looking for a significant alternative to this orthodox criminology. The discussions among them are confusing and not always free from intolerant and seemingly dogmatic denunciations of those of diverse persuasions or approaches (Taylor, Walton and Young 1973), which weakens the political impact of their ranks as a whole. Taylor, Walton and Young anticipate in this connection that in the near future empirical radical research will be minimal because the appropriate and correct departure points for research are not quite clear yet (1975: 28–29).

But adequate insight into the attempts to formulate an alternative criminological perspective can only be gained if they are examined together with the societal and organizational conditions which have promoted or hampered their elaboration and development. In the following paragraphs the author will try to give a bird's eye view of the process of political awareness in criminological thought in the United States, Great Britain and the Netherlands. Different sociopolitical arrangements have influenced the actual state of the alternatives to orthodox criminology in these countries.

3.1.

In the United States criminology has been taught by sociologists in the Departments of Public Administration; it has been regarded as an auxiliary science to general social policy rather than, as in Europe, merely to criminal jurisprudence and criminal policy. This, and the specific politico-economic structure of the US, may account for the fact, that more than in Europe, awareness of politics as an integrated part of the problem of crime has been shown by many criminologists. Although Tannenbaum has to be mentioned as one of the pioneers in this field, the work of Sutherland has drawn much more attention. In his widely used textbook on criminology he makes many caustic observations pertinent to the political influences on the phenomenon of crime. He writes about the social and political importance of the upper classes, who make the laws in such a manner that many of their own wrongful acts do not come within the scope of the penal law; the 'dark numbers' varying with changes in police policy; white-collar crime, the extent of which is unknown, because the white-collar criminals are respectable and of high social status, which enables them to avoid prosecution; law-breaking by the police; and especially the role played by the notorious 'political machine' which cooperates with law violators.

Notwithstanding his scourging philippics on US political and commercial mores, Sutherland, however, did not investigate the American politico-economic structure as such, as the major constitutive factor of crime, or search for ways to achieve politico-economic changes. Nor did he consistently impart priority to studies on those kinds of crime which he suspected to be prevalent among people of high social status and especially injurious to society, but of which the general public is less aware. Indeed, he did not confine himself to the study of the economically and politically powerless criminals, as so many criminologists do, and his pioneer studies on white-collar crime (1941, 1945 and 1949) are deservedly famous. Yet, in his textbook, when he argues for breaking crime into homogeneous units of 'behavior-systems' as holding the greatest promise for criminological research, he puts 'professional theft, circus grifting, drug addiction, racketeering, fraudulent advertising, and manipulations of corporate securities' on one and the same level (1947: 219), and it is the firstmentioned crime (on which he had published an also famous study (1937)) that he described in some detail as illustration of the procedure of studying behavior systems in crime, and not the last-mentioned. Furthermore, his theory of differential association attempts, as Cressey has explicated in his revision of Sutherland's book, to indicate 'the mechanisms and processes which are common to the rich and the poor, Negroes and whites, urban and rural dwellers, young adults and old adults, and the emotionally stable and the emotionally unstable who commit crimes' (Sutherland and Cressey 1960: 75), herewith blurring by abstraction the fact that crimes of political and economic powerholders may to a large extent condition the lives and behavior, including criminal acts, of the disprivileged, and not the other way round.

Nowhere in Sutherland's *theoretical* formulations on criminal etiology are his penetrating observations on the interrelationship of politics and crime reflected. This may well be related to his feeling that 'the (corrupt political) system has been operating for many decades and no person can change it very much' (1960: 183). Tracing supposed cause and effect relations produces findings *for* and *against*, as Seeley in his thoughtful essay has indicated. He reflects: 'In society, as in nature, everything is related to everything and in some ultimate metaphysical sense everything is the cause of any one thing. But by „the cause" or „a cause" we mean in science, as in practical everyday life, that particular thing which it would be most „convenient," economical or efficient to change in order to secure a desired change in what we are pleased to call an effect. Thus mosquitoes, if we do not mind exterminating them, are „the cause" of malaria in men; though apart from this canon of convenience we might equally have said that blood was the cause of malaria if we could do without it, or men, if we were prepared to exterminate them' (1963: 59).

From the discussion of Sutherland's views (exemplary for criminologists before the sixties) it has become clear that despite his keen observations of the criminal and criminogenic corruption in business and political organizations, he did not challenge the legitimacy of the established political system of liberal capitalism in the United States. Being devoid of socialistic ideas, he reflected the typical liberal critical stance in the line of muckrakers who helped to arouse a concern with social reform without, however, taking into account the total structures and presenting a fundamental social alternative, for the existing order seemed permanent (Bottomore 1969: 20–52). This was the kind of social criticism (mostly less telling than Sutherland's) expressed in criminological work and, with a few remarkable exceptions, in sociological treatises too, in those days. One of the exceptions was Wright Mills; worth reading is his essay 'The professional ideology of social pathologists,' first published in 1943, a review of textbooks on social problems current in the thirties and an indictment of their fragmentary, nonpolitical or opportunistic, non-theoretical and rural middle-class-biased approach. Wright Mills was the leading social critic of the fifties and worked to revive a classical tradition of sociological thought, created above all by Marx and Max Weber and which treated large-scale social and historical problems (Bottomore 1969: 54). Typically, the essence of the morality that directed his social science practice can be found in politically conscious assertions: 'All social scientists . . . are involved in the struggle between enlightenment and obscurantism . . . to practise social science is, first of all to practise the politics of truth. But . . . the truth of our findings, the accuracy of our investigations – when they are seen in the social setting – may or may not be relevant to human affairs (1959: 178–179). 'Intellectual work is related to power in numerous ways, among them these: with ideas one can uphold or justify power, attempting to transform it into legitimate authority; with ideas one can also debunk authority, attempting to reduce it to mere power, to discredit it as arbitrary or as unjust. With ideas one can conceal or expose the holders of power. And with ideas . . . one can divert attention from problems of power and authority and social reality in general . . .' (1967: 612). Wright Mills' moral and intellectual stature shows up all the more clearly against the background of the conservative and essentially uncritical American post-war society until the sixties, demonstrating in social science and everyday life a dominating organismic or functionalistic image of society, emphasizing consensus and equilibrium.

With Bottomore, the present author considers the Cold War, which after the struggle with the fascist states confronted the Western democracies with the USSR and the newly created communist states, as the major reason that during that period in the Western countries democracy as a form of society was sharply contrasted with those other forms, resulting in the overshadowing and neglecting of the sources of conflict within society. Bottomore adds: '. . . the importance of such conflicts may actually have diminished not only because the sense of national unity was enhanced by their involvement in external conflicts, but also because . . . (there was an) exceptionally rapid and sustained economic growth, which had undoubtedly affected . . . the relations between classes and between political groups' (1975: 21, 33 and 45).

Such a society is clearly unfertile soil for any consistent critical social science, whose adherents may even fall victim to officially supported paranoid nationalistic movements such as McCarthyism in the early fifties. It is only after the thaw of the Cold War set in that the latent conflicts in American society came to the fore and protest movements gained momentum. Three interrelated progressive movements, notably antiwar movements against irresponsible governmental policy; student protests reflecting democratic idealism in direct action; and black militancy vindicating civil rights against racial discrimination, conditioned the political turbulence in the sixties and early seventies (Skolnick 1969). As Bottomore asserts, 'it is in those periods when there is manifest conflict and contestation in society itself that, in the first place, the distinction between a conservative and a radical sociology is sharply delineated, and secondly, a radical sociology assumes a growing importance in the whole field of social thought' (1975: 14).

In the early sixties some studies on deviance were published by sociologists affiliated with the Society for the Study of Social Problems, applying an approach which later became known as the labeling theory or the interactionist perspective. They seemed to upturn the traditional conception of deviance in sociology and criminology as behavior objectively departing from or transgressing social norms, conceiving deviance as an act subjectively perceived and treated as such by others. In the wording of one of the leading publicists in this vein: '. . . deviance is *not* a quality of the act a person commits, but rather a consequence of the application by others of rules and sanctions to an „offender." The deviant is one to whom that label has successfully been applied; deviant behavior is behavior that people so label' (Becker 1963: 9). The 'labelists' focus attention on the process of labeling and its injurious effects on the moral character of the labeled persons, provoking them to enter deviant careers (Becker 1963 and 1964).

This approach was not altogether new. Notably Tannenbaum had already attempted a similar approach in his *Crime and the Community*, published in 1938 (and 1951). Under the chapter heading: 'Point of view,' he posited inter alia: 'The process of making the criminal, therefore, is a process of tagging, defining, identifying, segregating, describing, emphasizing, making conscious and self-conscious; it becomes a way of stimulating, suggesting, emphasizing, and evoking the very traits that are complained of . . . the entire process of dealing with the young delinquent is mischievous in so far as it identifies him to himself or to the evironment as a delinquent person. The person becomes the thing he is described as being. Nor does it seem to matter whether the valuation is made by those who would punish or by those who would reform' (1951: 19–20). Merton, too, had earlier called attention to the impact of social defining (lucidly elaborating what he called the Thomas' theorem: 'If men define situations as real, they are real in their consequences.') in his concept of the self-fulfilling prophecy (1957: 421–436). Lemert put the full emphasis on the social reaction in his *Social Pathology*, a systematic theory of sociopathic behavior published in 1951, among other things already distinguishing between the primary deviant, whose deviance is of marginal significance to him, and the secondary deviant, whose life and identity are organized around his deviance because of stigmatization, punishment, segregation and social control.

But none of them had any noticeable impact on criminological research or theorizing before the sixties. It seems that consistently critically studying the social reaction to crime plainly was not possible in the then existing social order and the accepted (political) power positions within that order. In this context it is characteristic that Tannenbaum, after ascertaining that a considerable quantity of crime in the community is made possible by the peculiar connection that existed between political organizations and criminal gangs, stated flatly: 'This is not meant as a condemnation of our politics. We cannot condemn our politics without condemning our community. They are so closely intertwined that the good and the evil go together . . . At present, evil and unhealthy as the relationship between crime and politics is, it is still to be taken as a typical, that is as a natural and inevitable, aspect of the kind of community we have' (1951: 129).

Only in the last decade, in a society where mass opposition against governmental abuse of power, authoritarian policymaking and discrimination was growing, did the critical posture toward official institutions which the labeling approach apparently implied, appeal to social scientists who had been getting weary of conventional criminology (Schur 1965, Skolnick 1966, Erikson 1966, Platt 1969, Cicourel 1968, Matza 1964 and 1969, Quinney 1970 are among the best known of the studies with the labeling approach that were then pouring forth).

A notable asset of these publications is that they have broken down the tendency of older criminology and social pathology to insulate themselves from the mainstream of sociological theory and knowledge. Studies wholly outside the scope of the traditional study of deviant behavior, which have influenced the labeling perspective and its development are among others: Mead (1934), Goffman (1961 and 1963) and Berger and Luckmann (1966). Empathy with and sympathy for the deviants under study, combined with criticism of the agencies of control, more or less explicitly exhibited, have been common to studies in this perspective.

In his presidential address at the annual meeting of the Society for the Study of Social Problems in 1966, Becker candidly argued 'that it is not possible to do research that is uncontaminated by personal and political sympathies and, therefore, that the question is not whether we should take sides, since we inevitably will, but rather whose side we are on' (1970: 99). He seemed to be defensive when he stated: 'We are, if we are proper members of the group, morally bound to accept the definition imposed on reality by a superordinate group in preference to the definitions espoused by subordinates . . . Thus credibility and the right to be heard are differentially distributed through the ranks of the system. As sociologists we provoke the charge of bias, in ourselves and others, by refusing to give credence and deference to an established status order, in which knowledge and truth and the right to be heard are not equally distributed . . . By refusing to accept the hierarchy of credibility, we express disrespect for the entire established order' (1970: 103).

The late sixties were the heyday of the labeling or interactionistic theory of deviance. Meanwhile fundamental criticism and radical alternatives were forthcoming.

Gouldner, for one, took issue with Becker's presidential address in a hard hitting reaction (1970a: 112–148). He distrusts the labelists' identification with the underdog: '. . . their pull to the underdog is sometimes part of a titillated attraction to the underdog's exotic difference and easily takes the form of „essays on quaintenes" . . . such an identification with the underdog becomes the urban sociologist's equivalent of the anthropologist's (one time) romantic appreciation of the noble savage (p. 121). . . Becker's school of deviance expresses the romanticism of the zoo-curator who preeningly displays his rare specimens. And like the zookeeper, he wishes to protect his collection; he does not want spectators to throw rocks at the animals behind the bars. But neither is he eager to tear down the bars and let the animals go . . . . The very empirical sensitivity to fine detail characterizing this school, is both born of and limited by the connoisseur's fascination with the rare object; its empirical richness is inspired by a collector's aesthetic (pp. 121–122). (Becker) has really given birth . . . to the first version of new Establishment sociology, to a sociology compatible with the new character of social reform in the United States today . . . It is a sociology of and for the new welfare state' (p. 132). '. . . Radical sociologists differ from liberals in that, while they take the standpoint of the underdog, they apply it to the study of overdogs. Radical sociologists want to study 'power elites,' the leaders or masters, of men; liberal sociologists focus their efforts upon underdogs and victims and their immediate bureaucratic caretakers' (p. 133). 'It is to values, not to factions that sociologists must give their most basic commitment' (p. 148).

It is this issue of values 'to which criminologists would be able to give their basic commitments' that Herman and Julia Schwendinger in point of fact discuss in their much-quoted article 'Defenders of order or guardians of human rights?' (1970). They fundamentally challenge the notion that 'the legal definitions of crime and the criminal are ultimate standards for deciding whether a scholarly work should be considered criminological, so that criminological studies should provide knowledge which is diachronically or synchronically related to legally defined crimes' (1975: 113).

Their main conclusions are that political events have now made it possible to define crime as abrogation of human rights; and that criminologists should identify those forms of behavior and social institutions which should be engaged in order to defend human rights. They must be able to identify the violations of these rights – by whom and against whom, how and why. This will entail the problem of priorities regarding different rights. Because the terms imperialism, racism, sexism and poverty are abbreviated signs for theories of social relationships which cause the systematic abrogation of basic rights, they can be called crimes (1975: 132–137).

The radicalization of other American criminologists has likewise advanced them outside all bounderies of conventional criminology. They are leaving legally defined crimes wholly aside, advancing to study the more comprehensive evil and socially injurious phenomenon of American capitalism and its immediate manifestations in legal and social control. This has been closely related to sociopolitical development and growing political awareness. The criminal character of governmental policy, and specifically its foreign policy, has become widely exposed by critical reporting in the mass media. The graphic details of government-instigated mass killings of human beings, of mass destruction of homes and property, the ecocide in a once beautiful and fertile country, have dwindled the significance of ordinary crime to nil. Besides the repressive domestic policy with regard to the opposition to this criminal foreign policy, the reaction to the unrest at the universities, and black militancy, have also been repulsively brutal. This process of radicalization can be traced clearly through Quinney's successive publications. These show choice and commitment parallel with a developing insight into a rotten capitalistic State (Quinney and Clinard 1967, Quinney 1969, 1970, 1972, 1973 and 1974). He exhorts in 1974: 'Much more attention has to be devoted to an understanding of legal repression as a counter-revolutionary force. . . . In critically understanding (and demystifying) our current historical reality we are in a position to act in a way that will remove our oppression and create a new existence' (1974: 197). He tells about his own radicalization in an interview (Goldwyn 1971). The process of radicalization of Matza and Platt, once two 'show-pieces' of interactionist sociology of deviance, is also described by them in interviews, both explicitly referring to Vietnam (Weis 1971 and Currie 1973).

Matza declares that he is not writing anymore about delinquency and crime. He now writes critically on topics such as poverty and youthful rebellion, and on a historical study on the building of an American conservative order in the years before the war (Weis 1971: 41–42).

Platt also dissociates himself from his *Child Savers* (1969), much lauded by academic criminology, because the book stops short at the really interesting questions: Why did the child saving reform movement develop at that particular time in the United States? How was it related to other reforms in the emerging welfare state, etc.? He is of the opinion that 'criminals' like Malcolm X, Eldridge Cleaver, Angela Davis and George Jackson have written better books on crime than the criminologists (Currie 1973: 26–27). In 1973 Platt reports that at the School of Criminology in Berkeley courses are given on racism, sexism, colonialism, Nixon's crime-politics, etc. The Union of Radical Criminologists has been formed with its own journal *Crime and Social Justice* (1975: 105–107).

3.2.

There exist excellent and easily available accounts on the recent developments of criminology in Britain with specific attention paid to issues of politicization, notably by Cohen (1971 and 1974), and Taylor, Walton and Young (1975: 6–62). They are the main sources of the following section.

Until the mid-sixties traditional criminology was as dominant as in the Netherlands. However, a number of young sociologists active in teaching and research in the field of crime and deviant behavior were attracted to the emerging interactionist sociology of deviance in America, which has a certain affinity with the British antipsychiatry school of Laing (1960, 1961). Besides, it should be noted that traditional British criminologists have also provided potentially disturbing insights into the inherent irrationality and injustice of official reactions to criminals in the name of law and order. Mannheim extensively treated the class character of legislation and criminality in his handbook (1965: 419–499) and Wilkins introduced the concept of deviation amplification (1964: 85). The young sociologists were turning away from official criminology because of ideological reasons, but probably even more owing to boredom. Also, apparent attempts by forensic psychiatrists, clinical psychologists and criminal lawyers to define criminology as a self-contained discipline, dominated by them, made these sociologists unhappy. Cohen reports: 'One had to get away from that scene, but being a sociologist wasn't enough, one had to find a separate subculture within the sociological world. The sheer physical isolation of many of us in small departments, teaching a subject with no colleagues in the field and few graduate students was another contributing pressure' (1974: 26). In July 1968, in the middle of a national conference on teaching and research in criminology, organized by the Institute of Criminology in Cambridge (bulwark of traditional criminology), seven of them decided to form a group, it seems primarily to provide some sort of mutual intellectual support. Without exception they had all been involved in orthodox political movements, like Anarchists, CND, Young Communists and International Socialists. The initial intention was to organize discussions around the work they were doing. In November of the same year, when the first symposium of the National Deviance Conference (NDC) was held in York, the group of seven increased to about twenty, discussing five papers. By 1973 NDC had held fourteen symposiums attended by some 1300 people. It was then 'one of the largest alternative quasi academic bodies in Britain, with over 400 members. In the organization of the British Sociological Conference on deviance and control in 1971 the NDC played a mayor role. NDC members have built links with activist groups like Radical Alternatives to Prison, Preservation of the Rights of Prisoners, the Squatters, *Case-Con* (the journal for revolutionary social work), *Red Rat* (the journal for alternative psychologists). Individual members have been insolved in various campaigns' (Taylor and Taylor 1973: 209–210). Two compilations of papers from the NDC have been published (Cohen 1971, Taylor and Taylor 1973). Cohen has attempted to analyze the attraction of the NDC for its first group of members. The stress on labeling, injustice, scapegoating, stigmatizing, the sympathy for the underdog, the implications of Laing's work, were found appealing because of the personal background of the group members. He states: 'Talking or doing something about deviance seemed to offer . . . a form of commitment, a way of staying in, without on the one hand selling out or on the other playing the drab game of orthodox politics . . . Such commitment was easier because the historical period was one of growing and visible militancy of deviant groups working outside the political structure. . . . These identifications were facilitated by personal involvement in some of these marginal groups. Some of the original members and even more of the later members were on the fringes of the „Middle Underground." Involved as participants, they couldn't resist to be observers and make a decent living from it. The romantic, voyeurlike appeal of the subject-matter was important; one doubts whether a similar group could have been formed in industrial sociology, educational sociology or community studies' (1974: 28). With the rapid growth of membership (besides sociologists a large group of social workers has joined NDC) the direction of further development, that is, deeper commitment to social action or to theoretical sophistication, has become more problematic. From the list of papers presented at the symposiums (Taylor and Taylor 1973: 211–214) the diversity in topics of interest and approach is also evident. Whatever the NDC may be, it has not at all constituted one school of thought concerning problems of deviance and control. Cohen states, despite attempts to work out a more general position: 'We are probably more agreed on what we are *against* than what we are for' (1971: 16). Nevertheless the seven papers in *Images of Deviance* do have a common starting point, notably the 'skeptical' approach to deviance, concerned with 'the reactions of society towards behaviour classified or classifiable as deviant.' The research worker must question and not take for granted the labeling by society. In Cohen's elaboration of this skeptical approach under six points (1971: 17–24) it appears to be quite similar to the interactionist perspective. Yet the first and last point may be additions to it. Under point one (on reaching the public) the necessity to be intelligible in explanations not only for fellow sociologists is stressed. Under point six (on the political implications of studying deviance) the range of evaluative, moral and practical suggestions implied by a conception of deviance, toward which the sociologist should consciously take a stance, is pointed out. The authors in *Politics and Deviance* deepen the sociological dimension of the approach; 'being not content with Becker, identifying the question of rules and their enforceability as political, they go on to examine in various ways and in different areas – why particular kinds of politically enforceable rules arise in particular periods, in particular cultures and in respect of particular behaviours' (Taylor and Taylor 1973: 8). So, evolving from individualistic interaction the study of deviance is then hardly distinguishable from an incipient sociology of criminal law (Carson 1974). The most vocal of British deviancy theorists, Taylor, Walton and Young, have at present dissociated themselves wholly from the 'skeptical' approach. More than Cohen, they emphasize that the most central concern of that approach was the defense of the authenticity of deviance. They consider the only innovative theoretical statement that *clearly* distinguished the early work of NDC from American deviancy theory to be the statement that rule-breaking activity is an attempt to assert some form of *control* (1975: 17). In their textbook, which perhaps should have been titled 'Toward a New Criminology' instead of, rather prematurely, *The New Criminology*, since it is mainly a critical review of previous theories, they still granted this feature central importance (1973: esp. 144–158, 169, 221, 267, 282). In the best review made of this already three times reprinted book, Currie refers to their overaccentuation of the rationality of deviance as simply turning bourgeois criminology upside down. Where traditional criminology regarded deviance as innately pathological, Taylor, Walton and Young regard it as innately healthy. This 'appreciative' approach comes very close to the 'hipromantism' of some interactionists. Currie urges us 'to analyze the sources and consequences and political significance of particular kinds of deviance *within the framework of an articulate set of political and moral values* (italics added). To do this, a political philosophy and a theory of history within which to assess the deviant act is needed' (1974: 139). However, in their overview of critical criminology Taylor, Walton and Young admit explicitly that the stress on rule-breaking activity as an attempt to assert some form of control 'is a crude and indeed false formulation according the deviant an unreal ability of transcendence.' As they see it retrospectively their former research concern was 'to demonstrate in detail and for a wide range of deviant „types" the diverse ways in which men might try to assert their own selves,' renouncing herewith the examination of situations and institutions which constrained the exercise of individual or collective control. In self-analysis they state that probably this development of skeptical deviancy theory was influenced by their own feeling of being powerless to affect the national culture, the politics of social democracy and that of the orthodox left itself. So skeptical deviancy theory can be seen 'as an attempt to look for alternative, less constrained agencies for change, as an identification by powerless intellectuals with deviants who appeared more successful in controlling events' (1975: 17). This analysis has the ring of sincerity and truth. Their present conception is called *materialist* criminology because they hold that the social processes involved in crime-creation are in the final analysis bound up with the *material* basis of contemporary capitalism (1975: 20). Normatively, this criminology should be committed to the abolition of inequalities in wealth and power, like they argued in *The New Criminology*.

This is a fine statement of the ultimate normative goal for all social sciences, which all leftist-oriented theorists would subscribe to. The theoretical problem (with practical impact), however, is how to proceed further in this inequal, exploitative world. Taylor, Walton and Young seem to adhere to the opinon that the first step is to formulate a specification of that utopian society of equal wealth and power, so as to make it specifically congenial to criminology. They argued forcefully in *The New Criminology*, and still argue, that their task and that of other criminologists is to attempt to create the kind of society in which the facts of human diversity are not subject to the power to criminalize (1973: 44, Young 1975: 91). This is a superfluous and imprecise formulation. It seems to say that in that ideal society nothing that is human will be considered criminal. Currie's remark that this is dodging important issues about crime and justice in revolutionary societies is to the point. Not the power to criminalize should disappear, but the class character of the definition of crime. Crime should be defined and treated on the basis of principles that are egalitarian and cooperative rather than hierarchical and exploitative. Perhaps the diversity that Taylor, Walton and Young are preoccupied with is not human diversity in general, but the diversity expressed by the specific groups of deviants with which they identified themselves during their early research work. This had brought about their idealistic view of the deviant's ability to transcend the exigencies of social life in general, according to their own statements referred to above. The abandonment of this idealistic view, as they point out, 'was occasioned by a change in the political orientation of both middle class practitioners and deviants themselves.' By this they mean the organization of social workers in *Case-Con*, of psychologists in *Red Rat*, of lawyers in *The Ass*, of sociologists and criminolo gists in the NDC, and their cooperation with and defense of groups of people such as those associated with People not Psychiatry (the anxious, the 'mentally ill'), the Claimants' Union (the unemployed), Radical Alternatives to Prison (prisoners), Womens' Liberation Movement and the Gay Liberation Movement (1975: 18). Against this social background it is indeed understandable why they changed their idealistic view about the deviant's ability to transcend the exigencies of social life, but it could also explain their continuing emphasis on human diversity with all the consequences thereof.

However, it would be more reasonable for criminologists not to ponder about one special aspect of ideal social life that criminologists could realize and be mesmerized by, but to think about how in their specific condition as criminologists they could contribute to the tactical and strategical reduction of arbitrariness as the manifestation of inequalities in power and wealth (which obviously encompass the criminalization of diversity that Taylor, Walton and Young reject).

Correctionalism, individual rehabilitation or tangential social reform should then not be condemmed a priori as was done by Taylor, Walton and Young (1975: 44), but, like the forms of deviant behavior and the criminological enterprise itself, should be evaluated as politically and humanely progressive or retrogressive.

For, as Fidel Castro once said, 'seeking the greatest social change doesn't mean that one can propose this maximum at any time. Rather, one can even propose a particular objective at a particular time – taking into consideration the level of development of awareness and of the correlations of strength. Once this objective is achieved, you can set yourselves another objective that is a little farther along' (1972: 67).

The task of materialist criminology, which Taylor, Walton and Young subsequently sketch, is not immediately related to the issue of diversity. It shows the trend away from sociology of crime toward sociology of (criminal) law, which Carson (1974) has noticed to be common in the newer approaches in criminology and it contains no innovative theoretical statements. Taylor, Walton and Young have a sociology of law in mind as professed by Marx and Renner (1949). It is summarized in the following compact declaration: 'Materialist criminology must set about the task of seeking to explain the continuance, the innovation or the abolition of legal and social norms in terms of the interests they support, the functions they serve to particular material arrangements or production in propertied societies, realizing that the legal norms in question are inextricably connected with the developing contradictions in such societies' (1975: 56).

Young's complement (1975) to his collective work with Taylor and Walton is interesting. He presents systematic retrospection on the new deviancy theory, contending that it reflects mirror-images of the false ideas of the conservative criminology that it has attacked and by so doing has become a crass inversion of the older criminology. He indicates among other things that in their attack on correctionalist criminology, which has developed a consistent practical concern and policy orientation, the new deviancy theorists have been strident noninterventionists, neglecting to provide pointers for practical struggle. Their aim was to show that the reaction of the State to threats to the social order by expressive deviants, was nevertheless irrational, amplifying deviance and at the same time contradicting its own democratic codes in the process of reaction. There was *no* clear conception of practice: power had really been discovered, but there was no desire to dirty one's hands in actual struggles. Young asserts that radical ideas by themselves are abortive unless linked to a wider analysis of the total society and tied into a wider struggle in class society (1975: 69–70). Treating the specific demands which should be on the program of a radical criminology, he posits among other things that criminologists should discriminate between kinds of crimes, they should 'separate out desperation from solution and relate the deviant solution to its effect on others (situating it historically in terms of a class struggle).' Also, social control of crime should be argued strategically; but such control must be exercised within the community and not by external policing agencies. For 'it is only in the process of struggle for control that the community can evolve out of its disorganized and disintegrated state.' The radical criminologist's task is to aid such struggles and projects. The task is not to romanticize illegality, it is to judge deviant action in terms of its relationship to the struggle, ignoring the classifications of legality and illegality created by the powerful in *their* struggle against the powerless (1975: 88–90). Young's remark, that it is a thousand times easier to become a radical academic than a militant shop steward, the first course of action leading to Penguin Books Ltd and the second to the blacklist (1975: 83), is relevant here.

The NDC, as an association of more or less radical criminologists, who reject agency-determined theorizing and research, has now become a power to be reckoned with, countervailing the British Society of Criminology, established in 1951 under auspices of the Institute for the Study and Treatment of Delinquents and the Home Office. Several like-minded criminologists from other countries attended the conferences, a few invited as speakers. Mainly at the instigation of the NDC, the European Group for the Study of Deviance and Social Control has been set up to challenge the orthodox organizations of international criminology, which are sponsored or supported by governments and their law enforcement agencies. The first conference of this group was held in Florence, September 1973, just before the seventh International Congress for Criminology in Belgrade.

3.3.

In the Netherlands criminological developments during the fifties seemed to hold promise for a politically critical criminology. It was the Utrecht school of Pompe, Baan and Kempe, held in great esteem by Nagel (1963a), which took a critical stance toward the governmental and social reaction to the criminal. Unlike the then internationally prevailing etiological criminology (appropriately dubbed criminology of measuring and weighing of factors by Nagel 1958: 77) this school argued in favor of approaching the criminal as a human being who develops himself through communication with others as a function of the reactions of the others (Kempe 1959). Recognizing the moral responsibility toward the people they studied, members of this school worked actively to humanize or make less inhuman the treatment of offenders, criticizing concrete governmental actions and treatment situations; they heralded the shift in criminological concern from etiology to social control. The leniency of the Dutch system of punishment, in comparison to the systems of the surrounding countries can be readily related to the efforts of this school. Nagel too argued that modern criminology should be a 'relatie-criminologie,' a criminology of relationships (1959: 22), and accordingly elaborated the victimological aspect of the criminological problem, strongly opposing attempts to divide it in two distinct parts: criminology and victimology (1959 and 1963b). A member of the Utrecht school published a collection of candid opinions of prisoners, an expression of their criticism about the way in which they were treated by police-, judiciary- and prison-functionaries. Introducing it, he wrote that it is time to reflect on the relationship between the public authorities and the offender, and to take seriously the experiences of the prisoner (Rijksen 1958 : XIII). Even before it was on sale in the bookshops, the book caused a commotion among officials, and the Department of Justice purchased the whole impression. Only discerning experts were able to buy the book from the Department. The Utrecht school protested, but complied with the Department's decision without attempting any 'socialization of the conflict.' This was a telling incident that partly explains why the ethical Utrecht school failed to pass judgment fundamentally on the communication between the State and the person officially declared a criminal and so often morally misshapen by that communication. Despite its radical conception of man and its practical experience, it acquiesced in the final authority of the State and the legal order of the Netherlands, according to the 'Zeit Geist.' Nagel's independent spirit has not taken the State and the legal order for granted, as has been shown at the outset of this paper. In 1958, speaking before Dutch and Belgian criminologists, he declared that the experts of parliament can provide the people with, or at least nurture them in, a Christian, a humanistic, a national socialist and a communist consciousness of law. It depends on the political constellation which consciousness of law is put on the menu for the people. The political constellation, different from what we say and hope, depends only for a small part on the will of the people. It is the result of a struggle between a small group of men ideologically interested or only interested in holding power (1959: 20). Notwithstanding all that, in his demand for a criminology of relationships, he only elaborated the relationship between the criminal and his victim and neglected the most important relationship, that between the State and the criminal. Also Nagel did then ultimately accept the State of the Netherlands and the Dutch Criminal Code by and large, living in a nation where there were no social conflicts about fundamental issues.

In the mid-sixties the harmonious social order of the Netherlands was stirred by mass disturbances in Amsterdam and Rotterdam. The police commissioner of Amsterdam was publicly censured because of the use of allegedly unlawful means to restore order (Frenkel 1966). In the late sixties student movements for democratization of the universities were very active. There was a rapid process of disenchantment with authority structures in once rigid religious organizations: jurists, especially criminal law jurists, spoke and wrote about a juridical crisis (Moedikdo 1974: 71–74). It seemed to be the start of new criminological developments when in March 1968, Bianchi organized a seminar on deviant behavior to introduce the American labeling approach and the *Nederlands Tijdschrift voor Criminologie* devoted a special issue to this seminar and the American developments in criminology. Yet, while politically critical criminology has rapidly developed in the USA and in Britain, the development of critical criminology in the Netherlands has been insignificant. The best-known criminologists, whose views can be regarded as politically critical in various degrees, are individual scholars without a real constituency which would enable and stimulate them to conduct research and develop theoretically their views in a consistent way. In a sense they are more like critical, individualistic literary men. This is not to depreciate their significance, for great men of letters have exerted wholesome political influence throughout history, but to denote the condition of critical criminology in the Netherlands. Despite the fact that all three of them (Bianchi, Hoefnagels and Nagel) have been directors of criminological institutes neither they nor any of their staff have ever published a significant report of research, based on their theoretical views.

This fact seems to be partly explicable by the historical position of criminology within the Law Schools, since criminology has been considered primarily or even merely an auxiliary of criminal jurisprudence. This has been successfully propagated by the IKV (Internationale Kriminalistische Verein) led by Von Liszt, who aimed at specific political goals in Bismarck-Germany (Kempe 1968). Until the mid-sixties criminologists were recruited mainly among jurists, like Kempe, Nagel,

Bianchi and Hoefnagels.

The development of USA-oriented sociology after the war was, however, formidable. Since then in academic circles the persuasion has grown that the quantitative and mathematical research techniques are the criteria for scientifically acceptable social research. Jurist-criminologists were not trained in these modern research techniques and they have gradually appeared as amateurs only; and it seems that most of them have also come to consider themselves as being dilettante social scientists, whose proficiency, based on experience, has been described as in the first place coordinating data presented to them by the various social sciences (Kempe 1967: 322–323). In any case even jurist-criminologists who started their career with for that time adequate sociological work, like Kempe (1938 and 1939) and Nagel (1949), have stopped doing empirical research since the rise of intricate quantitative research techniques.

With the rapid development of sociology, the odium of amateurism has been growing heavier, and since the mid-sixties, in order to pull criminology out of its amateurist conditions, the criminological institutes have gradually been staffed with experts in the new research techniques.

A vocal exponent of the view that criminology should be 'up-graded' by mathematical, deterministic models of interpretation to become a real science is Dessaur (1971a). Her position with regard to the exact, quantitative techniques remains ambivalent. In an interview, Dessaur tells that she has sleepless nights, thinking about how the more perfect the sciences become, the more controllable social life becomes, just as nature has already come to be more controllable. She then sighs that she therefore sometimes hopes that we will not receive too many subsidies and that we will not be too smart (Doomen, 1973). This is of course dodging basic issues of the enterprise of social science as she subsequently shows in the interview. Yet it highlights the fact that even the bringing forth, through quantitative techniques and 'nonethical,' mathematical models, of scientific products (which she wrongly alleges to be value-free because they are falsifiable, distinct from the heuristic process (Dessaur, 1974: 64–68)), always implies value judgements, moral choice and political commitment as Wright Mills (1959), Friedrichs (1966), Duintjer (1970) and others, and most fundamentally Habermas (1968), have exposed. Dessaur also seems well aware of this when she rightly denunciates criminological practice, which is drawn from the one ad hoc problem to the other ad hoc problem without any strategy with regard to theory-formation, and explicitly relates its dubious character with the unhampered practice of creative science in a society, which for the largest part is still primitive, intolerant, short-sighted and floating on primitive emotions, in a world which for the largest part is composed of dictatorships (1971b: 17). We are not suggesting here that quantitative research techniques should not be applied, but only that there is no stage in the practicing of criminology as a profession, wherein a criminologist is exempt from theoretical reflectivity and moral responsibility.

Anyhow, the influx of professional social scientists into the existing criminological institutes, has not resulted in a significant development. This is because the trouble with criminology is not that it has been insufficiently integrated into the social sciences, but that criminology has closely reflected the character of the social sciences as a whole, which in our time have been overwhelmingly bourgeois in their origins and assumptions (Currie 1974: 138). Furthermore the difference in professional and technical commitment has considerably impeded adequate communication between the older and newer criminologists in their collective endeavors. The latter perceive that which the former evaluate as socially significant, as not researchable; while the former regard as insignificant what the latter consider researchable. Feelings of insufficiency on the one hand and those of complacency on the other hand, related to the new earmark of professionalism in social science, that is, the mastery of the intricacies of quantitative research, might also have had an impact on the relationship. In most instances, the two parties have grown completelly apart in the fulfilling of their criminological tasks. So it has happened that Bianchi, Hoefnagels and Nagel speculate more or less abstractly about what they consider significant criminological issues, hereby outlining alternatives for traditional criminology, while in their institutes young sociologists or social-psychologists do traditional criminological research with modern techniques, in the manner of Buikhuisen.

Of course, the predicament of Dutch criminology has also been conditioned by the sociopolitical structure and culture in the Netherlands. Referring to the historian De Jong (1969), Kempe characterizes Dutch political culture before the war as paternalistic. He points out that the dominant attitude toward the then established political leadership was one of respect-in-confidence. This was also reflected in the people's attitude toward the paternal severity-in-justice of the penal court (1975: 5–10). He analyzes the major factors leading to the critique of society by the younger generation that has condemned the Establishment in the sixties and has brought on many noticeable alterations in society and in the administration of justice. Nevertheless he concludes that essentially nothing has changed, and states that the fundamental problem of the structurally determined, discriminatory feature of penal procedure is not resolvable in the society existing at present (1975: 11–19).

Kempe's realistic observation of Dutch society is in accordance with Lijphart's cogent analysis of party politics in the Netherlands, characterizing it as 'the politics of accommodation, the overarching cooperation at the elite-level of different, self-contained groups with divergent values and interests' (1968). For, Lijphart's analysis implies that the paternalistic structure of Dutch society before the war has not changed essentially, despite democratizational tendencies at the universities, spectacular secularization in the churches and subsequent movements in social and cultural life against the vertical integration of organizations on a religious foundation. Paternalism is also evident in the 'decriminalization' movement of which Hulsman (1972) is the acknowledged champion, and which is evaluated by many 'progressive' jurists and criminologists as a national achievement one can only be proud of (among others, Bianchi 1974a: 15). They seem to wholly neglect the fact that 'the process of decriminalization has important and ineradicable control-functions within capitalist society and that where it has occurred, it is a product more of bureaucratic strategies evolved to deal with an overloading of inmates or social work cases than it is a genuine attempt to recreate society,' as Young has pointed out (1975: 89). It is clear that Dutch society with its paternalistic structure and culture is not conducive to radical criminological theory or practice.

Although empirical research in the critical perspective is almost totally lacking, it is appropriate to give attention to the ideas of the three criminologists generally acknowledged to be critical in the Netherlands. For, as Wright Mills has said, 'social research of any kind is advanced by ideas; it is only disciplined by fact' (1959: 71).

Bianchi's source of inspiration has always been the *Bible*. In 1956, he spent much energy arguing that crime is a sinful act, invariably an act against God, besides being a punishable act, invariably an act against mankind (Bianchi 1956: 116–144, 194–207). Carried along by the waves of the secularization-tide in Dutch Christian theology with its critique on existing society in the early sixties, he elaborates an interesting critique on the prevailing doctrine about punishment as consciously inflicted suffering, based on the Biblical concept of 'tsedeka,' emphasizing among other things the liberative impact that any act of doing justice should have on the guilty (1964: 47–63, also 1974d). Apparently reacting against the role of the authorities during the mass disturbances in 1966, he publishes engaging critical essays on authority, law and order, also Biblically inspired, stating for instance that the most orderly epochs in world history have always been epochs with the most injustice, because the practicing of justice has paradoxically always been a deviation (1967: 84). It was not so strange that in 1968 it was Bianchi who introduced the labeling approach with its criticism of power-holding labelers, to Dutch criminology. In his somewhat phenomenological elaboration of the labeling approach, which seems to be less consistent than his elaborations of Biblical points of departure, he accentuates linguistic aspects of the labeling-process (1971, as does his Ph. D. candidate, De Back 1973). Proposing a new criminological, nongovernmental paradigm as contrasted with the governmental paradigm of traditional criminology, he seems to adhere to a subjectivist or relativist perspective, stating for example that the new paradigm serves to develop theories from a *derived* position and based on an *own* (italics added) ideological vision of man and society and confusingly adds that a nongovernmental criminology serves also as a *metacriminology*. Whatever is meant by his new paradigm, there is no mention of the fundamental issue of politics in its elaboration (1974c: 214–216).

Hoefnagels considers himself a member of the Utrecht school (1975 : 4); in any case, like the Utrecht school his attention is also mainly directed at the concrete action and negligence of authorities and functionaries, for instance at court procedure (1970), at the neglect to make industrial misbehavior punishable (1972), and at the probation and parole services (1973b). As a theoretical perspective he has taken the labeling perspective, and seemingly to its most extreme consequences as in his statements: 'De voornaamste groep benoemers zijn de machthebbers. Zij bepalen, desnoods tegen de vigerende waarden in, wat misdaad is. Daarom zal het voornaamste kriminologisch onderzoek van deze eeuw het onderzoek naar de benoemers zijn, ook als deze zelf misdadigers zijn' (The most important group of labelers are the power holders. They define, if need be contrary to the operative values, what crime is. Therefore the most important criminological research of this century will be the research about the labelers, even if they are themselves criminal.) (1974: 94). His views on what to do with criminals are however traditional. The criminologist, as the efficient chairman of a team of specialists from diverse sciences (among others: criminal anthropology, criminal psychiatry, criminal sociology, criminal jurism, criminal statistics, victimology, penology and social work theory), if concerned with an individual will speak of a *resocialization plan*, and when dealing with society, will draw up a *preventive plan*, the aims and methods of which will be stated as concretely as possible (1973a: 52 and 56–67). In 1974, Bianchi declared that the Utrecht school of the fifties is reproachable because of its lack of societal criticism and fundamental critical thought about penal law (1974b; 104). It should be noted that in 1956, Bianchi still defended such quaint opinions as 'crime is a sinful act and a punishable act,' 'a deficient deed, directed at an anticipation of the Heavenly Kingdom' (1956: 128 and 196–197). Hoefnagel's telling reaction to this moralistic reprimand is very instructive. Besides pointing out Bianchi's neglect of the sociocultural conditions and the concrete actions of the Utrecht school, he indicates that Bianchi's own interactionist, phenomenological approach is in fact not conducive to an adequate criticism of the societal system as a whole (1975: 12). Taylor, Walton and Young have also cogently discussed the limitations of the interactionist and phenomenological approach (1973). Indeed, we are not aware of any publication where Bianchi has significantly related society as a totality to the problem of crime. The point is that despite his pretensions he has either raised moralist or theological criticisms against societal structures, that is, without a relevant sociological analysis (1967), or, like Hoefnagels, he has not come beyond the restrictions of the interactionist and phenomenological approach in criminology (1971). Hoefnagels anyhow acknowledges his own reformist posture, stating candidly that to him the rule of law is still predominant in Dutch society, is still so frequently realized that he prefers using means acceptable to this society in changing it 'culturally.' He is concerned about a change of attitude of power-holders too (1975: 12). Both of them differ in this respect from Nagel, whose views have affinity with the more radical views in criminology.

Nagel does not reject the interactionist approach. On the contrary, before this approach had ever been applied in European criminology, Nagel, as already mentioned above, postulated a criminology of relationships (1959). But at the same time, unlike most of the interactionists, he has always critically related society as a totality and the legal order to the problem of crime (1956, 1958, 1959, 1971, 1972, 1974a, 1974b). By doing this he has been able to transcend the Dutch paternalistic culture and legal tradition and to perceive the State, the legal order with the legalized power positions in society, as essentially problematic, although recently more explicitly so, as already indicated in the first section of this paper. He is less interested in addressing power-holders on how to behave, in the way Bianchi and Hoefnagels do, than in facilitating the independent struggle for emancipation of the oppressed. His sympathy for such independent struggle is shown, for instance, in his treatment of terrorism, regarding terrorism by individuals as a possible reaction to terrorism by the State, at a time when decent people only abhor individual terrorism against which civil society is rather powerless (1972). His conception of political crime (1971), already mentioned above, highlights the problematic character of the State. Referring to the self-help of the oppressed, he asserts that it is possible for people to reach a point at which they should oppose the legal order, which in principle is their own creation, as if they stand against an enemy (1974a: 21). Nagel relates his criterion for criminal behavior explicitly to this self-help, stating that behavior, which impedes the process of human emancipation is criminal, even if this behavior is the choice of the existing legal order for socially adjusted behavior. He does not, however, take the direction of any reaction against oppression for granted, asking not without skepticism what course we hope the process of emancipation will take. In his answer, he specifies the orientation of his criminological efforts: it is in the direction of the liberation of the subjected people, the liberation from the superior power of individuals and States (1974a: 22).

So far, it is only clear that Nagel's thinking has gone parallel with that of the radical criminologists in the USA and Britain. Let us turn now very briefly to some of his victimological views which are likely to be able to add strength to the radical position, and also to prevent radical criminology from being uprooted out of its criminological ground.

According to Nagel, the fundamental discovery of the victimological notion is that criminals and victims are the products of each other and he approvingly cites Masaryk's words: 'as long as there are martyrs there will be tyrants' (1974b: 110 and 128). Radicals often tend to perceive oppression and exploitation too much as one-sided activities of the oppressors and exploiters while they are in fact dialectical outcomes. The end of victim proneness is the end of oppression and exploitation. The sociological study of the structure of victimization, the analysis of structural victimization, may support victims in devising strategy and tactics for self-liberation. In fact Nagel calls for continuous development of political awareness, political analysis and conscious political action of the people when he declares: 'A State which assumes the power from society so as to more equitably distribute that power, has the most power. History teaches us that the State often misuses power even more than societies. Nearly every State and society is more or less criminogenic and makes victims. Even the brand new State which we create in the place of the old ones . . .' (1974b: 113–114). In spite of the importance Nagel attributes to politics, unlike most radical criminologists he does not ignore the victims of ordinary crimes. It is his concern for the victims that seems to have prevented him from romanticizing individually or socially injurious acts, even if they are legally defined by the State as crimes. But he demands that 'in dealing with these legally defined criminals, we take into account the criminal victimisation which (they) have suffered at the hands of people and powers not brought to trial' (1974b: 128). It may be that if radical criminologists devoted more attention to the victims of ordinary crimes, also theoretically, they would be more able to discern rationally which acts made legally punishable are detrimental to the struggle for a humane society where the inequalities of power and wealth are abolished. Furthermore they would then not so easily, or even a priori antagonize people of the middle and lower classes living, rightly or wrongly, in fear of this kind of crime; after all, this would be bad politics.

Nagel's unique position in Dutch criminology can perhaps be related to his personal experience during the fascist occupation of the Netherlands. This war past has, since the late sixties, once again become a present, living reality for him (van Amerongen 1973, Meijer 1974). It was a time when the fascist legal system authorized an inhuman social order with the vilest discrimination against racial groups, State authorities were really dangerous criminals, persons opposing inhumane oppression were legally defined as grave criminals and small groups of determined individuals, protecting victims of discrimination and fighting the superpower of the criminal fascist State were not unsuccessful. It is this period that plausibly has inspired his profoundly skeptical perception of the established legal and social order, and his continuous concern with the abuse of power, the victimological problem and the (political) self-help of the subjected, while living in a relatively quiet and paternalistic society.

4.

In this essay, in which an attempt has been made to treat summarily aspects of the process of politicization among criminologists, the author is aware that he did not mention all relevant publications, nor could he do justice to those that have been referred to. But perhaps he has awakened the interest of some readers who were not already acquainted with them in studying these themselves; if they do so they can also find the many references that have been omitted. The very limited aim of this essay does not include making an original contribution to the debate among radical criminologists. It is even less an effort to present coherently the present author's own views on criminology, which is the subject of studies to be published next year.

The sole intention of this paper has been to elucidate the significance and implications of Nagel's insistence that criminologists should not stand aloof from politics, an aspect which has nevertheless been largely neglected by Dutch criminologists. An attempt has also been made to mention some aspects of social situations that have conditioned styles of theorizing. This suggests that significant criminology, implying political awareness, cannot do without theoretical reflectivity; and that it will develop adequately within an organizational setting which enables research and intellectual debate, and with a practical involvement in combating social and legal injustices together with disadvantaged groups of people.

However, the specific sociopolitical conditions of a country are the major factor in determining what kind of criminology is significant in that country. It is even conceivable that it would be altogether impossible in a country with a dictatorial oppressive regime to practice any meaningful criminology. In that case, leaving the profession would seem to be the only alternative.

REFERENCES

Bay, C., 'Politics and pseudo-politics: a critical evaluation of some behavioral literature,' *The American Political Science Review* LIX (1965) pp. 39–51; reprinted in Charles A. McCoy and John Playford (eds.), *Apolitical politics. A critique of behavioralism*, New York, 1967, pp. 12–37.

Becker, Howard S., *Outsiders. Studies in the sociology of deviance*. New York and London, 1963.

Becker, Howard S., *The other side. Perspectives on deviance*. New York and London, 1964.

Becker, Howard S., 'Whose side are we on?' presidential address at the annual meeting of the Society for the Study of Social Problems, Miami Beach, August, 1966; reprinted in Jack D. Douglas (ed.), *The relevance of sociology*, New York, 1970, pp. 99–111.

Berger, Peter L. and Thomas Luckmann, *The social construction of reality*. Garden City, N.Y., 1966.

Bianchi, H., *Position and subject-matter of criminology. Inquiry concerning theoretical criminology* Amsterdam, 1956.

Bianchi, H., *Ethiek van het straffen*. Nijkerk, 1964.

Bianchi, H., *De vliegengod: Opstellen over gezag, recht en orde*. Alphen aan den Rijn, 1967.

Bianchi, H., *Stigmatisering*. Deventer, 1971.

Bianchi, H., 'York en Florence; op weg naar een nieuwe kriminologie(?).' *Nederlands Tijdschrift voor Criminologie*, 16, 1974 (a), pp. 3–16.

Bianchi, H., 'Naar een nieuwe fenomenologische kriminologie,' *Nederlands Tijdschrift voor Criminologie*, 16, 1974 (b), pp. 97–112.

Bianchi, H., 'Goevernementele en non-goevernementele kriminologie,' *Nederlands Tijdschrift voor Criminologie*, 16, 1974 (c), pp. 201–126.

Bianchi, H., 'Das Tsedeka-Modell als „Alternative zum konventionellen Strafrecht," ' in *Zeitschrift für Evangelische Ethik*, 18, 1974 (d), pp. 89–110.

Bottomore, T. B., *Critics of society*. 2nd. ed., London, 1969.

Bottomore, T. B., *Sociology as social criticism*. London, 1975.

Buchholz, Erich, Richard Hartmann, John Lekschas and Gerhard Stiller, *Sozialistische Kriminologie*. 2. Auflage, Berlin, 1971.

Buikhuisen, W., *Criminologie en criminologisch onderzoek*. Assen, 1966.

Broom, Leonard and Philip Selznick, *Sociology. A text with adapted readings*. 5th. ed., New York and London, 1973.

Carson, W. G., 'The sociology of crime and the emergence of criminal laws. A review of some excursions into the sociology of law,' paper presented at the annual meeting of the British Sociological Association in London, April 1971; reprinted in Paul Rock and Mary McIntosh (eds.), *Deviance and social control*. London, 1974, pp. 67–90.

Castro, Fidel, *Fidel in Chile*. Major Fidel Castro's speeches during his visit to Chile. New York, 1972.

Cicourel, Aaron V., *The social organization of juvenile justice*. New York and London, 1968.

Cohen, Stanley (ed.), *Images of deviance*. Harmondsworth, 1971.

Cohen, Stanley, 'Criminology and the sociology of deviance in Britain,' paper presented at the annual conference of the British Sociological Association, in London, April 1971, reprinted in Paul Rock and Mary McIntosh (eds.), *Deviance and social control*. London 1974, pp. 1–40.

Currie, Elliott, 'Dialogue with Anthony M. Platt,' *Issues in Criminology*, 8 (1973), pp. 19–33.

Currie, Elliott, 'Beyond criminology,' *Issues in Criminology*, 9 (1974), pp. 133–142.

Dahl, Robert A., *Modern political analysis*. 2nd ed., Englewood Cliffs, N.J., 1970.
De Back, J., *Taal en afwijkend gedrag. Een analystische beschouwing*. Meppel, 1973.
De Jong, L., *Het koninkrijk der Nederlanden in de tweede wereldoorlog*. Deel I: *Voorspel*. 's-Gravenhage, 1969.
Dessaur, C. I., *Foundations of theory-formation in criminology; a methodological analysis*. The Hague, 1971 (a).
Dessaur, C. I., *Problemen en pseudo-problemen in de criminologie*. The Hague, 1971 (b).
Dessaur, C. I., 'Waardevolheid en waardevrijheid in de criminologie,' in Studium Generale Rotterdam 3: *Waarde, macht, kriminologie*. The Hague, 1974 (a), pp. 59–74.
Dessaur, C. I., *Criminal justice and conflict reduction*, paper presented at the English-Dutch Criminological Conference at Keele University, September 7, 1974 (b).
Doomen, Jeanne, 'Prof. dr. C. I. Dessaur (Andreas Burnier) hoogleraar criminologie Nijmegen. „Soms hoop ik dat we niet al te slim zijn," ' *Utrechtse Universitaire Reflexen*, 4 April 1973.
Duintjer, O. D., 'Moderne wetenschap en waardevrijheid,' *Algemeen Nederlands Tijdschrift voor Wijsbegeerte*, 62 (1970), pp. 22–44; reprinted in Theo de Boer and André J. F. Köbben (eds.), *Waarden en Wetenschap*. Bilthoven, 1974.
Erikson, Kay T., 'Notes on the sociology of deviance,' *Social Problems*, 9 (1962), pp. 307–314, reprinted in Howard S. Becker (ed.), *The other side. Perspectives on deviance*. New York and London, 1964, pp. 9–21.
Erikson, Kay T., *Wayward puritans. A study in the sociology of deviance*. New York and London, 1966.
Frenkel, F. E. (ed.), *Provo. Kanttekeningen bij een deelverschijnsel*. Amsterdam, 1966.
Friedrichs, Robert W., 'Choice and commitment in social research,' paper presented at the 6th World Congress of Sociology, Evian, France, (1966); revised version reprinted in Jack D. Douglas (ed.), *The impact of sociology*, New York, 1970, pp. 79–89.
Goffman, Erving, *Asylums. Essays on the social situations of mental patients and other inmates*. Garden City, N.Y., 1961.
Goffman, Erving, *Stigma. Notes on the management of spoiled identity*. Englewood Cliffs, N.J., 1963.
Goldwyn, Eileen, 'Dialogue with Richard Quinney,' *Issues in Criminology*, 6 (1971), pp. 41–54.
Gouldner, Alvin W., 'The sociologist as partisan: sociology and the welfare state,' *American Sociologist*, 3 (1968), pp. 103–116, reprinted in Jack D. Douglas (ed.), *The relevance of sociology*, New York, 1970 (a), pp. 112–148.
Gouldner, Alvin W., *The coming crisis of Western sociology*. New York, 1970 (b).
Habermas, Jürgen, 'Technik und Wissenschaft als „Ideologie," ' in *Technik und Wissenschaft als 'Ideologie,'* Frankfurt am Main, 1968, pp. 48–103.
Hoefnagels, G. P., *Beginselen van criminologie*, Deventer, 1969.
Hoefnagels, G. P., *Rituelen ter terechtzitting*, Deventer, 1970.
Hoefnagels, G. P., *Welzijnscriminaliteit. Een essay over criminele politiek en milieu-beleid*. Meppel, 1972.
Hoefnagels, G. P., *The other side of criminologie. An inversion of the concept of crime*. Deventer, 1973 (a).
Hoefnagels, G. P. (ed.), *Help, ik word geholpen*. Deventer, 1973 (b).
Hoefnagels, G. P., 'Macht, waarde en kriminologie,' in Studium Generale Rotterdam 3, *Waarde, macht, kriminologie*, The Hague, 1974, pp. 75–96.
Hoefnagels, G. P., 'Criminologie, fenomenologie en de Utrechtse School,' *Nederlands Tijdschrift voor Criminologie*, 17 (1975), pp. 3–14.
Hulsman, L. H. C., 'Kriteria voor strafbaarstelling,' in *Strafrecht te recht? Over dekriminalisering en depenalisering*, Baarn, 1972, pp. 80–92.
Kempe, G. Th., *Criminaliteit en kerkgenootschap*. Utrecht, 1938.
Kempe, G. Th. and J. Vermaat, *Criminaliteit in Drente*. Utrecht, 1939.
Kempe, G. Th., 'Vers une criminologie mieux fondée,' in Jacques Léauté (ed.), *Une nouvelle école de science criminelle l'École d'Utrecht*, Paris, 1959, pp. 81–94.
Kempe, G. Th., *Inleiding tot de criminologie*. Haarlem, 1967.

Kempe, G. Th., *Fransz von Liszt en de criminologie*. Amsterdam, 1968.
Kempe, G. Th., 'De publieke opinie en de strafrechter in de laatste halve eeuw: enkele inleidende opmerkingen,' in *Dilemma's in het hedendaagse strafrecht*, Utrecht, 1975, pp. 5–22.
Laing, R. D., *The divided self*. London, 1960.
Laing, R. D., *The self and others*. London, 1961.
Laing, R. D., *The politics of the family and other essays*. London, 1971.
Lemert, Edwin, *Social pathology*. New York, 1951.
Lemert, Edwin, *Human deviance, social problems and social control*. New Jersey, 1967.
Lijphart, Arend, *The politics of accomodation. Pluralism and democracy in the Netherlands*. Berkeley and Los Angelos, 1968.
Lipset, Seymour Martin, *Political man. The social bases of politics*. Garden City, N.Y., 1960, (quotation from the Anchor books edition, 1963).
Matza, David, *Delinquency and drift*. New York and London, 1964.
Matza, David, *Becoming deviant*. Englewood Cliffs, N.J., 1969.
Mead, George Herbert, *Mind, self and society*, edited by Charles W. Morris, Chicago, 1934.
Mannheim, Hermann, *Comparative criminology* (A textbook). vol. II, London, 1965.
Merton, Robert K., 'The self-fulfilling prophecy,' in *The Antioch Review*, 7 (1948); reprinted in Robert K. Merton, *Social theory and social structure*, New York, 1957, pp. 421–436.
Merton, Robert K. and Robert Nisbet, *Contemporary social problems*. New York, 1961.
Merton, Robert K. and Robert Nisbet, *Contemporary social problems*, 3rd ed., New York, 1971.
Meijer, Ischa, 'De rechtvaardiging van J. B. Charles,' *Haagse Post*, 61 (1974), pp. 38–63.
Millet, Kate, *Sexual politics*, Garden City, N.Y., 1970.
Moedikdo, Paul, *Sociologie en recht. Over hedendaagse opvattingen betreffende het strafrecht en hun maatschappelijke betekenis*. Meppel, 1974.
Nagel, W. H., *De criminaliteit van Oss*. Groningen, 1949.
Nagel, W. H., *Het strafrecht en de onmens*. 's-Gravenhage, 1956.
Nagel, W. H., 'Sociologische criminologie,' *Sociologisch Jaarboek*, XII, 1958, pp. 58–102.
Nagel, W. H., 'Victimologie,' discourse at the Belgian-Dutch criminological meeting, 20 Dec. 1958; reprinted in *Tijdschrift voor Strafrecht*, 68 (1959), pp. 1–26.
Nagel, W. H., 'De Utrechtse School,' *Tijdschrift voor Strafrecht*, 72, 1963 (a), pp. 322–355, Leiden.
Nagel, W. H., 'The notion of victimology in criminology,' *Excerpta Criminologica*, 3, 1963 (b), pp. 245–247.
Nagel, W. H., 'Critical criminology' paper presented at the VIth Congress of the International Society of Criminology in Madrid, Spain on September 24, 1970; reprinted in *Abstracts on Criminology and Penology*, 11 (1971), pp. 1–5.
Nagel, W. H., 'Terrorisme,' *Tijdschrift voor Sociale Wetenschappen*, 1972, pp. 135–156.
Nagel, W. H., 'Politiek en criminologie,' in Studium Generale Rotterdam 3; *Waarde, macht, kriminologie*, The Hague, 1974 (a), pp. 3–24.
Nagel, W. H., 'Structural victimisation,' *International Journal of Criminology and Penology*, 2, 1974 (b), pp. 99–133.
Phillipson, Michael and Maurice Roche, 'Phenomenology, sociology, and the study of deviance,' in Paul Rock and Mary McIntosh (eds.), *Deviance and social control*, London, 1974, pp. 125–162.
Platt, Anthony M., *The child savers. The invention of delinquency*. Chicago and London, 1969.
Platt, Anthony M., 'Prospects for a radical criminology in the U.S.A.,' paper presented to the 1st Conference of European Group for the Study of Deviance and Social Control, Florence, Italy, (1973); reprinted in Ian Taylor, Paul Walton and Jack Young (eds.), *Critical Criminology*, London, 1975, pp. 95–112.
Quinney, Richard and Marshall B. Clinard (eds.), *Criminal behavior systems. A typology*. New York and London, 1967.
Quinney, Richard, *Crime and justice in society*. Boston, 1969.
Quinney, Richard(ed.), *The social reality of crime*. Boston, 1970.

Quinney, Richard, 'The ideology of law: notes for a radical alternative to legal oppression,' *Issues in Criminology*, 7 (1972), pp. 1–35.
Quinney, Richard, 'Crime control in capitalist society: a critical philosophy of legal order,' *Issues in Criminology*, 8 (1973), pp. 75–99; reprinted in Ian Taylor, Paul Walton, Jock Young (eds.), *Critical Criminology*, London, 1975, pp. 181–202.
Quinney, Richard, *Critique of legal order*. Boston, 1974.
Rijksen, R., *Meningen van gedetineerden over de strafrechtspleging*. Assen, 1958.
Rock, Paul and Mary McIntosh (eds.), *Deviance and social control*. London, 1974.
Schur, Edwin M., *Crimes without victims. Deviant behavior and public policy. Abortion, homosexuality, drug addiction*. Englewood Cliffs, N.J., 1965.
Schwendinger, Herman and Julia Schwendinger, 'Defenders of order or guardians of human rights?' *Issues in Criminology*, 5 (1970), pp. 123–157; reprinted in Ian Taylor, Paul Walton, Jock Young (eds.), *Critical criminology*, London, 1975, pp. 113–146.
Seeley, John R., 'Social science? Some probative problems,' from a paper presented at a Department of Psychology and Sociology Colloquium at Brandeis University on November 14, 1962; reprinted in Maurice Stein and Arthur Vidich (eds.), *Sociology on trial*, New York, 1963, pp. 53–65.
Skolnick, Jerome K., *Justice without trial. Law enforcement in a democratic society*. New York, 1966.
Skolnick, Jerome K., *The politics of protest. A report submitted by Jerome H. Skolnick, director Task Force on Violent Aspects of Protest and Confrontation of the National Commission on the Causes and Prevention of Violence*. New York, 1969.
Sutherland, Edwin H., *The professional thief*. Chicago, 1937.
Sutherland, Edwin H., 'Crime and business' *The Annals of the American Academy of Political and Social Science*, 217 (1941), pp. 112–118.
Sutherland, Edwin H., 'Is „white collar crime" crime?' *American Sociological Review*, 10 (1945), pp. 132–139.
Sutherland, Edwin H., *Principles of criminology*. 4th ed., Chicago and New York, 1947.
Sutherland, Edwin H., *White Collar Crime*, New York, 1949.
Sutherland, Edwin H. and Donald R. Cressey, *Principles of criminology*. 6th ed., Chicago and New York, 1960.
Tannenbaum, Frank, *Crime and the community*. New York, 1951.
Taylor, Ian and Laurie Taylor, *Politics and deviance*. Harmondsworth, 1973.
Taylor, Ian, Paul Walton and Jock Young, *The new criminology: For a social theory of deviance*. London, 1973.
Taylor, Ian, Paul Walton and Jock Young (eds.), *Critical criminology*. London, 1975.
Taylor, Ian, Paul Walton and Jock Young, 'Critical criminology in Britain: review and prospects,' in Ian Taylor, Paul Walton and Jock Young (eds.), *Critical Criminology*, London, 1975, pp. 6–62.
Turk, Austin T., *Criminality and the legal order*. Chicago, 1969.
Van Amerongen, M., 'Verzet. De boze dromen van J. B. Charles,' *Vrij Nederland*, 34 (1973) 24 November.
Van Weringh, J., *Heeft onze maatschappij de criminaliteit die zij verdient?* Amsterdam, 1971.
Van Weringh, J., 'Een gesprek met de algemene adviseur wetenschappelijk werk van het Ministerie van Justitie,' *Nederlands Tijdschrift voor Criminologie*, 17 (1975), pp. 125–131.
Weber, Max, *Wirtschaft und Gesellschaft*. 5. revidierte Auflage, Tübingen, 1972.
Weis, Joseph G., 'Dialogue with David Matza,' *Issues in Criminology*, 6 (1971), pp. 33–53.
Wilkins, Leslie T., *Social deviance. Social policy, action and research*. London, 1964.
Wright Mills, C., 'The professional ideology of social pathologists,' *American Journal of Sociology*, XLIX (1943), pp. 165–180; reprinted in Irving Louis Horowitz (ed.), *Power, politics and people. The collected essays of C. Wright Mills*, New York, 1967, pp. 525–552.
Wright Mills, C., 'On knowledge and power,' *Dissent*, 2 (1951), pp. 201–212, quotation from reprint in Irving Louis Horowitz (ed.), *Power, politics and people. The collected essays of C. Wright Mills*, New York, 1967, pp. 599–613.

Wright Mills, C., *The sociological imagination.* New York, 1959.
Young, Jock, 'Working-class criminology,' in Ian Taylor, Paul Walton and Jock Young (eds.), *Critical criminology*, London, 1975, pp. 63–94.

Hans Hinderer

PERSONALITY RESEARCH AND ITS IMPORTANCE FOR CRIMINOLOGY AND CRIMINAL LAW

Offender personality studies are among the most important tasks of criminological research and the theory and practice of criminal law based on it. The crucial point in these offender personality studies is the identification of those personality features which, in addition to other factors, have played a more or less decisive role in causing the offender to commit his offense.

Studies on the personality structure of recidivists in the German Democratic Republic, for example, have in the main confirmed correlations also reported in the international literature. Recidivists are generally individuals with developmental deficiencies and problems in interpersonal relations, who try to compensate for their social deficit through offenses. The view that even aggressive offenders in reality demonstrate substantial maladjustment has been repeatedly confirmed – a fact which does not minimize their dangerousness in the acute offense situation. Identification of these personality data can supply exceedingly important information (also for social practice) when incipient criminal development can be successfully detected early and corrected by means other than those provided by criminal law. The objective of this correction is not to correct the deficiency, because the personal circumstances often make this impossible, but to develop and maintain the individual's ability to cope with these stresses and functional impairments, and to learn to act responsibly. These individuals usually turn to crime when their immediate environment fails to offer them the help which their personalities require, and when they lack the degree of self-esteem which every human being needs.

Criminological research in the German Democratic Republic focuses on the task of amassing research data which can contribute to an explanation of the crime phenomenon and to prevention of crime; a secondary task is to popularize these data in order to involve the entire society in this complex task. In this approach it is presumed that crime is for the most part socially determined. This basic concept, however, remains unaffirmed unless individual criteria are also taken into account and explained.

An important task in controlling crime is the control and especially the prevention of juvenile delinquency. If the above-mentioned characteristics of recidivists are to be utilized in juvenile delinquency control, it must be taken into account that among the young there is a group, only vaguely defined, that can become delinquent under unfavorable circumstances owing to certain disturbances in personality development. Evident social maldevelopment is involved in these cases. There are no methods of investigation by which the individuals in this group can be identified, because it is impossible to predict chance which is often the decisive factor in the turn to crime. Nevertheless, this predelinquency should be recognized, particularly in educational work, and government and society should take proactive and individualized sophisticated measures early enough to prevent its development into delinquency.

The solution to this task of practical crime prevention makes extraordinarily high demands on the empathy and understanding of all persons involved. This activity is guided by the constitutional principle expressed in article 90 (section 2) of the Constitution of the German Democratic Republic, which states that the control and prevention of crime and all other forms of unlawful activity is the concern of the entire society. This also encompasses, among other things, the resocialization of offenders who have served their sentence. We might note that in this context extensive and very effective activities have been organized in practice in order to meet this constitutional requirement. The constitutional principle has been taken into account in numerous legal regulations and also in various internal directives in businesses; in all these rules and regulations the responsibility of workers' collectives, managements and government organizations is clearly defined.

The obligation expressed in the Constitution of the German Democratic Republic is clear. The social responsibility in the fight against distressing and impeding phenomena does not release the individual from his responsibility for living in the community in accordance with the opportunities available to him, and for fulfilling his obligations in the community. This also creates the most favorable opportunity for developing his own personality. It would be a serious error to have delinquency-prone individuals rely exclusively on social activities, for this would not be conducive to the development of their own personality.

This self-responsibility also applies to convicted offenders. Legislation in the German Democratic Republic always affirms the expectation that the convicted offender will not passively 'suffer' his punishment but will make use of the time to draw useful conclusions from the events and learn from them to correct his life style. The constitutional principle applies without restriction also to the implementation of non-custodial sentences, e.g. probation. Moreover, through the various possibilities for serving a sentence in installments the law ensures that the individual's further development is not harmed.

In criminological research, special attention is focused on analysis of victims and their personality structure. This, too, serves the study of crime and the differentiated evaluation of criminal responsibility; but at the same time it protects the rights of the victims. A carefully premeditated murder cannot be properly evaluated unless the personality of the victim of the crime is carefully explored. In such cases the detection of personal peculiarities and characteristics of the murder victim is of no importance; what is important is the discovery of relationships and influences which led the offender to eventually commit the act.

These relationships and influences may have developed over a long period of time and the offense (e.g. the murder of a tyrannizing relative) cannot be properly evaluated if only the final phase of the tragic developments is considered in the investigation. A too narrow view of the course of events would not reveal the possibility of an affect with its consequences for the assessment of criminal responsibility and for the sentence. The criminal law of the German Democratic Republic recognizes the necessity of a differentiated evaluation of the offense, both with regard to determination of criminal responsibility and with regard to the appropriate sentence.

Victimological considerations ensure differentiated evaluations. In many crimes the offender-victim relationship is coincidental and this applies in particular to the numerous offenses against unknown victims (in order to minimize the risk of discovery).

Swindlers who commit the same type of offense frequently also operate in this way, applying only general criteria (e.g. age) in selecting their victims. Apart from the victim's personality, however, attention should also focus on persons who have some personal relationship with the offender without inciting him to crime or giving him aid, abetment or complicity in the technical sense of the law. The offender's behavior is influenced by numerous circumstantial factors. These include influences of all persons who affect the offender's development in some way. Criminological studies have shown, for example, that offenders often come from families which are disturbed in various ways. These disturbances in family life can have almost irreversible effects on the young, driving them to irresponsible behavior. It is possible to counteract these influences through social measures in principle: unless we accept this view, criminal responsibility could hardly ever be demonstrated in such cases. In exceptional cases, however, the unfavorable environment in which a juvenile was brought up can preclude the juvenile offender's culpability; and of course the responsibility of the juvenile offender can be precluded or reduced for the same reason in such cases.

In close personal relationships there are a variety of forces and influences. Reprehensible parental behavior does not always lead to similar behavior on the part of their children because their influence may be counteracted and suppressed by social influences and aids. This is probably an important result of the effect of the socialist society on its individual citizens, especially its youthful citizens. But there are also adverse influences and unexpected consequences with which one cannot reckon and which in fact seem quite impossible upon superficial examination. A child is not always a reflection of its parents. For example, a young person brought up in a home in which personal property and public property are strictly respected will as a rule follow this example and behave like his parents. But this is not an automatic process. Under some circumstances the good example may produce a paradoxical effect, as can be illustrated by the following example. When a child has a speech impediment which makes it difficult or impossible for him to establish personal relationships and friendships, and when in addition his parents are overprotective or humiliate him or hurt his feelings, it is quite understandable that he may seek to repress these problems in his own personality development by aggression aimed indirectly against his parents, e.g. in the form of theft.

Such aggression, which enters the sphere of delinquent behavior, can reinforce his self-esteem and minimize his feelings of inferiority. Aggressive acts are not exclusively aimed against the parents and their personal property; the young person may fear this directness of his aggressive behavior and its consequences, perhaps because he fears a final and decisive break with his parents – the only persons with whom he has any relationship. It is also possible for the juvenile to offset the model parental behavior (careful, thrifty and always self-denying) by being very generous with someone else's money. In this type of offense he creates distance between himself and his parents, whose views he does not fully understand and whose example he does not accept.

Of course the description of this example is an oversimplification; nevertheless it demonstrates an important fact: that development toward a criminal offense cannot be mechanically explained. It cannot be postulated that a certain type of parental behavior inevitably explains a certain type of behavior on the part of the child brought up by them. Such a 'carbon copy of a social behavior pattern' is conceivable, but it is not by any means inevitable. Our example has shown that an opposite type of reaction is also possible. The juvenile delinquent acts in contempt of the rules of social life in order to overcome the constraints of his parental home and switch off their influence on him. In this process of personality development, chance plays a certain role (in some cases even a decisive role); in our example the speech impediment and perhaps in addition the daily humiliations. These particular facts cause the adolescent to cope with his sooner or later inevitable separation from his parental home through antisocial behavior; after all, he must become independent some time.

It can thus be observed that the youngster's goal is justified and legitimate. What merits criticism is the manner in which he tries to achieve this goal. Leaving aside any assessment in terms of criminal law, we must observe that both sides of this conflict attest to social bungling. Not only has the youngster failed socially to cope with the situation in which he found himself, the adults involved, although they cannot be considered delinquent and are not criminally responsible for their faulty behavior, have in their role as educators also failed to cope with the situation. Perhaps they have in exercising their educational duties insufficiently recognized that their obligation to meet immediate needs and desires in their child is at the same time a contribution to the development of his personality. Under these circumstances they have not sufficiently seen and recognized the feelings, wishes and hopes, nor the disappointments and vexations of their child.

These considerations would seem to warrant the conclusion that, generally, the persons living in constant touch with the offender are of great importance in explaining his criminal development. It is therefore advisable to include in the criminological considerations the existing and ever-changing personal relationships and ties, with special reference to the position, dependency or dominant role of the person who has become an offender. What is important is not so much an all-round study of the personalities involved as an examination of their specific effects on the offender, which must be evaluated in this context.

Such a study may reveal the development of distinctive behavior discernible only in this relationship, perhaps induced by some negative factor but possibly also a consequence of many years of tension in a personal relationship in which both parties were fated to become entwined. In such cases it is quite evident that a study of the offender personality should include his relationship to other persons: otherwise the dominant conflict situation not only remains obscure but may be misunderstood as an individual trait without social background, and in extreme cases even as a biological or medical problem. In individual cases a relationship as outlined here can of course have psychopathological effects. The psychopathological effects, however, are only understandable and assessable in terms of practical prevention when the etiological factors are considered in the personality evalution. Otherwise a biological, psychological or medical interpretation of the offender personality, abstracted from the abovementioned determinants, would merely afford an explanation of the symptoms but not indicate the social conclusions which are needed for crime prevention.

It is hoped that this contribution will stimulate more intensive observation and assessment of the multiple interrelated factors in personality development. Undoubtedly, however, it is vital to recognize and apply the observations and assessments made by the social sciences and natural science in order to reach the right, concrete and direct conclusions for practical work in the prevention of personal maldevelopment.

It is by no means easy to draw these conclusions from the totality of developments in legal science, criminology, psychology, psychiatry, etc.; particularly because the mechanism of moral evaluation is not in principle confined to a differentiated and well-balanced assessment of scientific data but, in fact, often conceals gaps of knowledge behind prejudice. In legal evaluation, too, it is possible that these problems will arise. It is much easier to condemn certain behavior on the basis of generally accepted views than it is to confront the difficult problem of investigating the individuality of the behavior – confined of course to the basic elements – in a differentiated manner.

This problem can be solved only if jurists refrain from regarding themselves as the sole authorities in explaining deviant behavior. The diagnosis and prevention of human maldevelopment is a task of society, as it is in fact defined and viewed in the legislation of the German Democratic Republic.

Criminal procedure should take these aspects into account and take recourse to qualified assistance, e.g. that of psychological and medical experts. In law as in medicine, it is not only evaluation that matters but also prevention and cure; and this humanist approach cannot in principle disregard the individuality of the individual. This is the basic point which W. H. Nagel makes in his publication *Pönitentiäre Behandlung und die Gusseiserne Tautologie* (Penitentiary Treatment and Cast Iron Tautology) (Darmstadt, 1969).

A. Mergen

SEXUALITY AND CRIMINAL LAW IN TERMS OF ANTHROPOLOGICAL AND SOCIAL CONFLICT

The correlations and interferences between the biological and the social spheres, between what is called social reality and the needs or objectives of man, become evident in a study of the conflicts which sexuality poses for man in his society. Criminal law presents itself as an instrument of control and as a regulatory mechanism in these conflicts. Perhaps sexuality, more than any other phenomenon of human experience and behavior, is not only masked but also transformed by sociocultural influences. Biological, anthropological and psychological factors interlace on the sociologically created foundation. Since the Kinsey Reports of 1948 and 1953 we know that sexual reality differs substantially from the social expectations. From this discrepancy arises the self-perpetuating conflict which, in the final analysis, seems to be rooted in the antinomy between what is and what should be.

Sexuality is in the sphere of influence of vital needs and the requirements of society which in all cultures and at all times has tried to exert control over the sexual behavior of the group and of the individual. The precepts and prohibitions of criminal law have been introduced as instruments to enforce the desired human sexual behavior and prevent the undesired. Again and again it has been found that in the conflict which arises when biologically determined instinctive behavior is regulated by normative coercions the biological urges are the stronger. The protagonists of social control dislike admitting their partial failures. They close their eyes to reality; and when their eyes are forced open by a study such as Kinsey's, they side-step the facts in rationalizing their arguments or conceal the truth in a hypocritical attitude. They would rather not recognize the conflict. Yet the conflict is real, inevitable, and in fact necessary. Evolution is highly inconceivable without conflict.

The liberalization of criminal law with regard to the reglementation of human sexual behavior has required a long time of gradual realization. It has had to overcome obstinate resistance although it has from the outset not been clear which inalienable right or area of the law is really under attack or threatened (and therefore requires the protection of criminal law) when sexual activity does not endanger or harm either the individual or society. Consider, for example, the discussions concerning the decriminalization of homosexual behavior, the changes in the paragraphs on procuring and the treatment of sodomy as an offense and the recent heated, emotion-ridden debates on abortion. In all these instances the conflict grows. It becomes more acute as we are forced to recognize that the sexual behavior actually observable does not (or no longer) correspond to the postulated expectations; 'what is' reveals that 'what should be' is an illusion.

Sociologists, biologists, anthropologists and psychologists have offered a variety of definitions of sexuality, in accordance with their different disciplines. In all scientific disciplines, however, efforts focus on the identification of psychological phenomena and the determination of the dividing line between them and their biological foundations and sociocultural relations. The sociologists, and some anthropologists as well (Schelsky, Gehlen), vehemently refuse to accept sexuality as instinctive behavior rooted in biological processes. The behaviorists and ethologists (Lorenz, Tinbergen, Eibel-Eibelsfeld) on the other hand support this view. The reproach directed at the ethologists is that they commit the fundamental error of extrapolating the results of animal experiments to human experience and behavior. Without going into this controversy it can be maintained that ethologists do not simply extrapolate from one animal species to the other, or even to man. They merely make use of the working hypotheses obtained from animal models in their approach to human problems. It is Wicker's merit (1969) that he pointed this out again and again. Beach (1956) regards sexuality as something like a bundle of affect expectations. Wright (1968) characterizes the sexual urge as survival instinct. Masters and Johnson (1966, p. 139) define the sexual response as an instinctive activity arising from an undifferentiated condition. Depth psychologists – from Janet via Freud to Jung – have discussed, argued and debated the meaning and essence of sexuality. Some sociologists, past and present, go so far as to question the biological essence of sexuality. And Freud shocked laymen and scientists by describing the human infant as a sexual being of polymorphic perversities.

Criminal laws whose primary purpose evidently is to maintain the ideologies of a powerful minority, are criminogenic; they create conflicts and solve no problems. This is a reproach which criminal law must accept for vast areas of sexual legislation.

Before problems become legal problems they exist on an anthropological and sociological level. It is characteristic, particularly in Germany, for studies intending to suggest sociological solutions to conflicts of sexual-psychological determination (e.g. Schelsky, Gehlen) to concern themselves with the rejection of biological concepts for human application, and show a close relationship to obsolete philosophical anthropology and to the philosophical tradition of German idealism. Their opponents are the sexologists who draw upon natural science (e.g. Giese, Sigusch, Brocher, Bürger-Prinz) and the biologically oriented ethologists (Lorenz, Eibel-Eibelsfeld). Portmann and his school stand midway between these two fronts in their work. All this has led, not so much to clarification as to confusion. The question of the significance of the biological aspect for human sexuality is still controversial. The question whether human sexuality is based on a primary drive (Thomae 1965) is still moot, particularly for the sociologists. However, as long as all sociological studies on human sexuality are guided by the tacit hypothesis that man, in his biological existence and in the totality of his behavior, is subject to a special structural law (Gehlen 1958, p. 29; Portmann 1956), it will be difficult to bring these problems to a satisfactory solution. In the final analysis, all these efforts are made merely in order to prove the postulate of the totality of the special nature of man (Portmann 1956, p. 27). The situation remains hopelessly confused because there is no sign of agreement on the exact meaning of the drive concept. Jaspers (1959, p. 522) simply held that sexuality causes unrest in man. He probably meant the unrest which causes man and animal alike to look for suitable stimulus situations in which the drive can find gratification. Application of the drive concept to human drive phenomena poses problems in particular because of the smooth transition of its defined real elements along with all the possible human motivations and needs.

The entire problem revolves around the fact that the research findings to date with regard to the dividing line between congenital and learned cannot be brought under a common denominator acceptable to all disciplines. And this applies in particular to man and his sexuality.

All available facts seem to indicate, however, that human sexual behavior too, is based on well-defined, biologically determined basic patterns (cf. Lorenz 1963, 1967; Wicker 1969, p. 27). Despite all cultural transformation and despite the wide range of variation in human sexuality in all its individual manifestations, the biological aspect of sexuality is always apparent in sexual desire. Human sexuality does not simply represent a primarily unspecific basic need which receives its meaning and objectives only from society, as has been maintained by sociologists in particular, and also by anthropologists (cf. Lüth 1970, p. 2538). Intercultural comparison reveals that, in spite of the many different forms in which sexuality is expressed, it has a phylogenetic continuity and that the basic patterns of human sexual behavior show a high degree of similarity. Sociologists, too, should accept this. In their respective structures, all societies are founded on the biological difference between the sexes. In the social field, these biological immutabilities correspond to more or less firmly established role specifications for men and women. Even though the equality of rights of the sexes has become a matter of course in the law, the biological differences must not be forgotten. What Sumner wrote as early as 1927 remains true: 'No discussion, protest or rationalization can alter the fact that women bear children, and men do not.' Schelsky (1971, p. 148) maintains that our culture is based on opposite formations of the roles of the sexes, and that the growing similarity in the roles of the sexes will undermine the foundations of our traditional culture. Be this as it may, the problems are numerous, and fraught with conflict. Masculinized women and feminized men contribute to primitivization in the direction of uni-sex (which is really not desired either by woman or by man).

The disparate evaluation of masculine and feminine sexuality is based on sociocultural, and partly on religious concepts. Until recently, women were considered incapable of orgasm. Criminal law treated women unequally, for example by imposing a penalty on the homosexually active male, but not on the female who engaged in homosexual acts. Today the right to pleasure is granted to everyone, male or female. But even today the biologically determined sex role and the socially determined role of the male or of the female do not always correspond entirely. It is in fact very difficult to distinguish what is a psychosociological essential characteristic feature of the sexes, and what is really a sociocultural differentiating feature resulting from a certain ideal with regard to upbringing. In no culture, however, are there more than a few individuals who do not behave and experience themselves and the world in accordance with their biological sex (and in accordance with the expectations of society). This is confirmed by the minority of sexual deviates, who are either more or less accepted or completely rejected by the group. Everything seems to indicate that even the entirely socially determined behavior patterns are to some extent shaped by the basic biological patterns (cf. Murdoch 1949).

A fact which also points in this direction is that women very rarely commit violent crimes (they account for only 12–15% of all such offenses). Violent sexual offenses are committed only by men; women are the victims. Giese (1962, p. 209) was probably also referring to the sex-specific potential for aggression when he remarked that siring requires a different sexuality than conceiving. In the poetry of all cultures it is the men who sing and the women who are sung to. The muses are women, who inspire men. Sexuality is associated with aggression, particularly in the male. In the forms of his sexual activity, even if stunted as in exhibitionism, hypertrophic as in rape, or perverted as in sadism, man shows that every sexual aggression is accompanied by an experience of self-elevation and power over the sexual partner (which gives both partners pleasure). However, even apart from these specific manifestations of human sexuality in the range of abnormal or delinquent behavior, the genital potency of the male serves to confirm the value and special characteristic of the male individual in accordance with the social evaluations of a sexual performance society (Schelsky). Genital potency can become a demonstration of social potency. For both sexes sexuality, apart from all its sociological and anthropological meanings, is a means of self-experience, self-assertion and self-confirmation. Moreover, sexuality is in principle related to another individual and therefore to society, thus giving rise to reciprocal obligations of society and the individuals living in it. In every sexual partner relationship experienced, moreover, reciprocal responsibility and assistance arises from the dependency of 'Me' on 'You.'

Criminal law is directly and necessarily involved in this conflict in that it formulates enforcable rules for all citizens. Norms of criminal law have an absolute character, even though they have been made into law. The social and cultural norms have not been formulated by any legislative authority; they have simply developed, and are regarded as precursors of the law. It is left to the legislator to decide which sociocultural norms are to be elevated to generally binding legal norms. If social norms are habits, which have become second nature, as Gehlen maintains, then there is a risk that the legislator will indiscriminately preserve institutionalized norms without adapting them to the developments in a dynamic society. In that case a conflict arises between the social norm and the legal norm. When the legal norms are not shared by the general public but regarded only as protection of the norms of an elite group, they give rise to conflict. Another source of conflict arises when the punishability of a type of behavior is made dependent on a particular postulated image of man, rejecting other possible images. The prohibition of incest codified in criminal law has archaic overtones. There appears to be a general incest taboo, completely outside the control of criminal law. It should be self-regulating. Schelsky (1971, p. 159) holds that the incest prohibition is merely 'the negative side of the social precept of exogamy, which became necessary in all societies in order to attain and secure the social structure and cooperative coherence that extended beyond the ties of the family unit.' Incest was initially confined to parent-child and brother-sister relationships, but subsequently extended to more remote family relationships. The prohibition did not seem to apply to the ruling classes. Incestuous marriages between rulers were arranged by diplomatic negotiation, and served to establish or reinforce the reigning 'house.' A situation as ambivalent as that which the incest taboo creates, is unsuitable for regulation by criminal law.

Whenever there is a taboo on sexual behavior, it is self-regulating and not all dependent upon the control function of criminal law.

Criminal law regulates and controls the social behavior of the citizens. It should practice a strict hands-off policy with regard to morality, for 'morality' is not a juridical category. The law can make morality possible, as Radbruch maintained, but it can never enforce morality because the 'moral act can of necessity be an act performed in freedom only.' Criminal law should confine itself to its functions of order and protection and should refrain from codifying alleged ideal norms as if avowing its belief in some religion. Herbert Jäger (1962, p. 179) mentions the necessary demythologization of criminal law and states: 'A legislative conception which assigns to criminal law the function of maintaining social peace and protection is to be regarded as the only way to more objective, more valid solutions; only in this way can the defense against and control of harmful antisocial types of behavior (and not the maintenance of certain norms) become the teleological principle of legality.'

Before he becomes a social being, the human individual is a biological, and therefore a sexual, being. Sexuality is a biological fact, and is consequently not subject to any value judgment. The extent to which sexual activities can be subject to valuation is controversial, but criminal law would be well-advised to stand aloof from this controversy. It should refrain from all ideologies and moral conceptions, and should serve only as an instrument for the protection of all citizens and their state.

The problem of outside intervention with regard to sexuality persists, and remains conflict-laden. Schelsky (1971, p. 134) seems to evaluate the social regulation of sexual relations rather one-sidedly when he writes: 'The cultural transformation of sexual urges is certainly one of the most original cultural achievements and existential requirements of man, much like tools and speech; in fact there can be no objection to regarding this regulation of human sexual and procreational relations as the primary social form of all human behavior.' One might also ask: 'Hypocrisy included?'

Even if we accept Schelsky's hypothesis we must admit that both cultural and legal norms are subject to change and have the function of providing new objectives for action or of maintaining (while at the same time adjusting) the traditional concepts. The change begins when the discrepancy between the traditional and the actual, between the legislated and the experienced, between the social and the legal norms becomes so marked as to be intolerable.

Human sexuality cannot be shaped or formed by norms. It is what it is, as such existing and unique to human existence. It is only sexual activities that can be guided. Sexuality has its original purpose in itself; it is a source of pleasure and its aim is to maintain the species. It cannot be alienated from its aim, abused, suppressed or violated without punishment.

REFERENCES

Beach, F. A., 'Characteristics of Masculine Sex Drive,' in *Nebraska Symposium on Motivation.* 1956.

Eibel-Eibelsfeld, J., *Grundriss der vergleichenden Verhaltensforschung, Ethologie.* 1967.

Gehlen, A., *Der Mensch.* 1958.

Giese, H. (ed.), *Psychopathologie der Sexualität.* 1962.

Jäger, H., in Giese (ed.), *op. cit.*

Jaspers, R., *Allgemeine Psychopathologie.* 1959.

Lorenz, K., *Das sogenannte Böse.* 1963.

„ *Über tierisches und menschliches Verhalten.* II, 1967.

Lüth, P., 'Aspekte der Sexualwissenschaft und ihrer Disziplinierung,' *Deutsches Aerzteblatt,* 33 (1970) pp. 2479 ff.; pp. 2537 ff.

Masters, W. H. and V. E. Johnson, *Human Sexual Response.* 1966.

Murdoch, *Social Structure.* 1949.

Portmann, A., *Zoologie und das neue Bild des Menschen.* 1956.

Schelsky, H., in H. Giese (ed.), *Die Sexualität des Menschen.* 1971.

Sumner, W. G., *The Science of Society.* Vol. I, 1927.

Tembrock, G., *Verhaltensforschung.* 1961.

Thomae, H., 'Das Problem der Motivation,' in *Handbuch der Psychologie.* Vol. 2, 1965.

Wicker, H., in A. Mergen (ed.), *Kriminologische Aktualität.* IV, 1969.

Wright, H., *Sex and Society.* 1968.

Inkeri Anttila

A NEW TREND IN CRIMINAL LAW IN FINLAND

For hundreds of years the role of punishment in combating criminality has been a subject of public debate. Each age has attempted to find better answers which would have the appropriate effects. The more distant the time one is speaking of, the easier it is to see it in the light of only one movement: we speak of the classical criminal law of the 1800's, or the positivism of the first years of this century. We recall the main movements, those which gave the discussions of the time their typical flavor, either in Europe in general or at least in our own country. It is not quite as easy to dissect, for example, the main trends in criminal policy in Finland during the 1950's and the 1960's: we know more about these decades, we remember controversial debates and the polemics of experts. Even so, many are probably ready to agree that even these decades had their own central movements. One could simplify and emphasize matters by naming the 1950's the 'golden age of the treatment ideology' and the 1960's the 'age of the reevaluation of the role of the official control system.'

As we have now come to the mid-1970's, there is reason to ask if something new has been offered, something which in the future will be seen as the criminal law policy of the 1970's. Have we learned from our past mistakes, and have we been able to exploit research results to form a new trend in criminal policy?

The present author suggests that the answer to these questions is affirmative. The present decade does in fact differ from the previous ones, even though the discussion of new ideas still takes place principally in a limited circle of experts and only time will show whether the new ideas will find their way to the general public.

What, then, is so new about Finnish criminal policy thought during the 1970's?

If one limits oneself to dealing with the prevention of crime through criminal law, doubtlessly the most important feature can be seen to be the return to the belief that *the essential task of punishment is to function as public disapproval* – it demonstrates to the members of society what behavior is antisocial and thus to be avoided.

Naturally, these notions were not completely forgotten during previous decades; one could find attitudes in Scandinavian cooperation and in the literature of this author's country which were favorable toward the 'moral-forming function of the law.' However, for a long time, the interest of experts was directed elsewhere.

The difference in the general tendency of the decades can perhaps best be seen if the 1970's are compared with the1950's. Twenty years ago the main emphasis of the criminal policy reform movement was clearly on the supposed treatment effects of punishment, especially punishment which takes place in institutions. The intention was to 'individualize' the effect of punishment and measure its value to society only on the basis of how well one had succeeded in adapting it to each offender. This belief was naturally based on the ideology which held that a crime was always a symptom of a mental disease or of abnormality, and that therefore the purpose of punishment was to operate along the lines of treatment and cure: it should be prescribed as a medicine for an illness. Often the general support which punishment gives to social norms was not even mentioned, and if it was, it was often done so in a belittling manner. In speaking of the general deterrent effect of punishment, on the other hand, the usual one-sided connotation was the deterrent effect which some believed could be achieved through the use of a harsh level of punishment.

The shift from the treatment ideology of the 1950's to the new movement of the 1970's would probably not have been possible without the research and public debate of the 1960's. Severe criticism of the treatment ideology was needed, as were research results on the inefficiency of treatment and the weakness of legal protection of the targets of the ideology. It was necessary to have the general public clearly understand how sanctions which were in line with the individual ideology detracted from equality and predictability. It had to be demonstrated that punishment could no longer be reasonably justified on the basis of its supposed beneficial treatment effect. A new justification had to be found.

Furthermore, the focusing of interest on the entire field of punishable offenses had the effect of throwing new light on the matter. For example, the punishability or increased punishment of traffic or tax offenses, both of which have aroused an increasing amount of attention, were most difficult to base on treatment grounds. As often happens in such situations, one was satisfied in discussions of the matter to deal with some offence categories and offenders as exceptions to the general rule. In fact it became almost customary, for example, for drunken drivers or tax offenders not to be regarded as offenders at all; such groups did not fit the stereotyped image that was dominant for 'run-of-the-mill' criminality. The further the discussion on 'neocriminalization' progressed, the more difficult it proved to adhere to these premises. No longer did it seem feasible to divide offenders into two groups, the ordinary offenders needing treatment and the exceptional cases needing punishment. When the inefficiency of treatment became clearly apparent, the necessity of punishment had to be based on something else.

Regarding punishment principally as public disapproval did in fact lead the discussion in new directions. The discussion went from the individual to the general. A general deterrent aspect that had long remained relatively unnoted was emphasized, and therefore the new movement has at times been termed, with reason, a return to neoclassicist thought. As the shift has been gradual, the results of it so far have not been very apparent in the literature. Symptomatic of the tendency, though, is, for example, the fact that Sweden – the promised land of the treatment ideology – in 1975 organized a large international symposium on the general deterrent effect of punishment and its study, and the Parliamentary Criminal Law Committee of Finland in the preliminary drafts of its report in principle clearly leans toward the side of the new movement.

In emphasizing the public disapproval aspect of punishment, it certainly is not the intention to merely borrow a new – or 'neo-old' – label to head the discussion. It is a question of a deep-going reorientation, from which many practical conclusions can be drawn on the criminal policy level: some concerning the principles governing the drafting of legislation, others relating to the principles governing the application of legislation.

If one wishes punishment to serve as society's public reproach of an offense, society's control system should be regarded as an entirety so that criminal law norms support other social norms as far as possible. Especially in connection with sectors where it is a question of new criminalizations, and in which the genera sense of justice still presents limits, legislation should be clear and definitely limited. The difference between punishable and unpunishable behavior should be apparent to everyone. Legislation should be so structured that it censures specifically the act, not, for example, the offender's past history or personality in toto.

Even *in name* punishment should show that it is a question of norm supporting and warning. For this reason such present legislative terms as the 'dropping of charges' or 'suspension of the sentence' should be replaced with new terms that clearly show that the act is regarded as antisocial: some new proposals that have been made include 'court warning' or 'penal warning.' Under no circumstances should punishment or penal institutions officially be likened to treatment or care institutions. For example, the term 'juvenile prison' must be favored over such presently used terms as 'juvenile school,' 'juvenile reformatory,' or (an attempt at a neutral term) 'juvenile institution,' all of which lead tot misleading associations of ideas. An additional benefit from the use of exact terms is that decision makers, in drafting or applying legislation, cannot console themselves with the misconception that it is a question of something other than the intentional infliction of suffering on the offender.

In addition, punishment should be relatively rigid in order to maintain equality and predictability. Courts should not be granted the liberty of imposing widely differing punishments for similar acts within the limits of an indeterminate sentence; courts should in any case not exceed the normal punishment level; at the most they should impose a less severe sentence in the case of apparent exceptional mitigating circumstances.

Essential to the new system are legislated guidelines on sentencing which ensure uniformity in the application of the law and prevent the continuation of individual court practice, a procedure all too easily followed. It is equally important that the system not include sanctions which are connected with the general life style of the individual in question, and which would allow him to be held in institutions for a period exceeding the normal length of punishment. Thus, the new system does not accept, for example, an unusually severe sentence only on the grounds that the individual is a recidivist. On the other hand, the legislation on sentencing criteria may include unusually severe punishment for those whose exceptionally great amount of guilt shown in their offense (such as cold-blooded premeditation) displays a strong antisocial attitude.

As punishments are society's way of setting standards and supporting norms, they are part of what could be called an entirety of symbolic criticism resources. Because of this, punishments should be directed at acts which are perforce deserving of criticism. They should not be used for just any act, even though it may be a question, for example, of rather aggravating or unesthetic behavior patterns. *Indignation resources as such are also limited,* and so they should be used sparingly. If everything possible were punished, disapproval would lose its effect. Such inflation of indignation resources, then, should be avoided. Special care should be exercised in areas where indignation resources already suffer from an inefficient control system. For example, criminalizing attempts at suicide or passing a new law on prohibition would be poor decisions, as constant breaches of these laws despite the risk of severe punishments would lead to the feeling that the penal code in general is meaningless: everybody breaks it anyway, and only a few are brought before the court. Therefore correct directing of the indignation resources. should be accompanied by measures to ensure that the control actually functions. There can be no doubt that at times law can be ahead of the general sense of justice and thus guide its development; for example the prohibition by law of the corporal punishment of children despite the fact that a majority of the people approve its use could be an appropriate and successful criminal policy move.

Naturally, in view of the limits to the indignation resources their application should occasionally be examined. Criminalizations which are behind the times and no longer accepted by the general sense of justice are more detrimental than beneficial, as the old ideology behind them can easily lead to the entire criminal legislation being regarded as merely a forlorn attempt to support an outmoded system. And on the other hand, the fact that some acts which are well-deserving of reproach are not criminalized can lead to severe criticism of the penal system and to a decrease of the efficiency of society's disapproval of offenses. For this reason a flexible system is needed through which one can speedily criminalize, for example, new forms of undesirable behavior which have become current only through recent technical advances or an altered sense of justice. In such reforms, taking into consideration the limited indignation resources, one must continually keep things in balance by removing some old criminalizations when some new behavior is criminalized. Even though it is naturally important that new criminalizations not be made in the heat of the moment, but only after serious deliberation, in principle both decriminalization and criminalization are necessary. It has even been proposed that the penal code be given for a definite period of time only, for example for a five-year period, and that at the end of this period it be either reapproved as it stands, or in an amended format. This would force the legislators to examine the code at short intervals.

If punishment is regarded primarily as standard setting, there is *no other reason needed on which to base the justification and appropriateness of punishment.* Especially sanctions carried out in institutions – prison sentences – need not be based on the grounds that the offender himself will possibly benefit from the stay; and the length of time in the institution should under no circumstances be set on the basis of what is regarded as perhaps the most suitable period of treatment in that particular case.

The hypocrisy and inefficiency of the treatment ideology have already been clearly demonstrated during the past decades. And since we now know that research shows that the longer an offender stays in prison, the more antisocial his attitude becomes, there is no longer any excuse for the argument that an offender must be kept in prison until he is rehabilitated. Instead, we know that some offenders must be kept in prison even though they are not rehabilitated but become more and more maladjusted. For serious offenses, disapproval at least in today's society does not function without placement in institutions, even though it is known that the majority of offenders would be personally harmed less by some other type of measure. In other words, prison is not used to rehabilitate offenders and is not generally used because these individuals are too dangerous to remain in the free community, but because the very fact that they are imprisoned gives enough weight to the indignation apparent in the punishment.

Of course, what has been said above does not mean that offenders should not receive the treatment and, when needed, the care which is called for in each individual case. It goes without saying that prisoners have a right to the same medical services, including psychiatric services, as other members of society. And since prisoners have been sent to prison specifically to increase the moral influence of the punishment, as a warning to other citizens, it is no more than just to provide them in institutions with the assistance needed to withstand the often oppressive institution conditions and the length of the sentence, often damaging to mental health. It is also the responsibility of society, which is moreover strongly supported by reasons of expediency, to attempt to render assistance to those released from prison in such a manner that they do not become guilty of new offenses due to the lack of employment and housing. The new mode of thought, then, under no circumstances aims to remove treatment from prison. It only wants to emphasize that no one should be institutionalized as punishment so that he can be treated there.

As punishment by nature is public reproach, it should be appended rather rigidly to the performance of a criminal act. In the directing of the criticism, the offender is seen as a normal person who can be supposed to be affected by it. If the offender is seen as a very ill or abnormal person, for example, who is so incapacitated that he does not understand the significance of his act, the general sense of justice naturally allows him to go unpunished. How small an abnormality is taken into consideration in this respect depends on the general level of development of the society. Primitive societies were very rigid and severe in this respect. In modern times, we can afford to be more tolerant, as with the rise in the level of understanding we understand better than before that, for example, the mental deficiency of an offender can have a decisive influence on his actions. Therefore, the general system of standard setting and norm supporting functions in modern society even though some who behave abnormally are left unpunished, as long as nonpunishment does not become the rule.

In accordance with the new way of thinking, the indignation value of the punishment should be on a level with the act and the guilt shown therein. It is for this reason that the *criticism should not be applied in a cumulative way*, as this would be contrary to the sense of justice, and would place some offenders on an inferior level compared to others. One can reach many important conclusions from this principle. First of all, in the new system one should consciously avoid sanctions or official actions which have so far not been labeled as punishment but which are closely tied to the system of sanctions for offenses, and in practice also serve as punishment, i.e. reproach. For example, suspension or revocation of the driving license for a traffic offence, which is imposed as an additional sanction for the offense, should already be taken into consideration at the stage when the court sets the severity of the punishment, as this additional sanction has a different harshness for different people. In the same way, confiscation of a redemption, a tax increase or confiscation of property gained through an offense can prove to be more severe than the main punishment, and for this reason it is not right that matters be allowed to proceed on their own without allowing or obliging the court to take the entire situation into consideration. It is also quite common for punishment and other combinations of sanctions to be connected with, for example, disciplinary punishment of pupils, business licenses issued by administrative officials and compulsory care and treatment measures undertaken by welfare officials. In the new legislation on sentencing policy, therefore, more attention should be paid to the cumulative aspects of sanctions. In general, the best solution can be regarded as having the court deliberate the entirety of sanctions. Dividing up the sanctions so that different officials make their decisions at different times reduces the public reproach value of these measures, so that the present situation is inappropriate not only as regards the target of the sanctions, but also as regards the general aspect.

Punishment as indignation can be effective only if one knows which acts are criminalized and what punishment will be imposed. For this reason it is necessary that the penal code's punishment system be made known to all members of society in as simple and clear a form as possible. It is not satisfactory that it takes a complex method of deduction to term some act as punishable: the limits should be as clear as possible. It is not enough to vaguely guess that an act will lead to some sort of punishment: the severity of the punishment, and through that the degree of reproach of the act, should be apparent. The now-abandoned system where an offense bore a fixed sanction can, in this light, be regarded very favorably.

There are doubtlessly great problems in the *notification of norms.* At least in its present state, it is not arranged efficiently enough. The experts of the new criminal law movement should pay special attention to this question, for example by increasing the teaching of knowledge of norms in schools, vocational classes and in institutions of higher education. The literature on the subject which is used as a guide should be increased and be taken up from more angles, so that everyone is made conscious of the norms. It is very expensive to society if its members can only find out through personal experience what behavior is punished. Naturally, education in the subject should also be on general principles, and not just on the written format of separate, individual decrees. For example, a drawing away from the old way of thinking, where weight was only given to the consequence of an act and not to the subjective guilt displayed therein, has already become an accepted fact among experts and has been uniformly carried out in legislation; and yet it is still common to find popular opinions such as the one that drunken drivers should not be sentenced unless they have caused damage.

The appropriate directing and focusing of the entirety of society's indignation resources, according to the prevailing opinion, does not call for a high level of severity. Or stated more precisely: *the best results are achieved if the level is not very high.* Of course, the severity or mildness of the punishment level is still being debated, so that when we speak of a harsh level of punishment we are only referring to the level regarded as severe at this moment in European industrialized countries. If the punishment level is regarded as exceedingly severe, according to modern research many problems result. One of the most important is that people soon get used to severe punishments so they no longer have the intended effect. In order to keep the effect constant, therefore, one must continuously increase the punishments – something which is generally not possible in the long run. Needlessly inflicted punishment as such must be regarded as a social drawback and should be avoided.

Furthermore, overly severe sentences soon lead to the situation where the system's internal self-regulation mechanisms begin to function. If the punishment seems completely unreasonable, the number of cases where the accused is found not guilty will increase, or the number of cases where mitigating circumstances are artificially found in order to justify a milder sentence will increase. Or the control officials will ease their grip so that minor cases are not reported for the filing of charges. Under such circumstances the system does not function in a proper manner, as many cases deserving punishment – slight punishment, it is true – are left without the public reproach called for, while some comparable cases become targets of overly severe punishment due to chance or bad luck. Thus, severe punishments or changes which make the threat of punishment more severe should be used sparingly. This is even more desirable in view of the fact that social psychological research indicates that mild criticism often is more effective than severe criticism. One could say that severe criticism exceeds the mark – it is regarded as unjustified, and causes aggressive counteractions.

In the foregoing, the focus was on presenting one of the main principles of new criminal law. This is not intended to signify that modern criminal policy's only new movement is a return to the neoclassicist form of thought. Alongside of this, cost-benefit analysis, which has become important in all fields of social policy, has also become important in criminal law. When directing society's indignation resources, one must also ask the eternal question: what will all of this cost?

In criminal policy in this regard, one often comes across much undeveloped thought. Possibly the most astonishing fact is that one does not know or want to admit that even sentencing and the carrying out of sentences have a price, both in terms of money and of suffering of different people. Even some experts in the field, apparently without thinking the matter over any further, may recommend an increase in the length of imprisonment as a measure resulting in no costs whatoever. However, in fact it should be apparent to everyone that when it is a question of sanctions carried out in institutions, the mean number of prisoners is based on the number entering the prisons and the length of each prisoner's imprisonment, and even a slight increase in the level of punishment has an immediate effect on the prisons. This does not mean that the level of punishment should not be raised at times, but one should be aware of its effects. One must also bear in mind the other costs, such as those incurred by society in the care of released prisoners, and the social care given their families. In cost-benefit analysis, of course, decisive weight is also given to other than merely economic costs.

Criminal legal thinking during the present decade is centered principally on punishment, as it has been for many decades. In outlining the general directions of criminal policy, however, one is no longer very optimistic about the possibilities a pure criminal law system has of preventing criminality and decreasing the damage caused by criminality. Now one can see more clearly than before the limited potential of a criminal law system. The system is necessary, and its efficient functioning is important, but alongside it one needs other control systems, which could prove to be better than the old punishment system. This presentation has not gone into some matters which have caused much debate lately, such as plans on decreasing the opportunities for committing offenses, and of increasing grass-roots control, as well as debate on links between criminality and social planning. It is possible that it is these which in the future will be seen as the focal point of our present decade.

J. M. van Bemmelen

THE ACHILLES' HEEL OF THE CRIMINAL JUSTICE SYSTEM

According to a famous legend the mother of Achilles submerged her son in the waters of the Styx to ensure his immortality. In so doing she held him by his heel; as a result his heel was his only vulnerable spot and in the end he was mortally wounded by an arrow that struck it.

This legend has frequently come to my mind lately inasmuch as a ruptured Achilles' tendon has put me almost completely out of action for several months. These circumstances forced me to give up working on the article I was writing for this book in honor of Willem Nagel. All hope of completing the article, entitled 'The criminal judge between the demands of law and order and the data provided by criminological research,' had to be abandoned. There was nevertheless plenty of time to reflect on sentencing during my rehabilitation so I shall offer instead a few brief remarks on the sentencing process as the Achilles' heel of criminal justice.

Nagel came to the University of Leiden not long after completing his doctoral degree (1949). In 1956 he took over my task of lecturing in criminology at the Institute of Criminal Law and Criminology, where we worked in full harmony until my retirement in 1968. The many years we shared as colleagues have induced me to express some thoughts about the position of the government, in particular that of the criminal court judge, in the sentencing process, a subject in which Nagel too has always been greatly interested. His interest in sentencing is evident once again in his recent article 'Om de kwaliteit van ons strafrechtelijke systeem, of: opnieuw op de overloop' (The quality of our criminal justice system, or: on the landing once more). The article in question concerns not only sentencing, but the entire administration of criminal justice and the various agents who play important roles therein, namely the legislator, the prosecution, the judge and the prison administration. Nagel accords to the criminal judge 'a central position in the criminal justice system, in spite of the fact that his range of activity is limited on the one hand by the law and on the other hand by *expediency* – the phrase opportunity principle is somewhat unwieldy linguistically – of the administration, the other key figure in the criminal justice system'[1] (my translation-v.B.). Nagel is thinking here of the large degree of discretion given by the legislator to the judge in deciding the type and severity of punishment within the maximum penalties established for the various offenses and the general minimum of a 50 cent fine or a one-day prison sentence. 'It is,' says Nagel, 'partly because of this greater freedom that the criminal judge in our country meets with more opposition than in the United Kingdom. He enjoys much more freedom and therefore encounters more criticism.'[2]

However, the judge is also criticized in other countries, for example, the United

States. In a recent article 'A new look at sentencing,' Richard A. McGee, president of the American Justice Institute in Sacramento, Calif., and former director of corrections and administrator of the Youth and Adult Corrections Agency of the State of California, writes: 'Admittedly, probation, presentence reports and prosecutors and defense attorneys through the plea negotiation process also affect the outcome, but the trial court judge is still The Man. He carries the responsibility no matter who else or what else influences his judgment. This almost godlike power with relatively little oversight or review by higher authority vested in individual judges has been criticized by almost everyone involved for generations.'[3] McGee therefore, like Nagel, considers the judge to be the key figure in the criminal justice system and ascribes the frequently heard criticism of judicial policy in the United States to this fact. An entirely different tune is heard from Ch. J. Enschedé in his article 'De grenzen van de functie van de strafrechter' (The limits of the role of the criminal judge). He says: 'The judge has very little influence on prosecution policy. He can, after a complaint has been filed by an interested party, give orders to institute or continue prosecution proceedings (article 12 of the Dutch Code of Criminal Procedure), or, after an objection made to a summons or following notification of further prosecution, dismiss the defendant from prosecution (articles 250 and 262 of the Dutch Code of Criminal Procedure), but statistically speaking the number of these incidents is negligible. The total number of cases per year in which these articles are successfully invoked is less than 100, whereas the total number of cases prosecuted runs into the hundreds of thousands. The judge therefore *must* (my italics-v. B.) deal with the cases put before him by the prosecution. He is, in a sense, *the prisoner of the prosecution* (my italics-v. B.). Judicial policy can only be developed within the limits of prosecution policy'[4] (my translation-v. B.).

That is a striking difference. According to Nagel the judge is 'the key figure in the criminal justice system,' according to McGee 'The Man,' and in Enschedé's opinion 'the prisoner of the prosecution.'

If we also bear in mind that the prison sentences imposed by the judge can be implemented by the prison administration in greatly varying ways, on which the judge can exert almost no influence, there is very little left of the position of the judge as a key figure in the criminal justice system. Nevertheless, I see no reason to call the judge 'a prisoner of the prosecution.' It seems to me that we can say: 'Ni cet excès d'honneur, ni cette indignité.' The large degree of discretion accorded the Dutch judge with respect to sentencing is counterbalanced by the small amount of influence he has on the prosecution policy and the implementation of sentences imposed by him. One of the consequences of this ambivalence in the position of the judge is that criticisms of his sentencing policy are mostly directed at him exclusively, although the prosecution in many cases influences this policy by its demand for a particular sentence.

Enschedé has suggested that the influence of the prosecution should be further extended by forbidding the judge to exceed the sentence demanded by the prosecution and allowing him only to impose a sentence lighter than the one demanded by the prosecution.[5] Langemeijer has protested against this proposal,[6] and rightly so in my opinion. There really is no reason why the influence of the judge on criminal policy should be further weakened. Although the judge very seldom exceeds the demands of the prosecution, it should remain within his rights to do so. Should the legislator wish to put sentencing policy even more in the hands of the prosecution, he could do this better by giving the prosecution the power to deal with relatively minor offenses, for which only fines or short conditional sentences are indicated, out of court, in the same way in which this now occurs with lower court cases.

The judge would have to be called in only when the defendant lodges a complaint against the out-of-court settlement and does not accept it. That would at least be practical. The length of the criminal procedure could in this way be substantially shortened in a large number of minor cases.

Criticism of the sentencing is now directed at the independent judge. According to the new procedure, if the sentences imposed in minor cases are considered to have too little general preventive effect, the Minister of Justice would bear full responsibility. Also, we would be able to gain better insight into the reasoning behind the sentencing policy, for in the annual report that the prosecution would be required to submit the reasons underlying the decisions to settle a case out of court would have to be stated more fully. The prosecution would also have a better opportunity than it now has to make the defendant provide restitution for damages, by making this one of the conditions of a conditional out-of-court settlement.

In the system described here the problems concerning sentencing policy would by no means be entirely solved. In the first place, these problems, for judge and prosecution alike, are related to contemporary phenomena, for example an explosive increase in a certain type of crime. The criminal justice system is in fact never sufficiently equipped to deal with such problems. The sudden increase in a certain type of crime is accompanied by a call for harsher sentences for these offenses, even though our knowledge about their preventive effect remains limited.[7]

In the second place, the judge and the prosecution only have a limited number of sanctions at their disposal, mainly fines and prison sentences, conditional or unconditional. Although a great effort is currently being made to find alternative sanctions, such research is still in its infancy.[8]

In the third place, only a very limited number of offenders ever enters the criminal justice system; furthermore, very often they are not the really guilty parties. This is particularly apparent in the drug cases where the dealers and producers live abroad and go scotfree, while the users and go-betweens get caught.[9]

In the fourth place, a sense of fairness implies that offenders guilty of the same type of crime should be given similar sentences, which implies that minor offenses especially must be punished with light prison sentences regardless of whether the personal circumstances of some offenders in fact call for longer treatment in order to bring about profound changes in their life styles. Nagel has discussed this point at some length. He is afraid, and rightly so, that when we reach too readily for treatment measures, this will lead to long-term deprivation of liberty. We cannot do without punishment for, according to Nagel, the criminal law has *one* general function: 'to indicate and, in spite of the ceaseless efforts at improvement, to maintain the limits within which norm violations are prohibited and threatened with punishment'[10] (my translation-v. B.).

In my opinion a second general function of the criminal law can be discerned: the prevention of unrest in society and the prevention of self-help.[11] This function creates a fifth problem for the judge, especially in more serious cases: Should he aim for treatment in all those cases where this seems indicated out of a sense of fairness to the offender, because mental deficiencies or personality disorders imply diminished responsibility and thus a lesser degree of guilt or no guilt at all, or should he pronounce long sentences in these cases, because there is too much danger otherwise that the offender will be released too soon thereby causing unrest in society? The choice remains difficult and the dilemma is still unsolved.[12]

Finally, there is a sixth problem: imprisonment always has negative effects on the individual and stigmatizes him as well.

The Dutch judge, under the influence of these six problems, tends, like his fellow judges in several other countries, to a very lenient sentencing policy.[13] This certainly does not mean that it is generally assumed – as some criminologists would have us believe – that it is better to do nothing at all than to impose sentences which do not achieve their purpose.[14]

The task of the judge and the prosecution with regard to sentencing is highly complicated. If sentences are too light there is a danger that justice will not be done to either of the general functions of the criminal law, thereby discrediting the entire criminal law. The same holds true if sentences are too harsh, for then it is questionable whether justice has been done.

For this reason sentencing can rightly be seen as the Achilles' heel of the entire criminal justice system.

NOTES AND REFERENCES

1. W. H. Nagel, 'Om de kwaliteit van ons strafrechtelijk systeem, of: opnieuw op de overloop,' *Nederlands Juristenblad* 1975, p. 1213.
2. *Ibid.*
3. *Federal Probation*, 2 (1974), p. 3; 3 (1974).
4. C. J. Enschedé, 'De grenzen van de funktie van de strafrechter,' *Rechtsgeleerd Magazijn Themis*, 1974, p. 619.
5. *Ibid.* p. 622.
6. G. E. Langemeijer, 'De jurist op de terugtocht,' *Rechtsgeleerd Magazijn Themis* 1974/1975, p. 609.
7. See Charles W. Thomas, J. Sherwood Williams and Ineke Haen, 'Misdaadafschrikking,' *Nederlands Tijdschrift voor Criminologie*, June 1975. This article has also been published in English on the occasion of the 18th Conference in Corrections, Tallahassee, Florida, February 1973.
8. See the interview with W. Buikhuisen, *Nederlands Tijdschrift voor Criminologie*, June 1975, p. 127.

9. See the opinion of the American drugs expert Robert L. Dupont in an article in the newspaper *Volkskrant*, as cited in *Knipselkrant*, 9 September 1975. In his opinion the penalty for dealers should be two years instead of two weeks.
10. *Nederlands Juristenblad* 1974, ch. VI, pp. 1219–1220.
11. J. M. van Bemmelen, *Ons Strafrecht*. Part I, 5th ed., 1975 par. 9 and 14 .
12. C. P. C. M. Oomen, 'De terbeschikkingstelling op de keper beschouwd,' inaugural address at Leiden, 1974; D. Wiersma, 'Oomens keper,' *Delikt en Delinkwent*, 1974, p. 290; and G. E. Mulder, 'Vrijheidsstraf en terbeschikkingstelling,' *Rechtsgeleerd Magazijn Themis*, 1970, p. 452.
13. L. H. C. Hulsman, 'Criminal justice in the Netherlands,' *Delta, A review of arts, life and thought in the Netherlands*.
14. See also J. Taylor, P. Walton and J. Young, *The new criminology*, 1973, and D. Chapman, *Sociology and the stereotype of the criminal*, 1968.

Günther Kaiser

ROLE AND REACTIONS OF THE VICTIM AND THE POLICY OF DIVERSION IN CRIMINAL JUSTICE ADMINISTRATION

1. INTRODUCTION

The efficiency of public criminal prosecution and sanction practice has been disputed for a long time. The most important topics of the discussion are the deficiencies of law and order, the overcriminalization by penal law,[1] the stigmatizing consequences for offenders who have gone through criminal proceedings and prison, and the inadequate satisfaction of the victim's needs. Whereas steps toward humanization and rationalization with regard to the offender had been taken some time ago, the needs of the victim continued to be largely neglected. A draft of a law relative to the compensation of victims of violent offenses is now being debated in the German 'Bundestag' (the federal legislative assembly). All in all, however, the victim's situation has not changed much until now.

Criticism of the traditional criminal law system has led to the development of alternative conceptions of social and public reactions to crimes. Concepts such as decriminalization,[2] radical nonintervention[3] and diversion[4] characterize the new suggestions which aim at a more suitable and more human policy. Decriminalization and radical nonintervention are easily integrated into the spectrum of public criminal policy.[5] The acceptance and systematic integration of the concept of diversion, however, pose various difficulties in the FRG.

As is well-known, we are presently facing a problem which could be described as overcriminalization.[6] Yet, oversanctioning is much to the detriment of penal law; for penal law reaches its own limits of function[7] when offenses are committed and sanctioned in large quantities. A possibility for bringing these difficulties under control is decriminalization by the legislator. This course has been adopted in the FRG in criminal justice administration mainly in the field of traffic, demonstration and sexual offenses. The criminal justice system is in this way relieved by the complete elimination of criminal acts or by their redefinition as misdemeanors. With decriminalization the qualification for entering the criminal justice system disappears altogether.

This is different, however, with the concept of depenalization or even of 'radical nonintervention,' according to which a misdemeanor is not followed by any intervention so as to avoid negative consequences.[8] This strategy is characterized by an intentional abstention from sanctioning.[9]

Neither decriminalization nor radical nonintervention can successfully be used extensively as criminal policy approaches. Total decriminalization would be equal to the abolition of penal law. This would be contrary to the stabilizing- and order-function which rules certainly have. The concept of radical nonintervention or of extensive abstention from sanctioning is not based on the evidence of its own success but on a critical insight into the unintentional negative consequences of public sanctioning.[10]

The concept of diversion represents a strategy which aims to escape the negative consequences of the traditional sanction policy while at the same time trying to avoid facing criminal problems inactively, in the sense of 'laisser faire, laisser aller.' The concept of diversion, which originated in the United States in the late sixties,[11] has been newly introduced into the criminal political discussion during recent years. Considering the concept of diversion to be almost a kind of magic formula, we expect it to exclude the disadvantages of the traditional treatment of offenders and include an optimum of advantages. It is not amazing that it came to the fore of the criminal political discussion in the United States, since the recorded offenders belong to a larger degree to younger age groups, the percentage of prisoners in the population in the United States is more than twice as high as in European countries, and also because by European standards more cases have to be treated by fewer judges. It is therefore understandable that some of the large number of offenders are not submitted to the usual course of criminal proceedings but are turned over to other institutions outside the criminal justice system.

The problems of diversion, however, have been regarded up till now solely from the point of view that public authorities alone should decide the input into the system of criminal justice or into alternative, differently organized public systems.[12] The whole range of events preceding public authorities' concern regarding the offender has been ignored. Filtering and selection processes, however, already appear at the stage in which the breach of a penal rule becomes visible or perceptible. Accordingly, the victim of a crime makes the first filtering decision in the process of discretionary criminal prosecution by informing the police. The importance of the victim's position also becomes evident by the fact that about 90% of all reports to the police originate from private citizens. Only the remaining 10% can be attributed to the independent initiative of the police.[13] From this viewpoint, the victim, being the person who informs the police, is not a mere criminalistic phenomenon but also has definite importance as a criminal political problem. The victim, at any rate those groups which generally first come into touch with the offender, and not the police should be positioned at the decisive place concerning the effective organization of diversion programs.[14] Each diversion concept therefore must start from the reaction of the victim[15] because criminal proceedings are so often initiated by the person informing the police. No criminal political concept should therefore disregard the attitude of the individual directly concerned. This of course does not mean that each victim or each potential notifier is a 'diversion politician.' Simply 'ignoring' an offense, for instance by the decision of a police official, a public prosecutor or a judge to refrain from further criminal prosecution, means nothing but 'nonintervention.' Of special interest in this respect are those victim groups which renounce notifying the police but at the same time see to it that steps are taken against the offender by control systems other than criminal justice administration.

2. FINDINGS OF RECENT VICTIMIZATION STUDIES

The impact of the correlation between the situation of the victim and the act of informing the police has been especially illustrated by various recent surveys.

Such studies have also been undertaken in the Federal Republic of Germany during the last few years. In the town of Göttingen, for example, about every 100th inhabitant was asked in 1974 whether he had been a victim of certain offenses. The investigation showed that for each offense of larceny that had been reported to the police there were 15 thefts which had not come to the knowledge of the police; in the case of aggravated theft, the proportion was 1 : 2, in the case of damage to property 1 : 23. With a proportion of 1 : 55, hit-and-run-driving was on the top, whereas willful bodily injury, with 1 : 7, represented a much lower rate. In total, an average of 1 : 10 was computed for the proportion of reported to nonreported offenses. As reasons for nonreporting, 36% of the persons questioned stated that the damage was so slight that a report to the police was not worthwhile. Twenty-four per cent of the respondents did not expect any results from a police investigation, 8% thought it would take too much time to go to the police, and 5% were of the opinion that the police would not do anything about such a case anyway.[16]

A victimological study in Stuttgart in 1973 yielded similar results. The heads of households were asked whether they or members of their household had been the victims of offenses during the previous 12 months. Then the family members alone were asked whether they had been victimized. The interviews with the heads of the households showed 142 victimized households. This corresponds to 32.3% of all the persons interviewed. The interviews with members of the families revealed that 47.8% had been victims of offenses. Out of the 335 offenses mentioned during the interviews 153 (46%) had been reported to the police. As reasons for not reporting to the police, 49% stated that the damage was too slight and 26% felt that a report to the police would be futile.[17]

Summing up these findings, we see that the majority of victims refrain from informing the police. The fact that the damage is too slight is in Germany the most frequent motive for the decision not to report the offender or the offense to the police, but the assumption that the investigative authorities would probably not clear up the matter also plays an important role. The victim's attitude toward the offense, offender and criminal prosecution agencies is decisive for the input into the public control system, hence also for the question of what will become the basis of public diversion policy. Diversion models, therefore, which do not start from the information and the reports by the population will have to cope with problems concerning the attitude of the person reporting. If the aim of diversion is 'to involve social or community institutions' in order to enable crime control without formal stigmatization,[18] the community (as a potential victim and informer of the police) must assume this role in the process of diversion voluntarily. In view of the motives for reporting or not reporting to the police, it appears doubtful that the establishment of diversion instead of police stations would hold special attraction. On the contrary, this might have a negative effect on the attitude of persons potentially endangered, and in particular on the victims of crimes; for at the present time the latter sometimes already feel intolerably distressed by their needs.

Additionally, public prosecution may contribute to the victim's feeling of distress by staying proceedings. The victim's legal protection and his feeling of satisfaction are considerably diminished as a result.[19]

Beyond legitimate measures of self-help, the interests of the victim – whether organized or not – sometimes resort to practices bordering on lynching. Administration of justice usurped by private 'local guards,' denunciations in self-service stores, and the exposure of offenders to public ridicule, beatings, and other measures approaching lynching practices are demonstrative examples in our time. Diversion in such a way is of course not desirable in criminal policy.

There are essentially three significant prerequisites for diversion strategies of any kind: (1) general resolution of the conflict, especially between the offender and the victim, (2) appropriate support of the needs of the victim, and (3) a justifiable solution for the offender in accordance with a criminal policy aimed at avoiding negative consequences inherent in the traditional sanctioning concept.

Let us examine to what extent these conditions are fulfilled by the German institution *Privatklage* (private complaint and prosecution by the victim of the so-called complainant-offenses).

3. THE DISMAL STATE OF THE GERMAN SYSTEM OF PRIVATKLAGE. A CASE OF DIVERSION POLICY FAILURE

In the case of criminal acts which according to the legislator lack public concern and interest (see § 374, 1 Code of Criminal Procedure) the criminal procedure law of the Federal Republic of Germany leaves the decision regarding criminal prosecution to the victim alone. Public prosecution does not participate in this procedure. The victim in his capacity of complainant becomes a plaintiff. It is up to him to establish the facts, to have the witnesses called, and to make a charge.

The legal-technical frame of the law of private prosecution proceedings is such that its attempt at diversion may be considered as half-hearted because the citizen may not institute criminal proceedings until an attempt at reconciliation has been made by a so-called *Vergleichsbehörde* (arbitration authority). If such an attempt at reconciliation fails, the same penalties as in an ordinary criminal procedure are imposed provided sentence is passed. Accordingly, the formal proceedings run their course with only one difference, namely that public prosecution does not participate. Further peculiarities such as the possibility for the victim to withdraw the charges at each stage of the proceedings or to reach an agreement in order to conclude the proceedings without sentence are of interest from the point of view of diversion policy only in the sense of a 'minimization of penetration.'[20]

Some facts concerning the German practice of *Privatklage* (in so-called complainant-offense cases) were revealed by a study of 255 records of such cases brought before the *Amtsgericht* (district court) of the city of Bielefeld during the years 1966-1970.[21] This investigation showed an almost total nonsanctioning of those offenders accused by complainants. More than half of the cases that were brought in were not admitted to trial at all. In about 16% of all cases in which charges were preferred judgment was passed; half of these were sentences, the remaining half acquittals. Compared to these results, a little more than 3% of the official offenses (including so-called unsolved cases) coming into public prosecutors' hands are settled by judgment. Related to the total number of indictable offenses, however, the quota of judgments is as high as 31%.[22]

The majority of the sentences in complainant proceedings were fines between 50 and 250 marks. These sanctions were imposed mainly for offenses of slander and insult and to a very small extent for offenses of willful minor bodily injury and trespass on domestic premises. The charges had been withdrawn in 40% of all cases, almost half of them on the basis of an agreement by order of the court. Complainant-offense cases are already reduced to insignificance by the fact that they account for only a little more than 1% of all offenses.[23] The intentions of the German institution *Privatklage* (complaint and prosecution by the victim) as such may be good, but in practice the method must be considered as a case of diversion policy failure. Apart from the expenses which must be defrayed by the complainant, the person who is accused by the complainant, and by the judicial treasury, little can be said about the prosecution of complainant proceedings. Empirical investigations of a possible reconciliatory function of this procedure are not at hand. Little or nothing positive may be expected in this connection since the attempt at reconciliation by the arbitration authority is regarded as a mere formality preceding the real criminal procedure.[24]

Although the complainant proceedings are conducted before a criminal court, at least in practice the idea of punishment is minimized.[25] By looking at the organization of the German system of 'private prosecution' (complaint and prosecution by the victim), a similarity with the complaint in civil actions is almost evident. It is left up to the victim's initiative, whether and how he wants to assert his rights. From this point of view a transition to civil procedure by establishment of claims under civil law permitting a more adequate handling of the conflicts in so-called complainant-offense matters would be preferable.

4. SOCIAL REACTION TO SHOPLIFTING IN EAST AND WEST GERMANY

Shoplifting has increased simultaneously with the advancing self-service system in retail trade in the Federal Republic of Germany. Losses are estimated to be between 52 million and one billion marks per annum.[26] Big stores and department stores proceeded to establish their own control and sanction system a long time ago, since the police crime clearance activity did not seem to be efficacious enough and judicial decision making appeared too lax.[27] Increasedsu rveyability of store premises, concave mirrors and television 'cameras make better control and more effective deterrence possible.[28] In addition to this there are house-detectives and central registration of caught shoplifters.[29]

The Freiburg study on the frequency of shoplifting and the validity of penalty norm sanctions had the following results: out of 100 shoplifters, less than 5 were discovered, out of 100 discovered offenders, less than 50% were reported to the police, and out of 100 offenders who were reported to the police about 80 were sanctioned.[30] In spite of the fact that the department stores changed their policy with regard to reporting offenders in the course of 1966 – the store managements announced that they would proceed more severely against shoplifters in the future and report them to the police without exception – a comparative study of the records of thefts maintained by the stores and the police showed that in 1966 67% of all thefts had in fact not been reported to the police, and that in 1967 there was continued abstention from this reaction, i.e. still as many as 30% of the shoplifters had not been reported to the police.

Hence, it is obvious that a considerable part of delinquency is still settled by internal administration of justice.[31] What this means – or may mean – is shown by the usual treatment of shoplifters. The caught customer is asked to come into the office of the department manager. The evidence is collected. The stolen goods must be returned. Furthermore, the department manager has the possibility of banishing the shoplifter from the premises. There are until now no exact findings on the frequency of these sanctions.

Recently, many stores have proceeded to claim from shoplifters so-called processing costs or a fee fluctuating between 30 and 50 marks. According to the law, this procedure is extremely controversial.[32] The charging of processing costs or of a fee has certainly not been without repercussions on the subsequent treatment of the cases by the district courts. There appears to be a tendency to dismiss the case because of the insignificance of the offense after the offender has paid a fee, or the fee is deducted from the fine if such is imposed on the offender.[33] We may recognize here a certain willingness on the part of the administration of justice to support such a diversion of petty shopliftings.

In the new Penal Code of the Federal Republic of Germany, in force since January 1, 1975, the legislator only decided to make the prosecution of petty property offenses subject to the victim's request for prosecution. The proposal of the study group Alternative Draft of a Penal Code to sanction shoplifting in the future under civil law by means of the compensation claims of the shopowners, and thus transfer prosecution and sanctioning to the competence of the victim himself, was not accepted.

Similar considerations could also be observed in the discussion about the new Penal Code of the German Democratic Republic of January 12, 1968. The draft originally contained a provision giving the seller the right to claim a fine up to three times the damage as a disciplinary measure in the case of offenses involving the theft of articles of less than 20 marks in value.[34] This provision has, however, been dropped without apparent reasons. The private prosecution of shoplifting became effective in the German Democratic Republic as recently as 1975 with the introduction of the First Implementary Regulation on the Introductory Statute to the Penal Code. Shoplifting by customers in so-called 'socialist retail business' stores can now be sanctioned by the management of these stores with fines ranging between 5 and 150 marks together with identification of the offender, if the offense is petty and the intended damage or damage caused does not exceed the amount of 50 marks.[35] Shoplifting-offenses are usually dealt with by so-called societal courts (*Gesellschaftsgerichte*), with the exception of aggravated offenses.

The comparison of the reactions toward shoplifting by the control systems in the Federal Republic of Germany and the German Democratic Republic shows the same differences which may be observed between internal administration of justice at the place of work as it is practiced in the Federal Republic of Germany and the system of the societal courts in the German Democratic Republic. We generally encounter in the Federal Republic of Germany private help actions by the victims themselves. Their procedure is being tolerated and even approved, though with some hesitation, by the administration of justice, legislator and science. In the German Democratic Republic, however, the exclusion of petty criminality from the competence of criminal justice and the referral to other institutions is an intentional criminal political act by the legislator.

5. INTERNAL ADMINISTRATION OF JUSTICE AT THE PLACE OF WORK IN THE FEDERAL REPUBLIC OF GERMANY AND SOCIETAL COURTS IN THE GERMAN DEMOCRATIC REPUBLIC

Investigations of the reaction of industrial enterprises and employers in general toward norm violations by employees and workers in the scope of penal law and the law on *Ordnungswidrigkeiten** have shown that a relatively autonomous system of sanctioning offenders at the place of work has come into effect.[36] The extent of the evasion of public administration of justice is evident by the fact that about 20 criminal offenses per 1,000 employees are registered by industrial and other enterprises per annum, but only one third of the offenses and one sixth of the offenders on average are officially reported to the police by the employers.

From the point of view of predominantly economic considerations criminality at the place of work is of minor importance, at least as long as the management system and the business success are not jeopardized. Last but not least the fact that the costs and investments necessary to establish and develop control systems at the place of work would be higher than the presumed amount of loss due to internal criminality is a determining factor. The cost-benefit-analysis which is still missing in the public system of crime control and administration of criminal justice has been

* Petty offenses punishable only by a penance money penalty for which – contrary to a fine – imprisonment cannot be substituted in case of nonpayment.

reality in industrial enterprises for a long time.

The internal administration of justice at the place of work of course does not know procedural rules similar to the criminal procedure law. Normally, the personnel manager, as the representative of the management, and one representative of the workers' council take part in the decision concerning an offender. The following internal sanctions can be imposed: verbal and written reprimand, admonition and fine, exclusion from internal fringe benefits, threat of dismissal, and dismissal, in most cases together with a report to the police.

The dangers of overcoming criminality by internal proceedings, however, are obvious. The lack of legal guarantees and of legal control, for example the absence of defense counsel and the fact that there is neither legal hearing nor legal measures, give rise to substantiated criticism. Yet, internal control appears to be one of the alternatives available for overcoming criminality mainly by means of resocialization. In spite of the lack of uniformity in procedure and in spite of the selective sanctioning of only a fraction of employees who are offenders, the internal system of administration of justice is stabilized throughout. If the so-called administration of justice at the place of work, compared to the legal administration of justice, is more economical in the sense of the time-means relation, more effective in the sense of the cost-benefit analysis – i.e. in terms of the invested expenditures for reconciliation and resocialization – and more democratic in the sense of the fellow-workers' participation in the decisionmaking process, it unquestionably has the qualities of a functional alternative to the legal administration of justice in the field of petty offenses. Moreover, the internal administration of justice at the place of work, as a diversionary program, has the advantage of taking into consideration the immediate environment of the offender: his place of work. Accordingly, the internal administration of justice does not form a contrast to the situation with which the offender is confronted daily, but is a part of it.[37] Furthermore, internal control is an appropriate means of effectively relieving public prosecution and sanction institutions. The only prerequisite is that the proceeding must be legitimate and that it must not lose the advantages of the traditional administration.

The German Democratic Republic has specified the competence of so-called societal courts in the Conflict and Arbitration Commissions Law *(Gesetz über die Konflikt- und Schiedskommissionsordnung)* of June 11, 1968. These courts discipline minor breaches of the rules (petty offenses) on their own responsibility. The trial, however, leads primarily to an amicable agreement. If this should fail, the lay judges have the possibility of choosing appropriate measures from the following sanctions: (1) apology by the offender, (2) public revocation of an insult, (3) restitution of the damage, (4) reprimand the offender, or, as an exception, (5) imposition of a fine up to 150 marks.

In contras. to the so-called administration of justice at the place of work, the societal courts have a legal basis, are highly formalized, and have definitive normative sanction possibilities. The diversion of offenders is carried out by *order of a law* in the case of those offenses for which the societal courts are primarily competent. If the social rules are only insignificantly violated by an offense, the public prosecution authorities may transfer the case to the societal courts.[38] About 30-40% of all penal matters are assumed to be dealt with by these societal courts.

6. CASES OF AND TENDENCIES TOWARD 'LYNCH LAW'

The situation becomes precarious, however, when internal private help regulations of firms are regarded as approaching lynching and considered also a proof that the state is retiring, or perhaps already has 'resigned' from this field. Yet, there are great differences between internal private help regulations and the usual cases of 'lynch law.' Internal private help regulations try to control delinquency at the place of work and aim at reconciliation, resocialization or avoidance of recidivism, albeit for the sake of the company's own economic interests. 'Lynch law,' however, aims without exception to take revenge and to deter offenders.

The excesses in shoplifting prevention are part of lynch law tactics. Cases are known of Berlin shoplifters who were photographed and whose photos were displayed on bulletin boards in all chain stores of the enterprise in question.[39]
The display of offenders' addresses in store windows, informing about the offense and the facts of the case, of course falls into this category too. One department manager of a self-service store claimed an amount between 300 and 500 Swiss francs to be paid by 5 female customers who had been caught with stolen goods of a value between 90 Swiss centimes and 20 Swiss francs. He placed the claimed amount at the disposal of his company with the purpose of compensating for the other losses of goods in his department.[40] Such forms of abuse can by no means be justified or tolerated. They can often be qualified as cases of extortion.

In contrast to the internal private help measures of enterprises – which are generally unobjectionable – 'the man in the street,' who is not in a position to develop effective means of self-protection, often resorts to practices bordering on lynching. His acts are outbursts of his desire for revenge which may be connected with his assumption that criminality is steadily increasing and that public prosecution no longer copes with it. In the city of Wiesbaden, for example, a child molester was tied to a lamppost and exposed to public ridicule by the father of the victim.[41] Taxi drivers when robbed, sometimes pursue and catch the offender and use their fists to take revenge before police officers arrive. Presently, and perhaps in the near future also, these cases will remain exceptions in Germany. The profits, however, that stand to be made from the citizens' need for self-protection seem to be leading to a business boom for weapons dealers, if the figures on their turnover can be believed.[42]

7. ATTEMPTS TO UNIFY JUVENILE LAW AND THEIR FAILURE

Diversion attempts with respect to juvenile delinquents have the longest tradition. In 1923, special regulations for juveniles were established in Germany within the framework of the penal law: the Juvenile Court Law. This law, in its wording of August 4, 1953, provides special reactions to offenses committed by juveniles. Juvenile penal law serves primarily to guarantee (crime) control over 14-18 year old juveniles, and secondarily to make (alternative) resocialization possible.*

The inadequacy of juvenile penal law as a strategy and of its sanctions as measures of socialization are criticized. This criticism is directed toward the effects of the penal frame of reference and toward the unintended results of the process of control through juvenile penal law that intensify and accentuate existing socialization defects. For this reason, a further separation of juvenile penal law from general penal law, a far reaching detachment of juvenile criminal jurisdiction from general criminal jurisdiction and an individual analysis of juvenile corrections are demanded. The last is still marked to a much too high degree by the ideas of adult corrections. Such demands have resulted meanwhile in the semiofficial Discussion Draft of a Juvenile Aid Law *(Jugendhilfegesetz)* in 1973. This bill raises the age of relative responsibility from 14 to 16 years, and requires the applicability of juvenile penal law only in the case of serious offenses of 16 and 17 year old offenders. As a matter of fact, the Administration Draft of a Juvenile Aid Law (1974) has already dissociated itself anew from such principles. Therefore, the demand for a unification of the total juvenile law, abandoning all the effects of juvenile criminal law, remains unrealized, though it has been demanded ever since the beginning of the twenties.

Nevertheless, 'criminal' children are excluded from the field of application of juvenile penal law now in force. The sytem of youth protection also intervenes only if the provisions of §§ 1 III, and 3 I Juvenile Welfare Law, i.e. the child's right to education, are not or only partly fulfilled. Various kinds of individual educational assistance such as counseling, unstructured supervision or educational aid, and institutional training and reformatory education are provided. But upon closer examination of institutional training the question arises whether a purposeful diversion has really been provided by these institutions, or whether the old practice is merely being 'sold' under a new name. Institutional training is criticized to an increasing extent with respect to its low socializing efficiency.[43] This criticism refers also to the present treatment practice with regard to juvenile offenders, since there is an increasing demand to abolish reformatory schools and juvenile prisons completely and also to avoid diversion strategies that culminate essentially in education in closed institutions.

* In this field too the needs of the victim must be subordinate to the interest of the juvenile offender's education. The victim therefore cannot make a private claim on the juvenile (§ 80 Juvenile Court Law).

8. SUMMARY AND CONCLUSION

If these considerations are summarized, they lead to the conclusion that diversion strategies must be left mainly to the initiative of persons who have been victimized or are potentially concerned. The field of juvenile delinquency is an exception. The internal administration of justice at the place of work and moderate reactions toward shoplifting must in principle be estimated as justified and legitimate attempts to overcome crime by way of private help. The interests protected by these private help institutions certainly must be recognized as purely economic ones. Yet in the end, only the efficiency in achieving the criteria formulated at the beginning is of importance. Findings concerning efficiency are still lacking in this respect. The experience in the German Democratic Republic with the societal courts seems to be indicative of positive results.[44] The fact, that the legislator has made no provisions – with the exception of the unsuccessful system of *Privatklage* (complaint and prosecution by the victim) in the Federal Republic of Germany – to satisfy the incontrovertible need for relief of the criminal justice system by the substitution in some instances of alternative, better functioning institutions, deserves criticism. Primarily those areas in which private persons have taken the initiative must be reconsidered. This indeed does not mean that the private initiatives should be totally excluded. But at least the elaboration of directives in a legislative framework must be taken into consideration that will help to guarantee the general principles of the rule of law and of a 'fair social state' *(Sozialstaatlichkeit)*. Such directives should aim mainly at maintaining the principle of equality before the law when it has to be decided whether a diversionary measure is to be adopted or not. Besides this, the problem of a possible double penalty (e.g. internal sanction at the place of work plus a sentence imposed by the court) should also be solved satisfactorily.[45]

The victim questionnaire studies which have been carried out to date show that the confidence in the efficiency of public crime control by criminal justice agencies does not enjoy a high estimation. The situation in the Federal Republic of Germany is certainly very differentiated: the confidence of the citizens in the police seems to be less imperiled than in the rest of the criminal justice system.[46] This situation indicates a need for alternatives to the traditional treatment of criminality on the one hand; but on the other hand, the danger that the feeling of insecurity will be intensified and continue to increase if the retreat of public crime control is ill-planned and too far-reaching must not be ignored.

In the realm of reactions toward juvenile delinquency new efforts to decriminalize juvenile law in favor of a noncriminal youth aid law have failed. The lack of capacity and of methodical treatment strategies and the increasing juvenile delinquency have been serious obstacles to a wide-ranging diversion strategy.

In the end, however, the concept of diversion, no matter how well-meant and well-conceived it may be, cannot renounce the principles of the rule of law because diversion remains within the precinct of social control, regardless of what it implies or how it is labeled. For this reason it must not only face up to empirical research but also meet those rules and demands of criminal policy that apply to all strategies of jurisdiction and crime control: i.e. humanity, rationality, proportionality equality and efficiency.

NOTES AND REFERENCES

1. Compare R. T. Nimmer, *Diversion. The Search for Alternative Forms of Prosecution.* Chicago: American Bar Foundation, 1974; Law Reform Commission of Canada, *Diversion.* Working Paper 7, Toronto, 1975, p. 1.
2. See G. Kaiser, *Kriminologie. Eine Einführung in die Grundlagen.* Karlsruhe, 1973, p. 66.
3. E. M. Schur, *Radical Non-Intervention. Rethinking the Delinquency Problem.* Englewood Cliffs, N.J., 1973.
4. R. L. Smith, 'Diversion: New Label-Old Practice,' in *New Approaches to Diversion and Treatment of Juvenile Offenders.* Washington, D.C.: U.S. Dept. of Justice, 1973, pp. 38–57.
5. Compare D. R. Cressey and R. A. McDermott, *Diversion from the Juvenile Justice System. National Assessment of Juvenile Corrections.* University of Michigan, 1973.
6. S. Kadish, 'The Crisis of Overcriminalization,' *The Annals of the American Academy of Political and Social Science* 374 (1967), pp. 157 ff.
7. Kaiser, *loc. cit.*
8. For the problem of stigmatization compare G. Albrecht, 'Stigmatisierung,' in G. Kaiser, F. Sack and H. Schellhoss (eds.), *Kleines Kriminologisches Wörterbuch.* Freiburg, 1974, pp. 318–321.
9. For the concept of depenalization which is current in socialist countries see Kiraly, *Evolution of Methods and Means Employed in Penal Law. General Report of the XIth International Congress on Penal Law.* Section I. Budapest, 1974.
10. See, for example, C. A. Bersani, 'Book Review: E. M. Schur, *Radical Non-Intervention,' Journal of Criminal Law and Criminology,* 65 (1974), pp. 128–129.
11. The President's Commission on Law Enforcement and Administration of Justice, *Task Force Report: Juvenile Delinquency and Youth Crime.* Washington, D.C., 1967, p. 2.
12. From the extensive literature see, for example, U.S. Dept. of Justice, *New Approaches to Diversion and Treatment of Juvenile Offenders.* Washington, D.C., 1973; Cressey and McDermott, *loc. cit.;* Law Reform Commission of Canada, *loc. cit.;* S. Palmer, 'Pre-Arrest Diversion,' *Crime and Delinquency,* 21 (1975), pp. 100–108.
13. Compare H.-H. Jescheck, 'Rechtsvergleichung als Grundlage der Strafprozessreform,' *Zeitschrift für die gesamte Strafrechtswissenschaft,* 86 (1974), pp. 761–782; E. Blankenburg, K. Sessar and W. Steffen, *Die Staatsanwaltschaft im Prozess sozialer Kontrolle.* Freiburg, 1975; generally, H. Kerner, *Verbrechenswirklichkeit und Strafverfolgung.* München, 1973.
14. See, however, E. M. Lemert, *Instead of Court: Diversion in Juvenile Justice.* Washington, D.C.: National Institute of Mental Health, 1971, p. 68.
15. Willem H. Nagel has primarily contributed to this topic by discussing the wide-ranging aspects of 'structural victimization:' compare Nagel, 'Structural Victimization,' *International Journal of Criminology,* 2 (1974), pp. 99–132, esp. pp. 124 ff.:
16. H.-D. Schwind and H. J. Eger, 'Zwischenbericht zur Dunkelfeldforschung in Göttingen,' *Kriminalistik,* 28 (1974), pp. 241–245.
17. E. Stephan, 'Die Ergebnisse der Stuttgarter Opferbefragung unter Berücksichtigung vergleichbarer amerikanischer Daten,' *Kriminalistik,* 29 (1975), pp. 201–206.
18. Compare C. Schrag, 'Theoretical Foundations for a Social Science of Corrections,' in D. Glaser (ed.), *Handbook of Criminology.* Chicago, 1974, p. 738.
19. See G. Kaiser, 'Viktimologie,' in Kaiser, Sack and Schellhoss, pp. 380–385.
20. Cressey and McDermott, p. 8.
21. R. Koewius, *Die Rechtswirklichkeit der Privatklage.* Berlin, 1974.

22. Compare K. Sessar, *Die Staatsanwaltschaft im Prozess sozialer Kontrolle.* Mitteilungen aus der Max-Planck-Gesellschaft 1974, pp. 90–96; and E. Blankenburg, 'Die Staatsanwaltschaft im Prozess sozialer Kontrolle,' *Kriminologisches Journal*, 3 (1973), p. 182. (In the federal state of Baden-Württemberg trials and penal order procedures accounted for 26% of the judgments in 1971).
23. Compare Koewius, p. 166.
24. See H. Zipf, *Strafprozessrecht.* Berlin and New York, 1972, p. 218.
25. See Koewius, p. 166.
26. Institut für Selbstbedienung (ed.), *Millionenverluste durch Ladendiebstahl.* Köln, 1969, p. 5.
27. Compare H. D. May, 'Die Selbstjustiz bei Ladendiebstählen,' *Kriminalistik*, 20 (1966), pp. 570–574; in general with regard to the topic of 'larceny and crime control' from historical and comparative perspectives, D. Rössner, *Bagatelldiebstahl und Verbrechenskontrolle. Ein exemplarischer Beitrag zur Entkriminalisierung durch quantitative Begrenzung des Strafrechts.* Beiträge zur empirischen Kriminologie, vol. 2, Frankfurt/M., 1975.
28. On crime control in general by recasting its design O. Newman, *Defensible Space. Crime Prevention Through Urban Design.* New York, 1972; and J. L. Grenough, 'Crime Prevention: A New Approach - Environmental Psychology and Criminal Behaviour,' *Journal of Police Science and Administration*, 2 (1974), pp. 339–343.
29. Compare May, p. 571.
30. See E. Blankenburg, 'Die Selektivität rechtlicher Sanktionen,' in J. Friedrichs (ed.), *Teilnehmende Beobachtung abweichenden Verhaltens.* Stuttgart, 1973, p. 145.
31. For Switzerland, R. Stephani, *Die Wegnahme von Waren in Selbstbedienungsgeschäften durch Kunden.* Bern, 1968, p. 56, according to whom 75% of the offenders were not reported to the police.
32. See G. Arzt, 'Forum: Zur Bekämpfung der Vermögensdelikte mit zivilrechtlichen Mitteln-Der Ladendiebstahl als Beispiel.' *Juristische Schulung*, 1974, pp. 693–702.
33. Compare 'Amtsgericht Nürnberg,' *Neue Juristische Wochenschrift*, 27 (1974), p. 1668.
34. On this problem see T. Lyon, Kriminalpolitische Tendenzen und die „Massnahmen strafrechtlicher Verantwortlichkeit" nach dem neuem StGB der DDR,' *Jahrbuch für Ostrecht*, 1968, p. 88.
35. R. Gerberding and G. Materna, 'Neue rechtliche Möglichkeiten zur wirksamen Bekämpfung von Verfehlungen,' *Neue Justiz*, 29 (1975), pp. 191–193.
36. Compare G. Kaiser, 'Betriebskriminalität und Betriebsjustiz,' in *Strategien und Prozesse strafrechtlicher Sozialkontrolle.* Frankfurt, 1972, pp. 100–123; J. Feest, 'Betriebsjustiz: Organisation, Anzeigebereitschaft und Sanktionsverhalten der formellen betrieblichen Sanktionsorgane,' *Zeitschrift für die gesamte Strafrechtswissenschaft*, 85 (1973), pp. 1125–1152; J. Feest, U. Krautkrämer and G. Metzger-Pregizer, 'Betriebsjustiz. Eine Untersuchung über die soziale Kontrolle abweichenden Verhaltens in Industriebetrieben.' Unpublished MS, Freiburg, 1975; compare also K. Luhmann, 'Die Betriebsjustiz in der Bundesrepublik und die Ahndung von Verstösse gegen die sozialistische Arbeitsdisziplin durch gesellschaftliche Gerichte in der DDR.' *Jahrbuch für Ostrecht*, 2 (1973), pp. 97–109, who attempts to find a legal-theoretical classification of internal administration of justice at the place of work.
37. On this aspect of diversion programs compare LaMar T. Empey, 'Crime Prevention: The Fugitive Utopia,' in D. Glaser (ed.), *Handbook of Criminology.* Chicago, 1974, p. 1117.
38. On societal courts in general, H. T. Schmidt, *Die sowjetischen Gesellschaftsgerichte am Beispiel der RSFSR.* Köln, 1969; A. Eser, *Gesellschaftsgerichte in der Strafrechtspflege.* Tübingen, 1970; G. Metzger-Pregizer, 'Gesellschaftsgerichte,' in Kaiser, Sack and Schellhoss, pp. 112–115.
39. According to May, *loc. cit.*
40. See, for example, Stephani, p. 65.
41. Compare G. Kaiser, *Strategien und Prozesse strafrechtlicher Sozialkontrolle.* Frankfurt, 1972, p. 85.
42. See A. Stümper, 'Verlust des staatlichen Gewaltmonopols?' *Kriminalistik*, 29 (1975), pp

193–196.

43. Compare G. Kaiser, *Jugendrecht und Jugendkriminalität*. Weinheim-Basel, 1973, p. 88.
44. W. Hantsche, quoted from 'Nöllechen.' *Westf. Rundschau*, December 21, 1974, who states a recidivism rate of less than 10% of the offenders sanctioned by more than 25,000 societal courts existing in the German Democratic Republic. Compare also F. E. Zimring, 'Measuring the Impact of Pretrial Diversion from the Criminal Justice System,' *University of Chicago Law Review*, 24 (1974), pp. 235–241, who questions the successful data of American projects under methodic viewpoints.
45. R. Nijelski, 'Diversion of Juvenile Offenders in the Criminal Justice System,' in *New Approaches to Diversion and Treatment of Juvenile Offenders*. Washington, D.C.: U.S. Dept. of Justice, 1973, pp. 83–92.
46. Stephan, *loc. cit.*

John M. Steiner
Stuart C. Hadden
Len Herkomer

PRICE TAG SWITCHING

It has become commonplace within the social sciences to study criminal behavior such as rape, murder, skyjacking, theft and the like from the point of view of the threatened society. The common theme in this approach can be broadly characterized by the question, 'What causes people to engage in this particular behavior?' While this is certainly a pertinent inquiry, its advancement typically ignores the contextual and temporal relativism of social rules which define the activity as criminal or deviant in the first place.[1] Dependent primarily on social assessments of appropriate time, place, and participants, behaviorally identical phenomena (e.g. killing a person) can be considered on a continuum from justifiable and necessary to reprehensible and wanton. The failure to recognize such social processes at the assumptive level forces *a priori* consideration of 'criminal acts' and their perpetrators as qualitatively distinct phenomena from that considered conventional. Such a distinction necessarily restricts subsequent formulations by granting ontological status to pretheoretical categories.[2]

In the last decade, a substantial shift from the above perspective has gained credence in the general field of deviance with concomitant extension into the study of criminals and their behavior. Classified to some extent under several rubrics (e.g. labeling, interactionist, phenomenological theories) this latter focus rejects the notion that deviance is an inherent characteristic of any act or set of acts. Rather, the category designation of deviance is reconceptualized as a meaning set applied by particular groups to behavior engaged in by others. This conception does not deny an idea of a common morality but rather, takes cognizance of the fact that the lines between conventional and deviant behavior are matters of social meaning which change over time and between situations. By stressing the problematic character of social meanings as applied to behavioral sequences this perspective assumes that in the entire range of alternatives available to a person, 'criminal/deviant' activity is but one of an array of possible selections, imbued with meaning for that person within a social context. Consequently, research is directed toward processes by which meanings of a particular behavior are granted social legitimacy by the individual and involved others. As such, the 'fact' that the behavior is ultimately considered criminal or deviant becomes a condition to be dimensionalized rather than an *a priori* stipulation. In this sense, the phenomenon studied is rendered most simply as yet another arena of human activity with its supposed 'criminality' a possible variable.[3]

The present paper, utilizing this latter perspective, reports an exploratory study of a relatively little known 'criminal' activity – price tag switching. The intent is to develop both a descriptive and theoretical view of the phenomenon, cognizant of both self-definitions and organizational contingencies. The analysis is framed in terms of 'facilitants' which enhances a conjoint rendering of self, interaction and structural conditions and at the same time, connotes a sense of process – change over time.[4]

DATA AND METHODS

Price tag switching is a relatively new phenomenon in the United States which began to occur with some prevalence approximately ten years ago. Phenomenologically, the *modus operandi* of the price tag switcher is quite simple. The perpetrator removes a price tag from a less costly item and places it on a more expensive item which he desires. Even if the person's act is discovered at the checkout counter, it is next to impossible to prove that he, himself, performed the switch. The prevalence of this activity is indicated by the estimated multimillion dollar losses attributed to price tag switching each year in stores in the United States and to a lesser degree in Great Britain, the Federal Republic of Germany, Italy, and other countries in Western Europe.

To the knowledge of those involved in this study, no prior research regarding price tag switching has been conducted to date. Consequently, the research was entered without a readily specifiable population. This problem was compounded by the lack of police or judicial records on the act. While price tag switching is indeed illegal, there is no specific statute in the research locale under which price tag switching is singularly prosecuted. Rather, it falls within more general misdemeanor charges of petty theft, shoplifting, etc. This lack of specificity rendered official records virtually useless. However, even if specific records had been available, the authors would have been reluctant to use them exclusively since this would have confined the study to 'unsuccessful' (i.e. apprehended) offenders.

In consideration of the above situation, it was decided to solicit volunteers from the general public for interviews about price tag switching activities. To this end, the following advertisement was placed six times in the Sonoma State College newspaper, *The Sonoman*.

> Do you or people you know participate in the widespread phenomenon of price tag switching?
>
> If you do, Sonoma State College sociology professor, Dr. John Steiner, would like to talk to you about it. He has started a research project on what he calls, 'one of the recent phenomena in socially deviant behavior which has not sufficiently been researched to date.'
>
> Of course, all interviews or information would be strictly confidential.
>
> Professor Steiner has observed and interviewed numerous people who participate or who have participated in the activity but would like to talk to others before reaching any conclusions. If you have any information you would like to share with Dr. Steiner or his assistant you can see them in his office on campus at 2084 Stevenson Hall, Room C, Monday through Thursday, 11 a.m. – 3 p.m. or Friday, 10 a.m. – 6 p.m. He can be contacted by telephone at 795-2160.

Twenty persons with price tag switching experiences volunteered to be interviewed (See appendix). Since the small number would make statistical analysis specious, it was decided to treat such interviews as self-reported 'case histories' and to utilize the general method of qualitative analysis suggested by Glaser and Strauss.[5] This approach allowed for the isolation of major patterns of behavior and their constituent features without making untoward claims to a larger universe. The end product is a substantive model which can be modified as more information becomes available. Further recommending this particular methodology is the fact that the resultant model need *not* be restricted to a description of the substantive *unit*, price tag switchers. Instead, since the methodology centers on major behavior patterns as illuminated by the substantive unit under study, the focus not only enhances an understanding of price tag switching, but also allows for the possibility of crosscutting similar substantive areas at a later date.[6]

If immaculate description of price tag switching had been the task here, the smaller than desired sample, the reliance on volunteers, and the method of soliciting same would have prohibited generalizations regarding the social characteristics of the obtained sample to the unknown population of price tag switchers. However, the sample can and will be described below since several commonalities were noted which are suggestive for later consideration.

The sample consisted of thirteen males and seven females, all Caucasian, ranging in age from 17 to 40 years old (median age approximately 24). Economically, only one person classified himself as being from a lower than middle class background. Approximately 40% of the respondents reported annual parental incomes between $ 10,000.00 and $ 20,000.00; 10% indicated that income was below $ 10,000.00; 15% had parental incomes over $ 20,000.00; and 35% were not able to respond. Additionally, 50% of the fathers and 45% of the mothers of those persons interviewed had at least two years of college education.

Approximately two-thirds of the parents were characterized as having strong religious affiliations while approximately one-third of the interviewees professed religious commitments for themselves. Respective family relationships were classified as good (or better) by two-thirds of the respondents with the remaining one-third reporting broken or turmoil enmeshed homes. Geographically, one half of the subjects were raised in suburban areas; approximately one-fourth were raised in rural areas and the remaining one-fourth were raised in urban areas.

All but two of the respondents placed themselves on the liberal end of a sociopolitical spectrum with some professing a socialistic economic orientation. Almost all acknowledged obligations and responsibilities due society by individuals but most did not recognize authority as *ipso facto* position/status conferred. Rather, the majority of respondents tended to individualize the right of authoritative control over their activities by some method of subjective judgment, distinguishing between legitimate authority and authoritarian control (e.g. 'I must *respect* a person before he can tell me what to do.'). Approximately 50% felt they had control over their own lives; 25% felt they did not exercise complete control and the remaining 25% felt they had no control over what happened to them.

This sparse descriptive coverage of the sample yields an interesting model. The 'typical' price tag switcher of this study comes from a Caucasian, middle to upper-middle class family, including good, intact familial relationships and strong religious affiliation. He is likely to have a liberal sociopolitical orientation characterized by a desire for rational social change centering on humanistic issues (e.g. eliminate poverty, discrimination, etc.). In short, the demographic and attitudinal characteristics sketched are *inconsistent* with the imagery of criminal/delinquent activities suggested by the major theoretical approaches in the field. While this remains a rough assertion at this point, the following analysis of the price tag switching phenomenon and perpetrator will more fully illuminate this disjunction.

GENERAL CONDITIONS

In the following discussion it should be noted that we refer to price tag switching in terms of discrete acts and *not* as an activity which organizes a life-style or provides a primary identity. None of the respondents in our sample conceived of themselves or saw others as seeing them in any central manner as price tag switchers. Rather, their self-images were of student, teacher, etc. who, among other things, occasionally engaged in price tag switching. The activity demands little of their time, energies or organization of their social life.[7]

Consistent with this minimal intrusion into self-identity, a most striking feature of our interviews was found to be the constant report that price tag switching is a spontaneous activity. Participation is dependent on a situational conjunction of objective and subjective factors which help to define price tag switching as a readily available, viable behavior for actors. This holds for both the initial foray and subsequent switching activities. The spontaneity does not equate with random behavior however, and the facilitating factors can be codified. What follows is a brief outline of these facilitants.

Availability

Price tag switching as a possible activity is objectively available to most members of American society. Behaviorally, it requires little specialized knowledge or expertise apart from that necessary for day-to-day life. As one of the respondents succinctly stated, 'How much technique can there be in price tag switching?'

Most American stores are ideally structured to facilitate price tag switching. Among the characteristics noted and capitalized upon by our respondents were: stores with a large selection of marginally different items; with prices which are either hard to detect by unsophisticated sales personnel or where prices fluctuate often (e.g., sale items) with the same result. Additionally, larger establishments were sought out so as to minimize the chance of individualized service being tendered by store employees. All in all, these characteristics constitute a general description of a large proportion of American department stores, supermarkets, novelty shops, secondhand stores, and the like.

These lay assessments of retail outlets appeared central to our respondents' decisions on which items could be successfully switched in value and how much difference there could be between the original and substituted costs. Such decisions were primarily dependent on common-sense conceptions of what a sales person would and would not be able to detect based on the structures outlined above. Additionally, it was felt that these conditions provide an appropriate explanation if the price tag switch is detected. The perpetrator merely asserts that the store, not he, has accidentally mismarked the item – a charge difficult to disprove.

A second consideration of store organization for our respondents is the manner by which the items are tagged. The usual method in stores as described above is for the tag to be attached to the item by either glue or pins. The latter is most easily switched as it merely involves removing the pin and reaffixing a lesser value price tag. With glued price tags, it is often difficult to cleanly remove the original and complete a passable substitution.

The physical ease with which the tags can be switched and still maintain an 'authentic' appearance seemed to be crucial as the entire act, as reported by members of the sample, depends on being as unobtrusive as possible. A poorly switched tag was thought to draw unusual attention to this feature of the sales transaction, heightening the chance of detection. Correspondingly, it was felt that the 'unauthentic' appearing tag, if detected, decreased the credibility of the previous alibi which held the store responsible for mismarking the item.

The major efforts of the retail industry in combating price tag switching activities have been directed toward this latter structural feature – making the tags more difficult to remove without detection.[8] Several technologies are being explored, but all have the common theme of reducing the objective availability of price tag switching.[9] Thus, it appears that the retail industry is hoping to reduce the incidence of such activity by expanding the amount of knowledge/expertise required to successfully complete same.

Justification

Descriptively, respondents indicated their price tag switching activities were initially prompted by a very common human predicament. They wanted a given article but were either unable or unwilling to pay the set price for it. The latter case, being unwilling, was most often the case, for very few of our respondents reported instances where lack of funds was a motivating factor. A similar observation has been made by the chief security officer in a large California department store. Most price tag switchers he encountered were regular customers of the store, fully capable of paying the full purchase price of the tag switched item.[10] Tangentially, it seems items most frequently switched are luxury products such as household goods, sporting goods, electronic equipment, phonograph records, garments, cosmetics, pharmaceutical items, and more expensive food products - articles not absolutely essential for basic subsistence.

The alternatives usually perceived for obtaining an item in situations as above are: (1) pay the full amount, or (2) steal the item.[11] Price tag switching can be seen as a middle ground and will be examined in terms of respondents' justifications for its selection as compared to other alternatives.

As stated earlier, most respondents were unwilling to pay the listed price for the desired item. Usually the price was considered to be in excess of these persons' subjective assessment of the 'real' value of the article. These lower-than-price value assessments were either stipulated in terms of the cost of production/marketing of the item or the individual's desire/need for the goods. Price tag switching afforded an opportunity to secure the item, save money in the process, and if so defined, strike a blow for 'fair' prices.

Outright theft of the articles, on the other hand, was often ruled out by most of the respondents. The risk of getting caught and the certainty and severity of punishment were reported as the mitigating factors in rejecting simple theft. Subjectively, price tag switching was considered 'not really stealing' by the overwhelming majority of the sample interviewed. Correspondingly, most persons felt that if they were detected, price tag switching as opposed to outright theft would be more difficult to prove (see availability factors above); they would be less likely to be prosecuted and if charges were brought against them, they would be less severe. In fact, several respondents felt the most severe penalty they would receive would be a stern reprimand and consequent embarassment.

In setting price tag switching apart as 'not really stealing,' individuals revealed both cognition of the 'deviant' nature of their activities and their personalized definition of this behavior. In the first instance, the low risk involved for detection and the perceived assessment of minimal certainty and severity of punishment made price tag switching a subjectively safe 'deviant' act. At the same time, the act is obviously illegal and for respondents this facet of the activity provided an aura of excitement. 'Getting away with it' was an important adjunct to the meaning of the behavior for those involved. Most respondents indicated they perceived price tag switching as a challenge (albeit, with minimal risks), and substantial satisfaction came from successfully meeting this self-imposed 'test' of abilities.[12] Any moral qualms were 'neutralized' by the low risk factor and concomitant denial of victim.[13]

The denial of victim took essentially two forms. The first and most prevalent stipulated that no person (including the perpetrator) was getting hurt. Stores were, of course, incurring losses but such a perception was handled by conceiving of stores as objectthings as opposed to people. The second victimological explanation depicted the particular stores involved as deserving victims. The individuals perceived of themselves as subject to inflated prices and their price tag switching as an equalization of indignities, vis-à-vis the original perpetrators (the merchants).[14] Thus, with 'no victim' and relatively little risk, our respondents indicated the viability of price tag switching as a form of behavior bringing them satisfaction in terms of both attaining an instrumental goal (securing the item for less money) and providing an appropriate test of their guile, abilities, etc. The process is summarized in Figure 1.

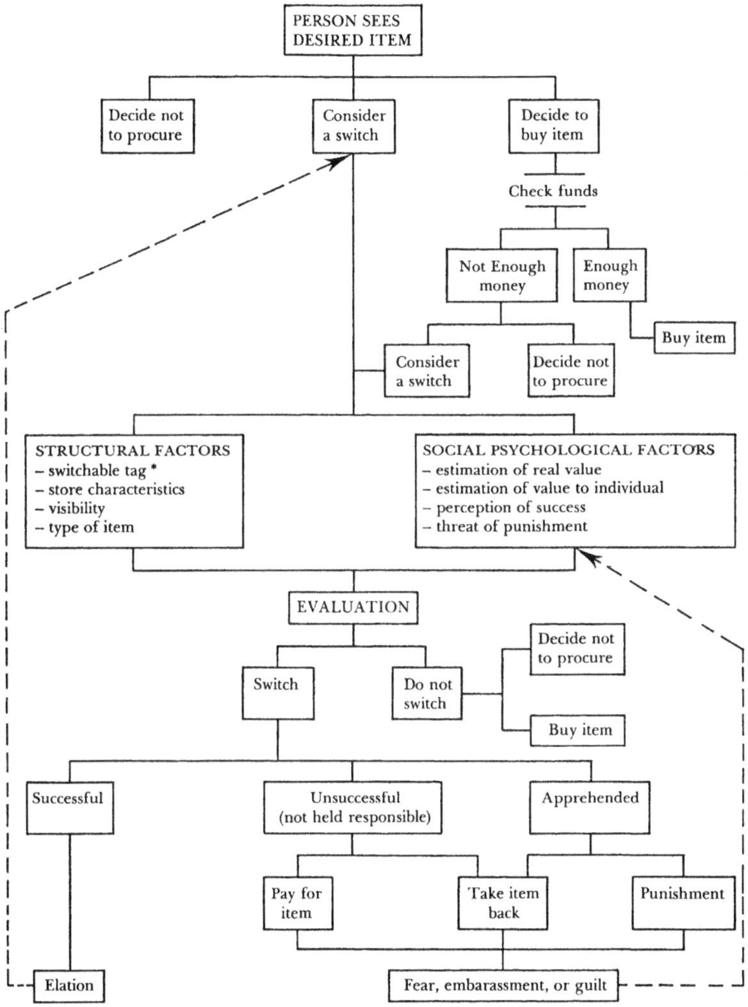

* This is the only factor that is particular to price tag switching. The rest apply to shoplifting as well.

NOTE: Broken lines indicate negative or positive reinforcement tendencies for future action.

DISCUSSION

Hans von Hentig, in his trailblazing study, proposed that in a sense, the victim stimulates the offender and his criminal act in their symbiotic interaction.[15] Furthermore, von Hentig observed that the interrelationship between the perpetrator and victim is not adequately reflected in criminal law, especially when it can be established that the offender has, in fact, been victimized. Similarly, Reckless draws attention to 'the victim proneness' which is to say that many victims tend to be victimized because they are in a sense responsible for provoking criminal behavior in the offender.[16] Following this line of reasoning, the evolving pattern of victim-aggression can be seen as anchored in precipitating social conditions in which normative interaction is no longer experienced as rewarding.[17]

Singelmann suggests that social interaction is a 'complex exchange of mutually rewarding activities in which the reception of a needed benefit is contingent on the delivery of a return favor. Needs, anticipations, and predictions of others' behaviors thus become important ingredients in a person's decision-making.'[18] In this sense, exchange has a larger dimension in the social structure, consistent with our concerns, that provides the opportunities and constraints based on what, by consensus, is deemed to be a 'fair' bargaining process. If, however, the actor at a given point in time/space is no longer able to agree on or submit to what constitutes 'fairness' in an exchange and has recognized an imbalance, he will covertly or overtly break the social contract. This will be done by manipulating the sources of reward to ensure a favorable outcome for him 'even against the resistance of others.'[19]

Unbalanced social conditions become further aggravated if those in authority have lost their credibility because they themselves no longer adhere to what they advocate as 'fair' exchange. Again, if we accept that a balanced exchange relationship is one in which a person needs the other's services as much as the other needs his, we will find that 'in an unbalanced relationship the benefits exchanged are of unequal value, which gives 'power' to the one who can provide the superior or more needed benefits.'[20]

Viewed from that perspective, price tag switching is essentially an act of protest pursued as an alternative response to experienced socio-economic inequity. For the most part, the respondents who have engaged in price tag switching tend to reject traditional public authority figures because they have experienced them as excessively constraining, unfair, and inept. As noted, approximately 80% of the respondents have price tag switched because they felt that they were being overcharged by department stores and not because they were unable to pay the listed price. The items switched were in the majority of cases not needed for basic subsistence but classified as luxuries. The majority of the respondents also felt that price tag switching was the only alternative recourse available by which they could defend themselves against excessive exploitation by large business corporations.

The department store corporate owners who are primarily the victims of price tag switching may inadvertently be playing conflicting roles by overstimulating the wants of the offender by advertising their goods thereby creating desires which, from a pecuniary standpoint, can almost never be fully satisfied. The price tag switchers respond by developing the desired wants from the corporate point of view but resent having to pay an 'unfair' price for such commodities. Induced by the victim, the continuously tempted offender responds by breaking the law. That is to say, the victims (corporate owners) with their carefully designed, target-oriented advertising practices, create a homo consumens without sufficiently considering the sociological, psychological, economical, and moral consequences of their practices when imposed on the customers' limitations. In short, the price tag switcher as consumer and target of the profit-seeker's exploitative and manipulative practices, responds with means at his disposal to defend his interests according to his understanding of fairness.

Phenomenologically, then, price tag switching is a syndromic novel response to: (a) consumerism, (b) educational and socialization specific norms, (c) including variables such as low functional exclusiveness. Seen from this perspective, switchers may prefer this middle of the road breach of law because the activity does not elicit intolerable feelings of guilt but renders an adventurer's thrilling experience (many switchers experienced elation during and after the act which provides satisfaction to them). It is important to know that the majority of price tag switchers, at the time of their activity, did not engage simultaneously in shoplifting. If, however, price tag switchers are strongly ideologically motivated, a correlation between switching and other behavioral areas, for example, protest activity, rebellion, and rejection of the establishment, might be found. More specifically, they might engage in the destruction of advertising posters, demonstrations, direct and indirect provocations against the power elite, and aggression against political authorities and corporate decisionmakers or other representatives of the establishment. As an expression of a still maintained and functioning bourgeois super ego, naive excuses for price tag switching given to us did not express this type of activism. Rather, they ran along lines such as: the others, but especially those in elevated power positions, are just as dishonest or crooked if not more so than I.

Price tag switchers do not assume, but seem to be escaping from, social responsibility and over-integrating social processes which render an autonomous existence difficult. Their notion of autonomy appears unrealistic. Instead of striving for optimal realistic integration with a rational degree of autonomy, they prefer to strike back with means which they condemn in others on whom they depend existentially. Finally, it is important to note that price tag switching is a direct response to experienced inequity. The majority of price tag switchers, in their spontaneous act, are responding to what they perceive as an alternative defense against a 'rip off' by corporate power and, in some cases, that of the political directorate. In most cases, price tag switching is not learned from others but a consequence of individual assessment and confusion of what, in their view, constitutes an alternative response to unfair practices. Thus, as Schafer has said: 'The functional role of man sets the limit of the accountable links in the chain of causes, and his instrumentality is the cause selecting factor for his responsibility. Crime is not only an individual act but also a social phenomenon.'[21]

CONCLUSION

As a result, from the foregoing analysis, we suggest the following categorization of offenses by consumers in stores which also allows for differing frustration-aggression variables, class, and subculture differentials which reflect the spectrum of high or low functional exclusiveness:[21] (a) Shoplifting as a more crass form of thievery; (b) Offenses based on philosophic or ideological motives in which the customer partially recompensates the store for services or goods rendered, that is to say, in which the social contract is not fully broken.

In his act, the price tag switcher reflects the recognition that switching is ideologically and morally a viable alternative to outright thievery and less risky in terms of possible apprehension. Further, it is a readily available activity requiring only everyday knowledge. This distinguishes them from acts committed by more seasoned and experienced property offenders. Our pilot study sample also shows that the more timid, burgeois, and intellectually inclined offenders tend to rationalize their acts more thoroughly than those originating from a lower social stratum. It is, therefore, questionable to what extent ideological reasons given by switchers are not a mere rationalization for a situationally proximate act when, in fact, fear or timidity may inhibit them from engaging in a more outright aggressive thievery. Our investigation clearly indicates that most switchers did not reflect any pronounced ideological commitment. Moreover, they viewed price tag switching as a compromise to outright thievery and, therefore, as a cavalier derelict.

NOTES AND REFERENCES

1. For a cogent development of this argument see Jack Douglas, *Deviance and Respectability*. New York: Basic Books, 1970, ch. 1.
2. See the similar critiques by D. Matza, *Delinquency and Drift*. New York: John Wiley and Sons, Inc. 1964, ch. I. and more extensively, D. Matza, *Becoming Deviant*. Englewood Cliffs, N.J.: Prentice-Hall, Inc., 1969, *passim*.
3. Implicit here is Zimmerman and Pollner's argument concerning the 'confounding of topic and resource.' Their central thesis is:
   'Sociological inquiry is addressed to phenomena recognized and described in common-sense ways, while at the same time such common-sense recognitions and descriptions are pressed into service as fundamentally unquestioned resources for analyzing the phenomena thus made available. Thus contemporary sociology is characterized by a confounding of topic and resource' (p. 81).
   For a full development, see D. Zimmerman and M. Pollner, 'The Everyday World as Phenomenon,' in J. Douglas (ed.), *Understanding Everyday Life*. Chicago: Aldine Publishing Co., 1970, pp. 80–103.
4. A 'language of facilitants' as opposed to a 'language of causality' is especially fruitful at the elemental level since it allows for a more detailed consideration of multivariate factors on an exploratory basis. For the logic of this approach and an application, see J. Lofland, *Deviance and Identity*. Englewood Cliffs, N.J.: Prentice-Hall, Inc., 1969, pp. 31–33 and *passim*.
5. This general approach, 'the constant comparative method,' is described in B. Glaser and A. Strauss, *The Discovery of Grounded Theory*. Chicago: Aldine Publishing Co., 1967, ch. V. Since such procedures are designed for 'discovering' conceptual categories, they are well

suited to the present purposes where the research as described above is concerned with an uncharted arena of activity.

6. The applied logic of this position is argued in B. Glaser, *The Patsy and the Subcontractor.* Mill Valley, Calif.: The Sociology Press. 1972, pp. vii-viii and ch. IX. Further examples of the logic in use are O. Bigus, 'The Milkman and His Customer: A Cultivated Relationship,' *Urban Life and Culture.* Vol. 1, No. 2, (1972), pp. 131–163 and S. Hadden, 'The Social Creation of a Social Problem,' Unpublished Doctoral Dissertation, Washington State University, Pullman, Wash.
7. As mentioned, no one in our sample had been apprehended at their price tag switching tasks. Had they been, the activity may have attained added importance for self-image. This latter instance is a major proposition of the labeling perspective and is aptly capsulized by Matza in terms of 'signifying.' For him, '. . . signifying makes its object more significant as we might expect. The object enjoys – or suffers – enhanced meaning. To be signified as a thief is to lose the blissful identity of one who among other things happens to have committed a theft. It is a movement, however gradual, toward being a thief and representing theft.' D. Matza, *op. cit.*, p. 156. See also M. O. Cameron, *The Booster and the Snitch.* Chicago: The Free Press, 1964, pp. 59–66.
8. To provide the *surveillance* necessary to correct the facilitating organizational characteristics (e.g., anonymity, marginal differences in goods, etc.) is seen as possibly offensive to potential customers.
9. Some of the technologies developed are described in 'Crime: They Would Rather Switch,' *Newsweek*, July 12, 1971, pp. 76–77.
10. C. Durant, 'Solid Citizens: New Style in Thievery-Price Tag Switching,' *Los Angeles Times*, Dec. 18, 1972.
11. It is interesting to note that except for specialized cases, the listed price is considered as firm. Exceptions take place in certain types of stores (e.g., second-hand stores) or with certain large commodities such as automobiles, where 'bargaining' is socially legitimated. In supermarkets, department stores, and similar retail outlets, bargaining is not seen as a viable alternative. However, at least one experiment demonstrates this 'common-sense' restriction can be violated successfully with items obtained for less than the listed price at such stores through bargaining. See H. Garfinkel, *Studies in Ethnomethodology.* Englewood Cliffs, N.J.: Prentice-Hall, Inc., 1967, pp. 68–69.
12. In this sense, price tag switching bears strong resemblance to Lofland's conception of the 'adventurous deviant act.' Here the act itself is an instrumental goal. See Lofland, *op. cit.*, pp. 104–116.
13. For more extensive development and general application of 'techniques of neutralization,' see D. Matza and G. Sykes, 'Techniques of Neutralization: A Theory of Delinquency,' *American Sociological Review* 22 (1967), pp. 644–670 and D. Matza, *Delinquency and Drift*, pp. 69–86. See also, Lofland's contribution in terms of 'conventionalization,' Lofland, *op. cit.*, p. 86.
14. Both the 'denial of victim' and 'deserving victim' explanations receive more extensive theoretical treatment in Matza, *op. cit.* pp. 171–176 and Lofland, *op. cit.* pp. 86–89.
15. H. von Hentig, *The Criminal and His Victim: Studies in the Sociology of Crime.* New Haven: Yale University Press, 1948.
16. W. C. Reckless, *The Crime Problem.* (3rd ed.) New York: Appleton-Century Crofts, 1961. pp. 21–22.
17. S. Schafer, *The Victim and His Criminal: A Study in Functional Responsibility.* New York: Random House, 1968, pp. 79–80.
18. P. Singelmann, 'Exchange as Symbolic Interaction: Convergencies Between Two Theoretical Perspectives,' *American Sociological Review*, 37 (1972), p. 416.
19. Max Weber defines power as 'the chance of a man or of a number of men to realize their own will in a communal action even against the resistance of others who are participating in the action.' From H. Gerth and C. W. Mills (eds.), *M. Weber: Essays in Sociology.* New

York: Oxford University Press, 1946, p. 180. See also Amitai Etzioni, *The Active Society*. New York: The Free Press, 1968, pp. 314–315.
20. Schafer, *op. cit.*, p. 152.
21. R. Dubin. 'Power, Function and Organization,' *Pacific Sociological Review* 6 (1963), pp. 16–23. Also see Schafer, *op. cit.*, p. 73.

John M. Steiner, the senior researcher, is indebted to Miss Charlsey Cartwright for her assistance in an earlier draft of this paper.

APPENDIX

Interview form for price tag switching

1. How do you switch price tags?
2. Do you have a favorite technique?
3. What determines which price tag you put on the items you want to buy? (Indicate desired price range differential).
4. When was the first time you engaged in price tag switching?
5. Were you worried about getting caught?
6. Did you plan to do it the first time?
7. Why did you do it?
8. At present, how do you view your p.t.s. activities?
9. Do you still engage in p.t.s.? If so, why? If not, why not?
10. In which stores do you prefer to p.t.s.?
11. In what size and type of store do you usually switch p.t.?
12. Are you a regular customer there?
13. Do you have a favorite time of the day in which you p.t.s.?
14. Does advertising affect your buying habits? If so, how?
15. Do you bargain hunt?
16. Do you prefer to wait until the items you need are on sale?
17. How many times have you p.t.s.?
18. Has p.t.s. become a habitual activity?
19. What items have you switched? (Luxury items or basic necessities?)
20. What was the extent of your need for these items?
21. Have you ever shoplifted?
22. If so, did you shoplift before or after you started p.t.s.?
23. Do you do both? If so, what factors determine what you do?
24. When and how did you find out about p.t.s.? (From relatives, peers, work associates, etc.)
25. Do you know others who p.t.s.? If so, who are they? What items are involved?
26. Do you know individuals who shoplift? If so, who are they? What items are involved?
27. How does p.t.s. differ from shoplifting?
28. After you have p.t.s. and left the store, how do you feel?
29. What do you feel you have accomplished by p.t.s.?
30. When you are in a store, do you ever get the urge to p.t.s.?
31. Do you enter a store with an intent to p.t.s.?
32. Do you intend to continue to p.t.s.?
33. If p.t.s. were prevented, what would you do as an alternative?
34. What are your friends' feelings toward your p.t.s.? If they don't know, how do you think they would feel if they knew?
35. How does your family feel toward your p.t.s.? If they don't know, how do you think they would feel if they knew?

36. What would happen if you were caught?
37. What would be your reaction?
38. How would your family and friends respond to this?
39. Do you talk to others about your p.t.s.? If so, to whom?
40. How old are you?
41. Where were you raised? (Metropolitan, suburban or rural area)
42. What is your ethnic background? (Foreign born, 1st, 2nd, 3rd generation American)
43. Do you have brothers or sisters? If so, what are their ages?
44. What is your educational background?
45. What is your marital status? If married, how would you characterize the relationship?
46. What is your father's profession?
47. What is your mother's profession?
48. What is their educational background?
49. What is their income?
50. Would you consider yourself to be in the lower, middle or upper class?
51. Do your parents own their own home or do they pay rent?
52. Are they/you religious? If so, with what denomination are they/you affiliated?
53. How would you characterize the family relationship?
54. Are you living with your family, by yourself, or with friends?
55. Do you own your own home or do you pay rent?
56. Are you employed? If so, where? What is your income? If not employed, what is your source of income? How much money do you receive?
57. How does the rising cost of living affect you?
58. What are your plans for the future?
59. What are your social or political beliefs?
60. How do you relate to authority?
61. With whom do you identify or relate most readily? (Models)
62. How do you view yourself? What kind/type of person do you believe yourself to be?
63. Generally, how do other people tend to view you? What kind/type of person do others believe you to be?
64. Is there someone who models his behavior after you?
65. Do you feel you are in control over what happens to you? Explain.
66. How do you feel about obligations and responsibilities?
67. Why have you volunteered to be interviewed?
68. How do you feel about this interview?

Denis Szabo

CRIME, DEVIANCE AND LAW IN POST-INDUSTRIAL SOCIETIES: PROFILE OF FUTURE TRENDS

TRENDS OF CRIME: IMMINENT CRISIS IN THE JUDICIAL SYSTEM

Based on current trends in crime and the development of criminal legislation, any estimate of future possibilities warrants the deepest pessimism. The increase in crime is alarming, and the means of dissuasion – prevention and punishment – seem cruelly inadequate. Neither our concepts nor our techniques have changed very much since ancient times, whereas society is ever changing. Traditionally, the law was an expression of the norms governing society's control over its members, but to all appearances, this control is being exercised less and less effectively. There is every indication that between now and year 2000, what we call the judicial system, which includes the police, the courts, penitentiary services and those concerned with juvenile delinquency, will collapse under its crushing load. Consider, for example, the recent prison revolts, the magistrates' and policemen's unions and their demands, etc. that have had to be dealt with.

BASIC FUNCTIONS OF THE LAW

The nature of law is, and always has been, a reaction to rather than anticipation of events. This means that the lawmaker, on the principle of precedent, does not specify norms nor provide sanctions until there are a sufficiently large number of known facts to necessitate his intervention. A social order that inspires unquestioned mores does not need a great many laws, since the people's behavior will be reasonably predictable.

As long as sin (individual morality), the mores (public opinion) and the laws (administered by justice) are one, (or nearly so), there is no crisis in the sense referred to here.

The problem arises when these three elements are divided: society has undergone a staggering transformation; many have observed that we have gone farther in the industrial and post-industrial era – in short, since the end of the eighteenth century – than during the whole of the neolithic upheaval which lasted thousands of years. Since the middle of the twentieth century, evolutionary leaps can be measured in decades.

It has been found that the legislator who translates the moral attitudes of society into law is having more and more difficulty finding acceptable criteria, not only for so-called moral crimes, but also those affecting persons or property. It is not only that homosexual behavior and prostitution have become less offensive in the eyes of the average man; in the face of the dangers of pollution, defective vehicles, aldulterated food, and drugs, it is more and more difficult to maintain the traditional criteria of social dangerousness with regard to murder, theft and common fraud. There is an increasing public awareness of electoral and political fraud, and provision has been made for punishment of economic and commercial offenses.

The close link between the political process, legislative action and the enforcement of the law by the judicial organizations, more or less independent of the political powers, becomes clearer as we get farther away from a consensus, however tenuous it may be, as to the legitimacy of the sanctions provided to strengthen the law.

The reactive nature of the law, as opposed to an anticipatory concept, is shown again in its inability to legislate in time with regard to a whole series of situations involving conflicts of interest that arise following rapid technical and socio-economic changes. The result is a paradoxical situation where, in certain respects (in the United States, for example), there is an excess of laws (the most ridiculous being those that abound in the area of sexual morality and alcohol), which tends to discredit them, thus rendering them ineffective. Despite this superabundance of laws, there is a deplorable lack of legislation in a whole series of vitally important areas, such as new techniques for artificial procreation; the protection of privacy against the electronic information systems of public and private administrations; human rights in the underprivileged milieus of society, for instance, the rights of prisoners or the aged; the rate of profits made by business or industry in a market economy largely subsidized by public funds, etc.

The law being reactive, it reflects interests and accepted values, and the attitudes these engender. Industrial society is based on these values. It is characterized by its emphasis on utility, its materialistic value system, its bureaucratic organization, its system of mass production and standardization, its subordination of the social organization to the mechanism of the market economy, etc. The new post-industrial society that is developing before our eyes, and which will predominate toward the end of the century, will have a technology, a social organization, mores and cultural preferences quite different from those we know today. Its legal system, then, must reflect these differences.

OLD AND NEW MORALITY: CHANGES IN VALUES

Victorian morality or the 'Wasp' mentality, which has had a profound effect on industrial society, has been described as being built on four cornerstones: 'achievement,' 'self-control,' 'independence,' and 'endurance.'

The new morality, which is now seeking definition and which will influence the society of the future, could be defined as being 'self-actualization,' 'self-expression,' 'interdependence,' and 'potential for enjoyment.'

It is very difficult to measure these values by applying positivist theories, but their existence and the increasing conflict between them are discernible to the naked eye. One basic value alone could dominate and rally the majority opinion of a post-industrial society, and that is 'enlightened self-interest' (Wilkins). The enlightenment could come from the social sciences – from criminology, where problems of law and order are concerned.

According to Toffler in *Future Shock*, societies can live without laws, for mores can mold behavior sufficiently to uphold the social order. On the other hand, no society is conceivable without order. In other words, it is social organization which makes it possible for the members of any society to anticipate the consequences of their own acts as well as those of others. And order – its criteria as well as its justification and legitimacy – depends on the values on which it is founded.

Caught up in a conflict of values that is creating a crisis in the functioning of the judicial system, the remedies envisaged are also open to question: therefore, 'more of the same' seems to be the rule. This means more prisons, that hardly resocialize and do not punish, more magistrates, whose sentences seem unfair to a large portion of the public, more policemen, when nothing is known as to their relative usefulness. There is also a demand for full employment, reforms in education, and social and mental health measures, when nothing is positively known as to the relationship between socioeconomic or psychosocial problems and the origins and development of criminal conduct. To resort to such remedies is like encouraging a fundamentally unbalanced growth by treating it with hormones, which can only lead to the destruction of the organism.

NEW PERSPECTIVES ON THE DEFINITION OF DANGEROUSNESS

The only way to get out of this rut is by making an effort to reevaluate the very criteria that make an act socially dangerous. And this brings us back to the statement made earlier, that the values ratifying collective legal action must be reexamined.

Another fact must be noted regarding the nature of the legal judgment: it is expressed in absolutes – 'true' or 'false,' a simplistic method that was suitable for past systems of social and cultural organization; the concept of 'law' used in science is now quite different from that used in jurisprudence. Scientific law consists in the formulation of a principle which accurately explains a certain number of facts or events that occur under a particular set of circumstances. Each new discovery adds to the universality and exactness of the law by making it possible to incorporate numerous variables. This does not occur in a law formulated by legal process; its universality is subject to rules of fairness inherent in the culture, and its enforcement based solely on approval or disapproval. Judgment is binary and absolute.

According to Toffler, there are two convergent trends in present-day society, and as they develop, by the year 2000, they will reveal the characteristicts of this post-industrial society. The first of these two trends is called diversity, the second transience. We shall sum up his argument in this order.

Diversity: the vast technological explosion has made many more choices available to most people. Contrary to the leveling effect of the industrial society which resulted from the technological revolution of the nineteenth century, this new revolution has resulted in a quite unexpected increase in the choice of consumer goods. Only a short time ago, the fact of having the telephone was hailed as a major step forward. Today, there are no less than 1,500 telephone models available.

The right to be different is made possible not only by the increased purchasing power of the masses, but by radical changes in the large social institutions, such as education. More and more, schools, classes and special teaching methods are being organized to meet the needs and aspirations of the very different groups that are proliferating in society. The same phenomenon is to be seen in the field of communications: while major magazines with a wide circulation are having a hard time surviving, they are being replaced by a mass of publications ranging from 'underground' newspapers to magazines specializing in sports, hobbies, etc. The introduction of the cassette has caused the same diversity – freedom of choice in the audio-visual field: anyone can tape the programs he wants on any subject he likes.

This 'destandardization' of tastes and preferences due to technical advances has some striking consequences in cultural areas. Regional or national values can be expressed in economic terms: there are linguistic, culinary or literary differences in innumerable subcultures but they do not prevent their adherents from having the benefits of advanced technology.

In the field of law, this 'diversity' naturally leads to a bewildering mass of litigation. All these varied segments of society, representing the most diverse subcultures, can no longer be governed by a code based on common sense or a morality fashioned by the industrial revolution of the nineteenth century. The differences in values, mentioned above, is clearly apparent here. Is it to be imagined, or even hoped, that this fragmented society of the twenty-first century can be held together and governed by laws that are ever increasing in number and always behind by several generations?

Transience is the other trend that characterizes the post-industrial society. It affects the field of law profoundly. The stability of the law throughout the thousand years of the neolithic revolution seemed almost to have become second nature to man in society. The relationships, rights and duties which had to be regulated were relatively few in number, Roman law being a transitional step between Sumerian law and Napoleonic law. But the rhythm of change has accelerated so much since the second half of the twentieth century that a kind of 'ad-hocracy' is replacing the rational bureaucracy developed during the nineteenth century. The dizzying increase in administrative and commercial laws, etc., and the settlement of a greater and greater number of cases outside the courts, show the direction the law (common law) has taken in the face of this growing 'transient' of the relations between individuals, groups and institutions.

People have such mobility, and the operations of multinational companies are so diversified and complex, that the law, designed for a stable social order, is finding it increasingly difficult to settle the conflicts that arise, or even deal with unprecedented relationships. Since the shift toward transience of social relations, freedom of choice has once more increased. It is possible to engage in many varied experiences and then leave them as soon as needs or curiosity are satisfied. The stability of the social order, that is, the relationships, actions and reactions of people, groups and institutions, is becoming problematic and unpredictable.

The effects of this second process on the law of today is as profound and injurious as those of the first. If 'diversity' leads to an excessive number of proceedings, growing transience lessens the need for reforms, adjustments and changes. Thus a paradoxical situation is created: the value of law has always depended on its stability and its ability to predict conformist behavior. When changes are too highly accelerated, it is robbed of its essential attributes. Sociocultural phenomena of such a divided and transitory nature can hardly serve as criteria for permanent legislative reforms.

FOR A NEW DEFINITION OF THE RULE OF LAW IN THE MODERN POST-INDUSTRIAL SOCIETY

Changes in values being related to these two processes, it is hardly surprising to see tension and conflicts between the judicial system of an industrial society and the social order born of a post-industrial society. These conflicts are a cause of deep disillusionment in different social groups whose aspirations are not met by these laws. Doubts about the legitimacy of the social and legal order are increasing, ambivalence toward the law is spreading, and more or less violent opposition is occurring and threatening to occur. The consequences of the reactive nature of the law are most serious during this period of change and rapid evolution toward a post-industrial sociocultural order. 'Deviations' occur so often and in such great numbers that neither the letter of the law nor the spirit of the law can take much note of these changes. In addition, the present system of administration of justice does not have the retroactive power to correct its own mistakes: techniques for the evaluation of administrative policies are very new, and in any case, the criteria for evaluation are still ambiguous and debatable. This situation further adds to the extreme instability of the system and the threat, already mentioned, of its collapse under the increasing strain.

The excess of laws, brought about by the increase and acceleration of the fragmentation of the social order, its breakdown into more and more diversified, interdependent subcultures having different and often opposite value-norms, only contributes to the crisis. And again we see the same pattern we criticized before: 'more of the same remedy.'

Increasing the number of punitive sanctions and heightening their severity does not seem to be a solution for the future either. More policemen, judges or prisons, charged with the same duties they have today, will only increase the financial burden of the community intolerably, without really assuring citizens any greater security. The values of a post-industrial society are not expressed in terms of 'general goodwill.' The decline of these values is already well advanced in the industrial society. Those who must protect the social order, the agents of social defense, sense the solid foundation of a feeling of legitimacy slipping from under their feet; but this feeling of legitimacy is essential for effective action.

We agree with Toffler's conclusion: even if we created a 'Commission of Anticipatory Law,' charged with discarding outmoded laws from the legislation every five years, and sounding out socioeconomic and cultural evolutionary trends in order to suggest new legislation, the problem of a social order endowed with social and legal mechanisms of control would not be resolved. We must look for a way to adapt the social order itself to the requirements of the post-industrial society.

PLEA FOR HAVING PRAGMATIC EXPERIENCES SHAPE THE UNFORESEEABLE FUTURE

If we believe that we are now at the end of 10,000 years of juridic history, characterized by attempts to have the numerous subtle mechanisms of social control subject to the law, we may assume that in the new era, the law will be subordinate to the social order.

The functioning of the law itself, and the mechanisms through which it exercises its power, could be achieved on a small community scale, or that of subcultural units, whose rapid increase and gradual diversification we have already pointed out. The proliferation of administrative jurisdictions today, the numerous 'boards' that in common law countries make up for the absence of centralized administrative jurisdiction, are an indication in this respect.

Juridic ethnology gives numerous examples of self-rule by a social order through recourse to the jury system, evaluation by one's peers, regulations often passed and administered by ad hoc organizations, but always very flexible. The essential point of this 'communalization' of the administration of justice is its 'de-professionalization,' its considerably reduced costs and its legitimacy, strengthened by the 'proximity' between 'judges' and 'deviants.' The People's Republic of China offers many examples of this type of thinking.

There are already numerous signs today on the North American scene of this trend to relieve the system of justice of an increasing proportion of the cases with which it is burdened. These run from the referral of certain delinquents to social aid organizations upon agreement between the police and the courts (for example, the Vera Foundation of New York), to simply doing away with juvenile detention services, thus making it necessary for the administration to find radical alternatives to the institutionalization (ineffective) of youth (as in the State of Massachussetts, for example).

Neighborhood surveillance could be undertaken by officers of the peace who are laymen, recuited locally from among citizens who would take turns doing this civic duty. The responsibility for reintegrating a former inmate into society, too, would be up to the services of his own community or receiving center.

Sanctions should be infinitely more varied. For a long time there has been criticism of the unjustifiable lack of imagination on the part of the lawmaker who has but two standards – time and money – for punishing criminal behavior. The equality of this is an illusion. The sociology of culture has frequently pointed out that the value of time is not the same for different groups or cultures; one does not have to be an economist to see that a $ 1,000.00 fine does not mean the same to a salaried person and to a member of a profession, a businessman, or industrial owner. This false theory that everyone has equality before the law has led to grave injustices in practice, considering the inequality of men and cultural values within communities.

Jean Fourastié has pleaded for a long time for an 'experimental' outlook and policy. The field of legal sanctions is ideal for its application. The principle is simple: if we would dissuade everyone from committing acts that infringe upon, flout or endanger the freedom of others, the sanctions that threaten us should truly instill fear in us. For example, vandals or looters of public property should be assigned to municipal repair shops, hit-and-run drivers to emergency clinics, parking violators to cleaning the roads. The man who steals should have to reimburse his victim by working, tax defrauders should be recruited for voluntary work in the social services, etc. All these measures have one trait in common: they have significance both as far as the life style and culture of the 'culprit' is concerned, as well as his environment and that of his victim. Hence anticipation of the consequences of a deviant act is made possible as well as reciprocal action as a consequence of a violation of the laws or regulations.

In conclusion, we must prepare for the social order of the post-industrial society that is taking shape before our eyes, and provide mechanisms of social and legal control that are appropriate for this new type of society. Profound changes in attitudes toward values have created a crisis in the field of justice that reflects a much deeper crisis in the social order, whose criteria and authenticity are being challenged by an increasing number of individuals, often for very different reasons.

Criminology and the social science researcher interested in a better quality of life in the industrial or post-industrial society, must set out on a combined mission of pragmatic empiricism, reflecting the trends in the social reality as it takes shape before our eyes, and of futurist forecasting leading to laboratory experiments to see what form the social order will take several decades from now.

Marshall B. Clinard

COMPARATIVE CRIMINOLOGY AND DEVELOPING COUNTRIES

A truly comparative criminology must approach existing data and conduct new research by using theoretical frameworks, propositions, or models that can be tested across various societies. For an adequate comparative criminology it is essential to ascertain whether similar social processes account for crime in technologically developed and less developed societies. For developed societies, such as the United States and the countries of Europe, the most important causal factors have been shown, generally, to be increasing urbanization and the persistence of slum areas. A universal process that crosses cultural lines is the migration of large numbers of rural people into the cities, where the subsequent process of urbanization modifies their behavior. The probabilities are high that many of these migrants and, if they are married, their children, who, if they had remained in their own rural homes, would most likely not have engaged in crime, will become involved in some sort of criminal activities in an urban context. If certain uniform social processes, such as urbanization, contribute to criminal behavior, existing variations can be assumed, conversely, to be related to variations in these processes, including urbanization.

A basic question is whether certain sociological theories of crime apply to the developing countries. They are, first, the theory of differential association, that is, the view that crime is learned in association with others, and, second, differential opportunity, a theory that, although based on the theory of anomie, proposes that differential access to certain goals in a society and to illegitimate means to achieve these goals accounts for crime. It is important to find out whether crime in developing countries is committed primarily by youth and learned from companions, as it appears to be in most developed countries. There is, furthermore, the question whether the types of crime of major concern in the countries of the developing world, including white-collar crime, are similar to those of the developed world. This study attempts to test the applicability of these frames of reference to less developed countries by organizing existing data and the findings of new studies carried out in Africa.

The goal of a comparative criminology should be to develop concepts and generalizations at a level that distinguishes between universals applicable to all societies and unique characteristics representative of one or a small set of societies.[1] To be applicable criminological theories must be tested, modified, retested, and again

From Marshall B. Clinard and Daniel J. Abbott, *Crime in Developing Countries: A Comparative Perspective;* Copyright © 1973 by John Wiley & Sons, Inc., pp. 1–13 and 254–262. Reprinted by permission of John Wiley & Sons, Inc.

modified until they can account for exceptions or at least predict exceptions. Durkheim recognized the importance of testing theoretical propositions in a variety of social settings as wide as is available to a scientific investigation.

> One cannot explain a social fact of any complexity except by following its complete development through all social species. Comparative sociology is not a particular branch of sociology; it is sociology itself, in so far as it ceases to be purely descriptive and aspires to account for facts.[2]

To obtain the objective of comparative criminological theory research should proceed, according to Durkheim's criteria of a comparative sociology, first in a single culture at one point in time, such as the United States, second, in societies generally alike, such as many countries in Europe which have similar cultural, economic, and technological conditions, and third, after proper modification, tested on completely dissimilar societies, yet sharing some common features such as those of many less developed countries. If any theoretical formulation in criminology is to be explained on a universal basis, it should be tested under all three conditions. In such comparisons it is not always necessary to use precisely similar research procedures providing the hypotheses and theoretical framework to be tested are the same. In this study, following Durkheim, we have tried to expand criminological research into the third stage, namely in developing societies that may be considered to be dissimilar to the developed countries of the world, particularly the United States and Europe, but, at the same time, are undergoing many similar processes.

For many decades comparative sociology tended to decline, despite the scientific need for it and the extensive comparative work of such pioneering sociological giants as Durkheim, Marx, and Weber.[3] In the last 20 years, however, there has been a revival of interest and work in this field by an increasing number of sociologists who have devoted themselves to detailed systematic comparisons and the construction of types in such areas, for example, as organizations, social stratification, political and kinship structures, patterns of socially significant behavior, and the analysis of total societies. Among the major factors that have stimulated the more recent interest in comparative sociology are developments outside the discipline in the comparative analysis of institutions by English social anthropologists like Radcliffe-Brown and Evans-Pritchard and the cross-cultural survey work in the United States of Murdock and the 'culture and personality' school of anthropology. Other major contributions to a comparative sociology have been the development of area studies, the foundation of the United Nations and UNESCO, and, as Merton has said, 'the emergence of new, self-conscious societies, and a growing sense of the interdependence of societies.'[4]

Although comparative sociology, as a whole, has been increasing, so far there has been only limited development in the area of criminology. In Marsh's survey of 1146 comparative sociology articles between 1950 and 1963, for example, only 29 dealt with deviance and only a small part of them with criminology.[5] DeFleur has stated that 'students of juvenile delinquency have frequently pointed to the urgent need for cross-cultural comparisons of youthful misconduct.'[6] On the whole criminologists have had an ethnocentric tendency to assume or to make claims that findings based on their work in one national culture are applicable to others. This is particularly true of most criminologists in the United States, where criminology is the most highly developed, who assume implicitly that findings from studies of American society and culture constitute generalizations applicable to others. Close examination of most basic books on American criminology reveals that they are based almost entirely on research done in the United States and thus are primarily descriptive of American society. There is an implicit but untested assumption that theories and research findings would generally fit other societies. Some European writers, however, have suggested that many of the American findings in criminal behavior are limited to American society because of the extensiveness of culture conflict, the frequency of horizontal and vertical mobility in the United States, and the fact that extensive immigration has disturbed the social stability of the country. American research findings would still be applicable elsewhere, however, provided that the conditions, factors, or variables discovered were found to apply to other societies.

In the use of cross-cultural criminological studies there have been a few notable exceptions; for example, the Philadelphia studies of Wolfgang on the subculture of violence as an explanation of such crimes as homicide and assault have been extended, with the collaboration of the Italian criminologist Ferracuti, to a comparative study of the subcultural violence in many cultures,[7] and both Clinard and Friday have made comparative studies of crime in Sweden in which they have applied theories of urbanization, differential association, and differential opportunity derived from the United States.[8] In England Downes has tried to replicate Cloward and Ohlin's theory of gang delinquency,[9] and several comparative studies of crime have been made in the Scandinavian countries through the collaborative efforts of Nordic criminologists. Joint studies of youth crime have also been carried out in Yugoslavia, England, and Poland, primarily by criminologists at the University of Ljubljana. In addition the Council of Europe has tried to develop collaborative European studies, particularly in the area of organized crime. Also important are the works of European criminologists Mannheim, Hurwitz, and López-Rey, all of whom have surveyed criminology from a comparative viewpoint but have concentrated heavily on studies from Europe and the United States.[10] The Social Defense Section of the United Nations has issued a number of reports on crime in less developed countries, but although they contain much useful descriptive material only a few of them attempt to test comparatively some basic propositions about crime. There have also been a few examples of comparative research: among the most important are Weinberg's work in testing United States-based urbanization and differential association theories of crime in Ghana and DeFleur's tests of North American gang theories in Argentina.[11] All of this is somewhat similar to the situation of comparative sociology in general. 'Many sociological propositions are, of course, stated as if the relationships and generalizations hold true for all societies, social systems, and even social action. However, such propositions have rarely been tested outside of modern American and Western European societies.'[12]

In many ways crime in the less developed countries is currently at a stage that provides a reflection of England, the United States, and other developed societies as they were at the time of rapid industrialization, urbanization, and development in the early nineteenth century.[13] Eventually men and women everywhere will be drawn into the modern world by urbanization, industrialization, the spread of mass education, and various mass media. In terms of observing and understanding the processes that lead to criminal behavior in various social environments, it is important at this stage of developmental world history to attempt cross-cultural research studies. Clifford has pointed out the significance of such research in connection with the rapid changes now taking place in Africa:

> In the years ahead even the imperfect attempts to study crime which we can make now may not be possible in anything like the same context. For the time being, we can find peoples in Africa comparatively unaffected by industrialization and economic development and we still have an opportunity to compare *their* standards and *their* methods of dealing with crime with those of larger city groups who are moving ever more rapidly to the urban pattern common to all developed countries. Everything indicates that this is a situation which will not last very long. As the years pass, more and more people in Africa are affected by the spread of education and by industrial change and urbanization. As the economies develop so will a more uniform pattern of living extend throughout these countries. Differences between the various communities will be reduced and information which might be gathered now may just not be available in the future. This, then, is the argument for not letting present opportunities slip by without doing the little we can. We may not have the background we require but even crude or speculative work at this stage may be worth a dozen carefully contrived and methodologically sound investigations later when the chance to compare societies has gone by.[14]

The problems in cross-cultural research in the less developed countries are formidable and might well account, in part, for the limited efforts in this field. There is the question whether differences encountered in comparing developing countries with one another or with the industrialized nations are based on unique cultural occurrences or on different levels of development.[15] Some writers feel that the direct transference of many criminological theories developed in the industrialized nations may well be totally inappropriate in a developing country, since initial conditions vary greatly from society to society.[16] Research in such cross-cultural settings may encounter unexpected problems and even resistance at each stage of the process. The overall project may be hindered by restrictions imposed by customs, taboos, and values or by political hierarchies of authority and prestige.[17] Many technical problems such as the inability to administer questionnaires to a largely illiterate population or to contend with local taboos about answering certain questions,[18] also exist, of course, in carrying out cross-cultural research, but in spite of the theoretical difficulties raised by the cultural diversity in the world today a basic set of commonalities in culture renders cross-cultural analysis a fruitful task.[19]

SOCIAL CHANGE AND DEVELOPING COUNTRIES

An understanding of the major forces and pressures that influence social change in these countries is imperative in any analysis of their crime situations. As the less developed nations attempt, in one or two generations, to bring about transformations that have culminated from several centuries of development for most of the industrialized nations, severe social repercussions are often evident.[20] At no other period, perhaps, in the history of the people of developing countries have values and living patterns undergone such extreme alterations over the span of one lifetime.[21] The magnitude of the social revolutions taking place throughout the world clearly signifies an intensive period of societal transformation. The resultant disruptions are greatly intensified when 'social change is disorderly, when the degree of social change is high, and the creation of new institutions is great.'[22] Among the 123 countries that are members of the United Nations 81 are considered definitely 'underdeveloped' and 20 to 25, borderline. As viewed by the United Nations, 'underdeveloped,' 'less developed,' or 'developing' refers not to cultural development but rather to the country's failure to 'develop' an adequate standard of living.[23] The concept of 'development' encompasses such a broad spectrum of social, economic, and technological factors that it defies clear definition. The term is imbued with ideological and value overtones that alter its interpretation in each economic and political system.

Merely associating the concept of development with the idea of 'progress' introduces a set of considerations that effectively blocks the possibility of a consensus. Culbertson refutes this concept of economic development as a single-track idea of inevitable human progress born, he says, in the optimism of the 1950s.[24] The critical social phenomena circumscribed by the concept of development refer to a more limited sphere of activity than the broad inferences in the term 'change.' Human development implies specific categories of change that can be evaluated as better or worse over time, reflect the quality of the human condition, and retain their significance in cross-cultural comparisons. Any enumeration of basic elements associated with the use of the concept development must necessarily reflect, to a certain extent, the assumptions of its author.

Although food, shelter, and health, and the substructures required to provide them, must be included in the perspective of human development, any exploration of the enormous societal upheavals which trace their origins to the transformations that occurred two or three centuries ago in England and Western Europe must be cognizant of productivity, human aspirations, and political participation. The unparalleled expansion of technological capacities available to many societies, plus the continued contrast between the 'haves and the have-nots,' renders economic change the most prominent, visible, and discussed feature of the twentieth century. A principal source of thrust in the struggle toward economic parity is the ground swell in humanity for a better standard of living and a particle of influence in the decision-making process.[25] The response to this explosive world awakening reveals enormous inconsistencies in every society. Development may flourish in one sector while suppression or regression is characteristic of another.[26] Nonetheless, the unique combination of technological mastery and the concomitant, to a certain degree resultant, expansion of human horizons marks a period in human development generally termed 'modernization.'

The growth of industrialization affects the direction and nature of urbanization and both, in turn, affect the growth of modernization. Physical, organizational, and financial facilities required to support an expanding industrial sector become concentrated in cities, and vast population shifts to urban centers occur as a response to the economic and social stimulus.[27] The urban population growth in developing countries has been a continually accelerating process. From 1940 to 1960 the population in urban areas of 20,000 or more in Latin America increased from 19 to 32%, from 7 to 13% in Africa, 8 to 14% in South Asia, and 13 to 20% in East Asia.[28] Latin America's urban population grew from 25.2 million to 67.8, Africa's from 13.8 to 36.4, South Asia's from 50.5 to 116.1, and East Asia's from 81.6 to 160.5. These changes signify a doubling or tripling of the urban sector in a 20-year period, a transformation that is part of a worldwide expansion of the population proportions in urban environments.

In relation to their population proportions, urban areas often achieve much higher levels of influence in developing countries than their counterparts in developed countries. One city, or a few cities at most, becomes dominant socially, economically, and politically and is thus termed the 'primate' city in the developing country. Concentrated in this urban sector are the government, commercial centers, transportation and communication facilities, and even the administrative talent crucial to industrial development. Investment funds flow into it, job opportunities are centered there, and it becomes the major target of migrants seeking a better or a different way of life.[29] Since the large city is the ultimate destination for extensive population movements as well as the main contact with the outside world, it serves as primary initiator for an entire country's changing goals, values, and normative patterns. Acting as it does as a focus for world observers, pressures are understandably acute to have the primate city present an appearance of affluence and success. Large sums of money are poured into projects such as impressive national monuments, government buildings, and prestige hotels, and short-term rather than permanent employment positions are created. Resources are diverted from the construction of industries or their supporting infrastructures. At the same time increasing numbers of migrants are drawn to the city because of its growing splendor, modernity, and complexity. Thus the ability of the economy to generate urban employment is reduced, whereas the probability of a greater influx of untrained manpower is enhanced.

Heightened expectations plus inadequate physical, organizational, and financial resources conspire to foment an extensive degree of 'overurbanization' in most of the less developed countries. Both the push of the burgeoning rural population and the pull of the city inundate urban areas with unskilled migrants who cannot be absorbed into the more slowly expanding industrial sector. Subject to continual unemployment or underemployment, destitute migrants gravitate toward the only housing available–the vast tracts of physically depressed living structures. The plight of the urban dweller is in sharp contrast to his mental set which rejects the fatalistic acceptance of a poor environment and demands the means to pursue his own destiny in more human conditions.[30]

One immediate result of these industrialization and urbanization trends is a complex division of labor and a growing differentiation among the people. Although the strong push toward industrialization has been accompanied by an equal emphasis on literacy and education in developing countries,[31] few newly independent nations have educated and trained their own technical and administrative personnel to build a rapidly expanding industrial economy. Governments have launched comprehensive programs to fill the needs of their own citizens and to remove the stigma of illiteracy. As education becomes the key to wealth and status, there is a strong impetus in the urban environment to pursue these goals with impassioned vigor and high hopes. Only a comparatively small percentage of the population can expect to attend a university and achieve high positions in the economic or political structures, but students with some secondary education often cannot find employment at a level they consider commensurate with the education they have managed to acquire. With even a few years of primary education students may have changed their self-images and their goals to such an extent that they may refuse to farm the land.[32] As a result, large concentrations of partly educated youth in urban areas cannot obtain employment, yet they refuse to leave the city. The emphasis on education, with the relatively few possibilities of success, produces social structural conditions that create deep feelings of alienation in many young.

Communication in developing countries undergoes radical changes with the advance of mass media even to their most remote sections. The expansion of social horizons creates a transformation in the individual, and, according to Lerner, generates the development of 'psychic mobility,' or empathy, the capacity to see one's self in the other fellow's situation.[33] This empathy does not connote sympathy or concern but is merely the inner mechanism that enables the newly mobile person to operate efficiently in a changing world. As the individual becomes increasingly aware of his total society, he wants greater participation in its affairs. Whether a society chooses the 'mobilization' or the 'reconciliation' system, as described by Apter, the individual plays a more active role.[34] In the former he is absorbed into a political system in which many qualities similar to a religion demand total allegiance. In the latter he is part of a complex web of groups, each of which freely makes demands on the political system. He is 'transformed from being defined as his father's son into a citizen.'[35] Increased responses to the mass media and interest in national affairs serve to augment the material expectations of the people to make them increasingly dissatisfied with their poverty and living conditions, and to incite them to make demands on their governments to provide greater amenities.

Concomitant with the impact of urbanization and industrialization are basic changes in social institutions. The urban environment has a secularizing effect on man's beliefs and relationships as contact with modern science minimizes strict adherence to traditional religious views and practices. Goode has stated that whenever any movement toward industrialization occurs the family moves toward some kind of 'conjugal' pattern; that is, few kinship ties are kept with distant relatives and the emphasis is on the nuclear unit of husband, wife, and children.[36] The heterogeneity of the city also brings the people into contact with varied patterns of living. The need for skilled labor and management often decreases the amount of traditional nepotism in business and government. Modernization brings increased concern with health problems. Broad strides have been taken to combat such diseases as malaria, smallpox, and tuberculosis and to reduce infant mortality. Since decreases in infant mortality are not generally accompanied by a declining birth rate in developing countries, sharp increases occur in the growth rate of the population.[37]

Modernization also fosters the development of a set of values and attitudes generally associated with modern man. Moore claims that certain value changes are essential to extensive economic transformation, since 'economic growth necessitates high individual mobility and a placement system based on merit.'[38] Based on the underlying logic of industrialization and urbanization, attitudes and values which are constant across cultures, supposedly develop.[39] In a cross-cultural study of six developing countries Smith and Inkeles attempted to construct an instrument for rating a degree of modernism that would be valid for all emerging societies. By giving batteries of questions to samples in the respective countries and employing factor analytical and correlational techniques, they isolated a set of items with high cross-cultural reliability.[40] In an extensive attempt to measure these values empirically Kahl found seven factor scales that reflected the value system of modern man.[41]

The international effect of the recent push toward modernization has been analyzed by Lagos in a discussion of what he has called 'atimia.'[42] This concept refers to inconsistency in the status of nations. Although they are formally equal to developed nations, independent and full voting members of the United Nations, they are not equal in economic power or prestige. The resultant overriding concern with rapid economic development and preoccupation with presenting an acceptable image to the world impinges on the consciousness of political élites and becomes a critical factor in governmental decision making. Developing countries, however, face formidable barriers as they attempt economic modernization. Comparing the preindustrial phase of the developed countries with the presently less developed countries, Kuznets points out that when the developed countries began to industrialize they had a much smaller population and a lower population growth rate.[43] Basic financial and market substructures were already apparent, and political independence was a reality in most of the industrialized nations. In most cases the per capita income was several times higher than the current per capita income of many of the less developed countries. These factors combine seriously to retard governmental efforts to generate the savings necessary for capital investment and to attain a sustained economic growth which surpasses population expansion. Political leaders are driven toward policies of forced saving among people who already live close to subsistence and who have greatly increased their material desires by the dual efforts of aspiring politicians and the deluge of products from industrialized nations.

In summary, the development process includes industrialization, urbanization, and concomitant changes in the values and structures of most social institutions. In the less developed countries serious asymmetries tend to appear as societies seek to propel themselves into the modern world:

(1) An imbalance between the concentration of modernization and economic power in urban areas and the backwardness of the rural population.

(2) An imbalance between population growth and the ability of the economy to create employment.

(3) An imbalance between the demands for talent by the economic sytem and the development of skills.

(4) In urban areas a reduction of the role of the family and elders as the main socializing agents of youth without adequate social control replacement by other institutions, resulting in the development of behavior patterns among youth that differ radically from family expectations.

(5) Changes in values that reject a fatalistic acceptance of the relatively impoverished conditions under which people traditionally have lived.

INCREASE OF CRIME IN DEVELOPING COUNTRIES

Despite the variations in the adequacy of statistics and the criticism justly leveled at official crime reports, data concerning the extent and serious nature of the crime problem almost unanimously substantiate the generalization that criminality is rapidly increasing in less developed countries. The president of the Ivory Coast supreme court stated in 1968 that 'the more a country develops, the more crime increases. There is a relationship between the economic development of a country and the struggle against crime.'[44] This relationship is a reality that governmental elites cannot ignore. Using a series of social indicators to rank a large number of countries as developed or developing, Wolf, for example, compared their ranks from 1958 to 1962 in crimes reported to Interpol (International Police Organization).[45] He concluded that crime rates increase with the developmental status of a country, compared with other contemporary nations.[46] This does not imply that increases in the amount of crime are greater in less developed countries but rather that the rate of increase is more acute at this point in their history.[47]

In 1970 the United Nations Congress on the Prevention of Crime and the Treatment of Offenders came to the following conclusion:

> As any country begins to open up, outgrow its traditionalism and respond to outside influences or new ideas by modernizing, industrializing and concentrating people in certain areas, its people and particularly its younger generation seize the many new opportunities. And in doing so, a small but progressively increasing number of them succumb to temptations and seek illegal satisfaction through crime.[48]

Even as far back as 1955 a United Nations report stated, with reference to Africa, Asia, and Latin America:

From observation of experts and from limited statistical data in such areas, it can be said that juvenile delinquency became a problem of concern in those countries when industrialization has increased and where urban centers have been established.[49]

Juvenile delinquency was then becoming more pronounced as a social phenomenon, particularly in Latin America. The report went on to point out that there were only a few regions of the world, such as various islands in Polynesia and Melanesia, Brunei, Sarawak, St. Helena, and some limited areas of Africa, in which juvenile delinquency was slight or did not exist at all. In these areas cities either did not exist or they were small, and close family, community, and tribal organizations had not yet been disrupted.

Recent reports collected by the United Nations in countries in Asia, Africa, and Latin America indicate a continued increase in crime rates,[50] and current United Nations studies in Chile, India, and Zambia report a progressive growth in both the volume and serious nature of juvenile delinquency.[51] Arrests in Thailand, for example, rose from 146,270 cases to 648,142, or a 350% increase from 1940 to 1964, whereas during this same period the population increased by about 72%.[52] Convictions for serious crimes showed a somewhat similar pattern. This profound change does not appear to be simply a reaction to additional categories of crime or increased ratios of arrests to crimes. In fact, 'it is highly probable that because of present conditions there are actually fewer arrests now than at some previous time.'[53]

In Venezuela, from 1953 to 1956, reported crimes against property increased from 20,477 to 24,243, or approximately one-fifth.[54] From 1950 to 1965 the city and province of Buenos Aires experienced a rise in juvenile crime rates more serious than those of Argentina as a whole, crimes against property representing a predominant 70% of the total.[55] In Puerto Rico cases of juvenile delinquency increased sevenfold between 1956 and 1964, although the population increased only slightly.[56] A Puerto Rican study has commented as follows on these various changes:

The Commonwealth of Puerto Rico has for many years been experiencing an extremely accelerated rate of social, economic and political change. Indices of these changes are many, including the rate of population growth, the rate and degree of internal and external migration, the change in the economy from agrarian to industrial, the increased urbanization of the island, the changing family roles, the rise in income levels, the change in the occupational structure, the emphasis on material wealth, and the like. Another important indicator of change, however, and one less optimistic, is the increase in various types of individual and social pathology which generally accompany such change and which are often generated by it.[57]

Accurate statistics for the Arab countries are not available, but their representatives at various meetings have expressed concern for what appears to be a serious increase in crime. The Second United Nations Seminar for the Arab states on the Prevention of Crime and the Treatment of Offenders, held in 1969, contended that serious increases in juvenile delinquency are a problem of paramount importance in all Arab countries.[58] Algeria has had a steady increase in new cases of crime: 19,049 in 1963, 41,898 in 1966, 62,379 in 1967, and 123,638 in 1969.[59] Between 1965 and 1970 cases of juvenile delinquency increased 200% in Madagascar, and in Ghana criminal cases reported to the police per 10,000 population rose from 84 in 1959 to 97 in 1964.[60] A Zambian study of delinquency between 1939 and 1962 showed a great rise in juvenile delinquency (229 offenders in 1939, 441 in 1950, 837 in 1955, and 1979 in 1962), but it did not find a positive correlation between it and an increase in police activity.[61] Although his findings were not conclusive in this respect, Clifford concluded that they did 'strengthen the view that juvenile crime is a real social problem which is growing.'[62]

THE PREVENTION AND CONTROL OF CRIME IN DEVELOPING COUNTRIES

In this comparative criminological study available data about crime in developing countries have been analyzed in terms of several important frames of reference, all of which are significant in any explanation of criminal behavior in the developed countries: urbanization, slums, differential association, and differential opportunity. Some conclusions have been reached about the applicability of these frames of reference to the less developed countries and the nature of crime. Before analyzing the significance of this problem in terms of programs of controlling and preventing crime in these countries, it is important to summarize some of the findings on which any program of criminal policy must be based.

Among the many general aspects of the developmental process, which encompasses the combined effects of urbanization and industrialization, migration and the resultant growth of slums, increased availability of consumer goods, and the extensive changes in normative standards of behavior, a sharp increase in property crime in nearly all the less developed countries is most prominent. The almost unanimous findings, despite some uncertainties surrounding statistical reports gathered from the developing countries, support the generalization that crime, particularly property crime, is rapidly increasing and becoming one of the major problems of the developmental process. The current crime rates of most of these countries are rising more rapidly than those of the developed countries. Although not increasing rapidly in absolute numbers, the rates of increase are more acute at this point of development in those very countries that have had previously rather low rates typical of most traditional societies.

Because of the increase in crime in developing countries, urgently needed developmental resources must be diverted to crime control. Additional manpower, transportation, special equipment, and buildings must be provided for police, courts, and prisons. In some instances street lighting is being improved, largely to guarantee more adequate security. Perhaps of even greater importance is the fear generated for the security of persons and property, a situation that had not been anticipated as a concomitant of independence.

Until now the rather sharp increases in crime in the less developed countries have been misleading because they are limited to that comparatively small proportion of the population in the cities where crime is concentrated. The dominant feature of the developing world is the accelerated rate of urbanization; characteristic village life is rapidly replaced by urban living patterns. Not only are the urban areas growing at a rate two to three times the rate of population growth, but population expansion in the developing countries gives them a greater potential for urbanization. Urbanization in the less developed countries today is proceeding much more rapidly than it did in the developed countries and the circumstances surrounding it differ distinctly; the tendency is to concentrate in large primate cities. Urbanization in the Third World represents, first of all, a generally high birth rate, a marked drop in the death rate, and an increasing and unprecedented expansion of Western education and culture into the most remote rural areas. The burgeoning rural populations force the young to seek alternate means of existence in urban areas, and the cities themselves draw many of them because of the fuller life they offer.

A series of factors combines to aggravate the crime problem in the developing countries. Vital resources for the drive toward sustained economic growth become concentrated in the primate cities, and once this process has been initiated investment naturally follows. The forces of modernization therefore control population movements and maximize the criminogenic effects of urbanization. In addition, the urban way of life in the developed countries characterizes the present situation in many primate cities of the developing world – heterogeneity, anonymity, rapid social change, competitiveness, emphasis on material goods, and individualism. Although small enclaves remain in which people carry on some of their traditional ways, they are constantly being exposed to the larger urban world. The heterogeneity and density of the city force people into slum neighborhoods with which they have little affinity or basis of understanding. The lack of intimate ties, plus the protective cover of impersonality and anonymity, radically reduces both internal and external control of criminal behavior. The city offers greater opportunities for theft and greater possibilities of collaboration with other offenders and with 'fences' for the disposal of stolen goods. Urban areas generate the motivation, rationalization, skill, and low risk of detection.

The migrant is faced with the difficult choice of accepting the urban way of life or attempting to recreate some semblance of a traditional life style in an unfamiliar setting. Although the sense of community, self-importance, and belonging is often weakened or lost in migration, the impact of drastic changes in social environment can be mitigated by contact with settled relatives or friends in the urban area. As they, in turn, however, have become affected by the anonymity of the city, this help tends to decline. New social alignments based on urban criteria of status and importance emerge. Many migrants choose the alternative of a short-term commitment to the city and even return to their villages if and when their economic goals are fulfilled. For those who stay on there are many impediments. Work is hard to find and may involve a frustrating and fruitless search of many months, during which time all needs must be met with cash money. At the same time the migrant is exposed to contrasts in life style unparalleled in the village. Ultimately many of them are drawn into some type of criminal activity.

Since not all migrants nor all urbanites commit crimes, this study has attempted to isolate and understand the backgrounds of those who were more likely to commit them. The analyses proceeded on two levels, first, the factors on the individual level and, second, the factors that affect crime rates in different urban communities. It is only by understanding the problem of criminality on both levels that realistic suggestions for crime prevention and control can, hopefully, be formulated.

What clearly emerged as a dominant factor in the background of the Kampala offender, compared with the nonoffender, was the comparative absence of experiences and supportive agents that could prepare him for urban life. The offender more often had only village life as a frame of reference before arriving in Kampala. When he did make his way to the city, he seldom had relatives or friends to offer him food and shelter and to guide him in his adaptation to city life. Furthermore, even when the offender did have relatives there, he tended to avoid them and to a much greater extent found close friendships outside his own tribal group. The offender was somewhat of a paradox, for he did maintain his connections with his village kin and he often owned land there. The offender thus seemed to be a person who maintained his village identification but who failed to form social ties that would enable him to make a successful adjustment to this new style of urban living.

As in the developed countries, the slum is the main focus of crime in the developing countries. Crime is committed by its residents and most of it occurs within its confines. Not all slums have high crime rates, however. Factors such as physical conditions, socioeconomic status, or population stability do not distinguish between slum communities with high and low crime rates. The low crime rate community appears to have a much higher degree of unity, expressed by a higher incidence of visiting, participation in local organizations, restricted friendship patterns, and stability in family relationships. By cultural homogeneity and strong emphasis on tribal and kin ties members of the low crime community manage to evade the heterogeneity, impersonality, and anonymity that prevailed in areas of high crime. The predominance of primary bonds in a neighborhood reduced the propensity to steal from a neighbor and made the unnoticed entrance of a stranger less likely. Older persons demonstrated a critical capacity to maintain the unity of the population and helped to enforce compliance to community rules.

Modernization also has a great impact on criminal behavior in less developed countries, some forms being more, others less, common than in the rest of the world. Property crime, which makes up nearly all crime in any city in all countries, increases sharply because of a marked decline in informal social controls, greater opportunities for theft, and the rising prestige of material possessions, however small, as status symbols. Since even the simplest object, such as a used shirt, a light bulb, or a piece of iron pipe, represents a desirable increment in wealth, the potential market for stolen goods is much greater than in almost any developed country. Also the opportunities for theft are greater because of the difficulties of protecting property and the absence of security measures. Special markets, usually regarded as regular establishments, are often readily available in the cities for the disposal of stolen goods.

As a country develops, robbery with violence and the threat of violence increases. In the developing countries armed attacks, which represent a growing problem in isolated nonurban areas, are made on homes, motor vehicles, and buses on the highways, and the spread of industrial, banking, and business enterprises requires the transportation of large sums of money, usually with few guards. The increase in robbery is due in part to the training acquired among growing prison populations, since more and more offenders are being taught sophisticated criminal techniques in their willingness to resort to force.

Auto theft in general occurs less frequently in developing countries because of the scarcity of automobiles and the inability of many persons to operate them. More frequent is the theft of parts and accessories for which there is a ready resale market, particularly when import restrictions are heavy. Those who do steal automobiles, however, usually have a fairly high level of sophistication, having learned how to elude alarm systems, trigger steering column locks, and evade private guards. Theft for the sole purpose of a short ride is much less common, as is vandalism by youth. As these countries become more highly developed, however, such offenses will undoubtedly increase. Also increasing in number and significance will be such offenses as check forgery, embezzlement, and the use of stolen credit cards.

Certain offenses, such as the use of children for illegal purposes, are more common in the developing countries. Theft by servants is also a common offense, since the availability of cheap manpower enables even persons of quite modest means to hire them. When the victim is a commercial employer, it is impossible to say whether employees steal more in the developed or the less developed countries. Other offenses that may be more frequent in the less developed countries are food adulteration, cattle theft, begging, certain political offenses, black marketeering in money, rioting over food shortages, village disputes, and political grievance protests. Most of them can be expected to show decreased rates with increased development, although the record of some more highly developed countries in the sphere of political crimes has not been good.

Many developing countries report much higher rates of violent crime, such as homicide and assault, than the developed. When the probable high degree of under-reporting in less developed countries is considered, the gap may be even greater. Violence is generally a subcultural phenomenon associated with specific cultural factors in its use to settle disputes, as, for example, the emphasis on 'machismo' in Latin America or certain African tribal definitions. As in the developed countries, the most frequent offender tends to be a young male in his twenties. Again, as in developed countries, the evidence indicates that violent acts generally originate in disputes between relatives, friends, and acquaintances. Prostitution is probably less common in the developing countries largely because it is an urban phenomenon and they are still predominantly rural. In the cities, on the other hand, it is often greater because of the abnormal sex distribution in many of them and the scarcity of economic opportunities for unattached women, which leads them into some sort of temporary sexual relationship or prostitution. The modal characteristics of prostitutes in these countries vary by marital status and in the motivations for entering this occupation, although most of them are migrants from rural areas. The status of the prostitute in the cities probably carries less stigma and is more open and less organized than it is in the more developed countries.

Corruption in business and government appears to increase as a country becomes modernized, being most prevalent in the intense phases of industrialization. It is generally agreed that corruption of government officials is an acute problem in most countries of Asia, Latin America, and Africa and that many persons and their families have amassed large fortunes by holding political office. Common forms of crime by businessmen in developing countries include the violation of income tax laws and import, export, and currency control regulations and embezzlement. An elaborate system of kickbacks often accompanies every phase of governmental activity, including even small purchases by government agencies, and graft is associated with the granting of licenses and privileges of all types. The extensiveness of corruption grows out of nepotism, for the transition from a traditional to a rapidly modernizing industrial society has not yet resulted in the transfer of village loyalties to a serious dedication to an emerging nation. Corruption of officials in high places frequently comes from the industrial and commercial classes who seek special privileges.

Numerous studies indicate the importance of companions and gang membership in the promotion of criminal behavior in cities of developed countries. Crime also appears to be transmitted and committed by groups in developing countries, although these groups vary by organization, size, and nature of their behavior. Gangs and other criminal groups furnish an alternate source of support in place of family units which are often severely disrupted by the effects of urbanization. In the Kampala study the offenders reported closer friendships with persons who had been in trouble with the police. Their attitudes and activities reflected their associative patterns. They were essentially more isolated form experiences that might negatively define criminal behavior, but at the same time had greater contacts and activities that would be more likely to reinforce these patterns.

IMPLICATIONS OF EXPERIENCES OF DEVELOPED COUNTRIES

Most Western European countries, as well as the United States and Japan, have serious crime problems: even a highly affluent and socially progressive country like Sweden has trouble of this nature. The picture presented to the planners of developing countries who, hypothetically, must expect more crime to accompany urbanization, an increase in productivity and per capita income, and literacy, is a discouraging one. Because of the rapidity of urbanization, with sudden shifting from the traditional to the modern, it is quite possible that crime and delinquency may present more acute problems in the developing countries than in the developed countries. They may even become greater. Yet this situation may not, and need not, be so discouraging as it may seem. The high crime rates of developed countries are products of almost no long-term planning in the area of crime control. The situation in most countries has gradually become worse, and little in the past has been done to correct it, mainly because of inadequate knowledge of the cause of crime or of measures, other than punitive ones, to deal with it.

Persons from developing countries often fail to realize that extensive and rapidly rising crime rates, general poverty, rural living, extensive migration of young males to the cities, and the growth of slums, all were characteristic of the developed countries 75 to 125 years ago. In England and France, for example, the failure of their economic and social systems in the nineteenth century to adjust rapidly to the great increase in city population was related to the increase in crime at that time. There had been much internal migration in the first half of the nineteenth century, towns were growing rapidly, and the people lived in a world of flux. Most criminals resided in certain slum areas, were under 20 years of age, and engaged in criminal activities either in casual groups or in organized youth gangs. In the early period of industrialization, up through the 1850's, older criminals made use of children in their crimes.

> Indeed, if we are to look for a parallel in the field of crime with the England of the first 60 years of the nineteenth century, it is not to the England of the twentieth century that we should look, but to those countries that are today undergoing the experience of industrialisation and urbanisation . . . The people of nineteenth-century England, like the people of many parts of Africa and Asia today, were not only building physical assets for their descendants. They were, slowly and painfully and at no small price, developing a new way of life. They were learning to live in an urban, industrialised society.[63]

The rapid changes in urbanization and industrialization in England had great impact on the original residents of the towns and on the young migrants. The increase in urban population brought about changes that directly or indirectly affected everyone in the large cities. The young unmarried migrants who lived in lodging houses were particularly exposed to criminal and other deviant influences, but the social atmosphere of the large cities had potentialities for deviance for most youths. Since many of these people were poor, it was assumed by many that poverty made them criminals. A careful study of crime in nineteenth century England concluded, however, that the crime rate of that day, particularly in the urban areas, was not to an important extent a consequence of their poverty nor in the sense of the immediate pressures of need. 'It was not usually poverty that governed the operations of the criminal class, and the adult honest poor did not, as a general rule, turn to crime, however straightened their circumstances.'[64]

Perhaps it is because there has been a lack of consensus about what causes crime that the developed countries on the whole have not been successful in dealing with it. Many omissions and mistakes in crime control have been made over the last century or more. A lack of adequate criminological theory for effective planning has accounted for some of these problems, as it does today in those countries in similar stages of development. These errors have not only resulted in the growth of extensive and sophisticated criminal behavior patterns, which are transmitted to each new generation, but they have been extremely costly; for example, much effort and money has been wasted in the developed countries on their individualistic approaches of personal maladjustment that requires the use of expensive psychological and psychiatric treatment facilities. Although this approach has been shown to be invalid and the treatment largely unproductive, it continues to be proposed as a sound program by some in the field. On the other hand, only recently has the importance of slum living to crime and of the police in their relations to the public been more thoroughly recognized. The use of severe prison sentences to deal with crime is only now being seriously questioned in overall crime programs. Capital punishment, widely employed from time immemorial, has been almost completely discredited as an effective method of controlling crime.

William Clifford, a well-known United Nations expert who has worked in various attempts to control crime in a number of developing countries, has pointed out some of the basic fallacies underlying many current programs in crime control in developed countries:

> It is assumed, for example, that raising living standards, increasing income, eliminating unemployment, providing social welfare services, improving housing and offering medical or psychiatric services, where necessary, will reduce crime – or, at least, will prevent the commission of more crimes. As yet, however, there is little proof of this. Not only does the training for these services lack validation, the services themselves have not yet fully established their effectiveness in crime prevention. As an example, affluent societies seem to have more crime rather than less; the spread of education has been accompanied, as a rule, by an increase in delinquency. As for treatment doubts have been cast on the effectiveness of social work. However, none of this is really conclusive yet and these measures may be preventing more crime than is known. Nevertheless, such reports encourage a healthy skepticism about preventive or treatment measures popularly thought to be effective.[65]

All effective social defense measures in the long run must be predicated on a valid theory of human behavior. Without it, one can hardly suggest what specific social defense measures should accomplish in the prevention and treatment of crime and delinquency. Extensive worldwide evidence now exists to support the position that criminal behavior involves the learning of norms in the same manner as noncriminal behavior is learned. Criminal norms are acquired primarily by group association and participation in deviant subcultures, such as those existing in the slums, in youth gangs, and in certain occupations. When criminal behavior becomes more developed, that is, moves from primary to secondary deviation, persons acquire more distinct social roles, self-conceptions, and rationalizations and participate in wider deviant subcultures. Within this theoretical framework we can understand why crime is much more likely to occur among young urban slum-resident males. Basically, crime is related to social and group factors, and this fact is extremely important and highly relevant in national development planning for the area of social defense.

These modern concepts, along with the previous failure to curb or prevent crime, and the adoption of some measures, such as improvements in police administration, better education, and better municipal administration, as in some Western European countries and the United States, should enable any kind of society to plan more effectively for crime control. Still, city growth has been left largely to chance, and the social consequences of migration, particularly on the young have not been entirely anticipated. Today developing countries should be able to foresee more adequately and to plan for the problems associated with migration and urbanization. The recognition that crime, for example, is primarily a problem of the young in all countries may make it possible for the developing countries to do a number of things. The United Nations has stated that crime prevention depends largely on the adoption of an adequate and comprehensive policy for a nation's youth. This is truer, they state, for countries in which more than half the population is in the young age range. The participation of youth can provide development planning and its implementation with the drive and dynamic quality that will more adequately ensure the success of the plan and is the greatest promise for crime prevention.[66] The young can be more effectively incorporated into decision-making bodies. In the United States and in Great Britain, for example, the voting age has recently been lowered to eighteen, and in the United States several states have lowered the age of responsibility to eighteen. Theoretically such approaches to youth will promote a greater interest in national development and engender wider compliance with the law. Some countries, such as Tanzania, have initiated national service programs for youths, and similar programs are integral parts of the government of the People's Republic of China.

NOTES AND REFERENCES

1. Reinhard Bendix, 'Concepts and Generalizations in Comparative Sociological Studies,' *American Sociological Review*, 28 (1963), pp. 532–539.
2. Emile Durkheim, *Les Règles de la Méthode Sociologique*, translated by S. A. Solvay and J. H. Mueller in G. E. G. Catlin (ed.), *The Rules of Sociological Method.* Chicago: University of Chicago Press, 1938, p. 139.
3. Comparative sociology has been characterized by Eisenstadt as 'the investigation of the distribution of social phenomena in different societies, or types of societies, or the comparison of such „total" societies or of major institutional spheres in terms of their development, persistence, or changeability.' Shmuel N. Eisenstadt, 'Social Institutions: Comparative Study,' in *International Encyclopedia of the Social Sciences*. New York: Crowell Collier and Macmillan, 1968, Vol. 14, p. 421.
4. Robert Merton, 'Foreword,' in Robert M. Marsh, *Comparative Sociology: A Codification of Cross-Societal Analysis*. New York: Harcourt, Brace & World, 1967, p. v. Andreski has similarly noted an increasing interest in comparative sociology. See Stanislav Andreski, *The Uses of Comparative Sociology*. Berkeley: University of California Press, 1965.
5. Marsh, *Comparative Sociology*, pp. 5–6.
6. Lois B. DeFleur, 'A Cross-Cultural Comparison of Juvenile Offenders and Offences: Cordoba, Argentina, and the United States,' *Social Problems*, 14 (1967), p. 183.
7. Marvin E. Wolfgang and Franco Ferracuti, *The Subculture of Violence*. London: Tavistock, 1967.

8. Marshall B. Clinard, 'The Relation of Urbanization and Urbanism to Criminal Behavior, in Ernest W. Burgess and Donald J. Bogue (eds.), *Contributions to Urban Sociology*. Chicago: The University of Chicago Press, 1965, pp. 541–558, and Paul C. Friday, 'Differential Opportunity and Differential Association in Sweden: A Study of Youth Crime,' unpublished Ph. D. dissertation, University of Wisconsin (1970).
9. David M. Downes, *The Delinquent Solution: A Study in Subcultural Theory*. New York: The Free Press, 1966.
10. Hermann Mannheim, *Comparative Criminology*. Boston: Houghton Mifflin, 1965, pp. 92–94; Stephen Hurwitz, *Criminology*. London: George Allen & Unwin, 1952; Manuel López-Rey, *Crime: An Analytical Appraisal*. New York: Praeger, 1970. See also Friday, 'Differential Opportunity and Differential Association in Sweden,' Durkheim, *The Rules of Sociological Method*, Ruth Shonle Cavan and Jordan T. Cavan, *Delinquency and Crime: Cross-Cultural Perspectives*. Philadelphia: Lippincott, 1968. For comparative surveys of various forms of deviance, but with little on crime, see S. N. Eisenstadt, *Comparative Social Problems*. New York: The Free Press, 1964 and Vytautas Kavolis, *Comparative Perspectives on Social Problems*. Boston: Little, Brown, 1969, Introduction.
11. S. Kirson Weinberg, 'Juvenile Delinquency in Ghana: A Comparative Analysis of Delinquents and Non-Delinquents,' *Journal of Criminal Law, Criminology, and Police Science*, 55 (1964), pp. 471–481; Weinberg, 'Female Delinquency in Ghana, West Africa: A Comparative Analysis,' *International Journal of the Sociology of the Family*, March (1973); Weinberg, 'Urbanization and Male Delinquency in Ghana,' in Paul Meadows and Ephraim H. Mizruchi (eds.), *Urbanism, Urbanization, and Change: Comparative Perspectives*. Reading, Mass.: Addison-Wesley, 1969, pp. 368–379; Lois B. DeFleur, 'A Cross-Cultural Comparison of Juvenile Offenders and Offences: Cordoba, Argentina, and the United States,' pp. 483–495, and 'Alternative Strategies for the Development of Delinquency Theories Applicable to Other Cultures,' *Social Problems*, 17 (1969), pp. 30–39.
12. Marsh, *Comparative Sociology*, p. 6.
13. J. J. Tobias, *Crime and Industrial Society in the 19th Century*. London: Batsford, 1967.
14. William Clifford, 'Problems in Criminological Research in Africa South of the Sahara,' *International Review of Criminal Policy*, 23 (1965), p. 18.
15. Adam Przeworski and Henry Teune, *Logic of Comparative Social Inquiry*. New York: Wiley, 1970, p. 8.
16. DeFleur, 'Alternative Strategies for the Development of Delinquency Theories Applicable to Other Cultures,' p. 30. Much the same argument has been made by Evans-Pritchard who feels that comparative social science should not range beyond societies that are culturally and geographically similar. E. E. Evans-Pritchard, *The Comparative Method in Social Anthropology*. London: Athlone, 1963.
17. B. B. Hudson, M. K. Barakat, and R. LaForge, 'Problems and Methods of Cross-Cultural Research,' *Journal of Social Issues*, 15 (1959), pp. 5–19.
18. J. M. Stycos, 'Sample Surveys for Social Science in Underdeveloped Areas,' in R. N. Adams and J. J. Preiss (eds.), *Human Organization Research*. Homewood, Ill: Dorsey, 1960, pp. 375–388.
19. George P. Murdock, 'The Cross-Cultural Survey,' in F. W. Moore, *Readings in Cross-Cultural Methodology*. New Haven: HRAF, 1961.
20. Gustavo Lagos, *International Stratification and Underdeveloped Countries*. Chapel Hill, N. C.: University of North Carolina Press, 1963; Simon Kuznets, 'Underdeveloped Countries and the Pre-Industrial Phases in the Advanced Countries,' in Amar Narain Agarwala and Sampat P. Singh (eds.), *The Economics of Underdevelopment*. New York: Oxford University Press, 1963.
21. For a graphic example of such change, see the description of a small Turkish village in Daniel Lerner, *The Passing of Traditional Society*. New York: The Free Press, 1958, ch. 1, pp. 19–42.
22. James Bennett, 'Criminality and Social Change,' in Simon Dinitz and Walter C. Reckless, (eds.), *Critical Issues in the Study of Crime*. Boston: Little, Brown, 1968.

23. In actuality, economic progress, according to Culbertson, is not inevitable. He regards change as being more closely linked to population growth, economic efficiency, environmental destruction, and variations in the standard of living. John M. Culbertson, *Economic Development: An Ecological Approach*. New York: Knopf, 1971.
24. *Ibid.*, p. 296.
25. William McCord, *The Springtime of Freedom: The Evolution of Developing Societies*. New York: Oxford University Press, 1965.
26. Irving L. Horowitz, *Three Worlds of Development: The Theory and Practice of International Stratification*. New York: Oxford University Press, 1966, p. 60.
27. Wilbert Moore, *Social Change*. Englewood Cliffs, N. J.: Prentice-Hall, 1963, pp. 97–101.
28. Population Division, United Nations Bureau of Social Affairs, 'World Urbanization Trends, 1920–1960 (An Interim Report on Work in Progress),' in Gerald Breese (ed.), *The City in Newly Developing Countries*. Englewood Cliffs, N. J.: Prentice-Hall, 1969, pp. 21–53.
29. W. Arthur Lewis, *Development Planning*. New York: Harper & Row, 1966, pp. 68–70.
30. Horowitz, *Three Worlds of Development*.
31. Fully one-half of the Bolivian national budget was allocated to public and private education. Cuba and Brazil promise universal free education through high school by the 1980's. Ivan Illich, 'The False Ideology of Schooling,' *Saturday Review*, October 17, 1970, p. 56.
32. René Dumont, *False Start in Africa*. London: Sphere Books, 1966, p. 73.
33. Daniel Lerner, *The Passing of Traditional Society*. New York: The Free Press, 1958, chs. 1–3.
34. David Apter, *The Politics of Modernization*. Chicago: University of Chicago Press, 1965.
35. Daniel Lerner, 'Comparative Analysis of Processes of Modernization,' in Horace Miner (ed.), *The Modern City in Africa*. New York: Praeger, 1967.
36. William Goode, 'Industrialization and Family Change,' in Bert Hoselitz and Wilbert Moore (eds.), *Industrialization and Society*. New York: Mouton, (UNESCO, 1963).
37. Philip Hauser, 'Urbanization: An Overview,' in Philip Hauser and Leo Schnore (eds.), *The Study of Urbanization*. New York: Wiley, 1965, pp. 37-38
38. Moore, *Social Change*, p. 93.
39. Clark Kerr et al. *Industrialism and Industrial Man*. Cambridge, Mass.: Harvard University Press, 1960, ch. 1.
40. David Horton Smith and Alex Inkeles, 'The OM Scale: A Comparative Socio-Psychological Measure of Individual Modernity,' *Sociometry*, 29 (December 1966,) pp. 353–377.
41. Joseph Kahl, *The Measurement of Modernism*. Austin: University of Texas Press, 1968, p. 21.
42. Gustavo Lagos, *International Stratification and Under-developed Countries*. Chapel Hill: University of North Carolina Press, 1963, pp. 22–30.
43. Kuznets, in Agarwala and Singh, *The Economics of Underdevelopment*. 1963.
44. Criminalité et Développement, Documents Présentés au IV Congrès des Nations Unies pour la Prévention du Crime et le Traitement des Délinquants. Milan: Fondation Internationale Pénale et Pénitentiaire Societé Internationale de Défense Sociale, 1970. See also Walter A. Lunden, 'The Increase of Criminality in Underdeveloped Countries,' *Police*, 6 (May-June 1962), pp. 30–34.
45. Interpol has published *International Crime Statistics* for some 20 years.
46. Preben Wolf, 'Crime and Development: An International Comparison of Crime Rates,' *Scandinavian Studies in Criminology*, 3 (1971), pp. 107–121.
47. Comparisons of crime statistics across national borders involves great risks. National statistics are affected by variations in the definition of criminal behavior, by differing judicial procedures, and by alternate procedures for classification of criminal acts. See Marvin E. Wolfgang, 'International Crime Statistics: A Proposal,' *Journal of Criminal Law, Criminology, and Police Science*, 58 (March 1967), pp. 65–69.
48. Fourth United Nations Congress on the Prevention of Crime and the Treatment of Offenders, 'Social Defence Problems in Relation to Development Planning,' Working Paper Prepared by the Secretariat. New York: United Nations, 1970.
49. *International Review of Criminal Policy*, July 1955.

50. Second United Nations Congress on the Prevention of Crime and the Treatment of Offenders, *Report Prepared for the Secretariat.* New York: United Nations, 1960, pp. 1–18; United Nations Report, *Social Change and Criminality,* Report by the United Nations Congress on Crime and the Prevention of Criminality. Stockholm: United Nations, August 1965; B. N. Mullik, *Criminality Resulting from Social Changes and Economic Development.* Government of India, Intelligence Bureau, 1956; Fourth United Nations Congress on the Prevention of Crime and the Treatment of Offenders, Report Prepared by the United Nations Secretariat. New York: United Nations, 1970.
51. United Nations, 'Trends in Studies of Juvenile Delinquency,' SOA/SD/C.S.1-5, 1966.
52. Walter A. Lunden, 'Crimes in Thailand,' *Police,* 12 (January-February 1968), pp. 41–48.
53. *Ibid.*
54. Andres Aguilar Mawdsley, *La Delincuencia en Venezuela y su Prevención.* Caracas: Ministerio de Justicia, 1961.
55. Oscar C. Blarduni, 'Juvenile Delinquency: Sociological and Juridical Considerations,' *Revista del Instituto del Investigaciones y Docencia Criminologicas,* 9 (1965–1966), pp. 11–50.
56. Franco Ferracuti, 'Juvenile Delinquency and Social Change in Puerto Rico,' Paper presented for 1966 Meeting of the American Psychological Association, New York.
57. Lenore R. Kupperstein and Jaime Toro-Calder, *Juvenile Delinquency in Puerto Rico.* Rio Piedras: University of Puerto Rico, 1969, p. 105.
58. United Nations Publication ST/TAO/SER. C/42.
59. Fourth United Nations Congress on the Prevention of Crime and the Treatment of Crime and Delinquency, p. 17.
60. Robert B. Seidman and J. D. Abaka Eyison, 'Ghana,' in Alan Milner (ed.), *African Penal Systems.* London: Routledge & Kegan Paul, 1969, pp. 59–88.
61. William Clifford, 'Juvenile Delinquency in Zambia,' United Nations Publication SOA/SD/CS.3, April 30, 1967, p. 15.
62. *Ibid.,* p. 17.
63. J. J. Tobias, *Crime and Industrial Society in the 19th Century.* London: B. T. Batsford, Ltd., 1967, pp. 49–50. Reprinted by permission of Schocken Books. Inc.
64. *Ibid.,* p. 244.
65. William Clifford, 'Training for Crime Control in the Context of National Development,' *International Review of Criminal Policy,* 24 (1966), p. 9.
66. United Nations, 'The Prevention of Delinquency in the Context of National Development,' United Nations Publication ST/SOA/SG/CG.2/WP.1, Geneva, 1968.

H. H. Bloembergen
A. R. Hauber
C. W. G. Jasperse
L. G. Toornvliet
H. M. Willemse

CRIMINALITY AND MACRO-SOCIAL CHARACTERISTICS: A REPORT OF TRIAL AND ERROR

SUMMARY

In an explorative attempt to establish the relations between criminality and macro-social variables data on 21 predictor variables (e.g. economic, demographic, traffic, mental health and social welfare variables) and 15 criterion variables (e.g. prison population and crime rates) were collected from official statistics. The data over 10 years and 14 countries were analyzed by means of factor analysis, multiple regression analysis and canonical discriminant analysis. Although many results were inconclusive, large differences in relations between countries and years were found and the presence of a general 'growth factor' is suggested.

FOREWORD

This contribution is a result of trial and error. Firstly, the subject matter of the research report is itself a result of trial and error, a matter that will be reported on in the paragraphs hereafter. Secondly, writing this report has been a process of trial and error.

The staff of the Institute of Criminology of the State University of Leiden wanted to make a collective contribution to this book, edited in honor of Willem Nagel on the occasion of his retirement as Professor of Criminology and Penology and Director of the Institute. It was decided to submit a report on a research project in which the entire staff, consisting of two psychologists, one sociologist, one sociologist/psychologist and one jurist, could participate. This is a rather unique enterprise in the field of criminology, and also an ambitious one. To synthesize the diverse opinions of the collaborators and to write a collective report proved to be difficult. It can be pointed out here that in general, criminology would benefit from research carried out by a multidisciplinary team. Even if this project has not entirely yielded the results that were hoped for, the team that produced it has proved to itself and to others that it is possible for an interdisciplinary team to reach a degree of unanimity that provides a sufficient basis for collaboration.

The results of the present research project are presented here in a shortened version. Any additional information will be gladly furnished by the authors.

STAFF CRIMINOLOGICAL INSTITUTE

Address: Institute of Criminology, Hugo de Grootstraat 27, Leiden, Holland.

The authors wish to express their appreciation for the help received in the course of this project from a number of law students majoring in criminology, notably Ms. M. F. T. Schrijver and Mr. J. A. Klok.

1. INTRODUCTION

This report describes an empirical, comparative and macro-sociological research effort in the field of criminology. This particular type of research was chosen after the following considerations.

In the authors' opinion there is a shortage of *empirical* criminological research. This is due mainly to the fact that empirical research is laborious, expensive, and hampered by serious problems especially with respect to the collection of data.

Comparative research is very necessary with regard to the scientific aim of generalization (Radcliff-Brown, 1957). One of the oldest and still actual comparative studies is *Suicide* by Durkheim (1966). Clinard (1956, 1959) has repeatedly stressed the necessity for comparative studies using theories derived from one society and applying them as exactly as possible to other societies, this being in his opinion the condition for the development of criminology as a science (See also Clinard, 1973). Friday (1973) points out the serious problems that should be mastered before one embarks upon cross-national research. The number of comparative studies, particularly in the field of criminology, remains rather limited. This is all the more remarkable when one considers the increased possibilities for quick exchange of information between countries. Despite the continual proliferation of scientific and nonscientific publications, showing striking differences between social phenomena in various countries, systematic attempts to investigate these differences are rare. For instance, some countries show great discrepancies between their relative number of prisoners. Discussions about the causes of this well-publicized fact, however, are based on speculations rather than on systematic explorations, not to mention empirical research. A second important aspect of comparative research must be mentioned here. Comparative studies that do appear are often limited to comparisons between countries, and rarely contain comparisons in time even though the social phenomena studied are also embedded in the dimension of time. Consequently, when one investigates these phenomena, this dimension should also be taken into account, in order to come not only to geographical generalizations, but also to generalizations in time.

In studying human behavior *macro-social* variables may never be ignored, especially not in criminological approaches. The influence of these variables can be perceived as very unequally divided over individuals. Not everybody is limited in the same way with respect to his behavioral alternatives.

The research project

An attempt is made to find significant relations between macro-social variables and criminality, using official statistical data as a source of information. These data have been gathered for a number of countries over a number of years. Although at the outset hypotheses were formulated, it appeared that these hypotheses could not be tested for a number of reasons. Subsequently, the data were analyzed in an explorative manner.

The reason why *official statistics* were used is that the preferable alternative of collecting original data was too expensive and time-consuming. Although the criticisms of the use of official statistics for scientific research are well-known (e.g. lack of uniformity in definitions and classifications, crudeness of the figures), it seems unreasonable to ignore completely these masses of information that do exist and are readily accessible. It seems unlikely that these data would be of no use at all.

Especially crime statistics have been subjected to heavy criticism. Some criminologists reject the use of this type of information completely (e.g. Wootton, 1959). The most important objections are those concerning the existence of the dark number, the legal definitions, the seriousness of the offenses and the methods of data collection and registration.

With respect to the comparability of legal definitions it can be pointed out that, in view of the remaining imperfections of statistical data, it is perhaps also profitable to look for possibilities to compute correction factors in order to enhance the usefulness of the existing statistical data in addition to trying to improve the quality of the data themselves through better international statistical agreements.

This research covers a *number of countries* in order to make more generalizable statements possible. This means that statistical data of these various countries have to be compared. With that in mind, the abovementioned arguments against the use of statistical data become even more cogent, especially the lack of uniformity in definitions.

A certain *number of years* should be included in order to bring to light changes in the relation between the variables in the course of time. When collecting data over a number of years one is confronted particularly with the fact that the definitions of the variables are subject to change and that there are changes in the methods of data collection.

The authors consider that *macro-social variables* are more worth looking at than has generally been done in recent empirical research. Several 20th century Dutch criminologists have pointed out the importance of the role of sociocultural systems at the macro-level in the explanation of criminal behavior (Bonger, 1916; van Weringh, 1971; Schuyt, 1973). Luckily statistical data that can be considered as indexes of macro-social structures are amply available. The importance put on macro-social variables in this research does of course not imply that these variables can by themselves sufficiently explain criminal behavior: macro-, meso- and micro-social, biological and psychological variables and their interaction all play a part.

A great number of the hypotheses that were formulated a priori, at the onset of the study, as should be done in every research project, sprang from study of the literature and the conceptions and personal ideas of the investigators. During the data collection process it was discovered that these hypotheses could not be tested properly either because the necessary data were not available or because the data available were not complete enough. This fact means that the study must be characterized as *explorative*. Therefore, it seems unnecessary to mention these hypotheses in this article.

The reader may wonder why it was decided to use statistical data for this research in view of the historical and recent criticisms of them. With respect to the use of statistics as a source of information the following remarks seem interesting.

In the days of the first statisticians, around the year 1800, a great deal of comparative research took place (e.g., Quetelet, 1831; Guerry, 1833). The statistical data used were of dubious quality because of the non-uniform methods of data collection. Also, simple, mainly descriptive, statistical methods were applied. Nevertheless, countless statements were pronounced on this basis that appeared to be fully justified in those days. After about 1880 an acceleration in the methodological development of behavioral sciences took place. This development was part of the reason why criticisms of the above described type of comparative research grew enormously. This may have kept a new generation of researchers from doing this traditional type of comparative statistical research at all.

Nowadays not only the statistical techniques, but also the data themselves, have greatly improved. For one thing, many data are collected today by international bodies, like the OECD, UNESCO, Interpol, World Health Organization, which has certainly made the data more suitable for comparison.

Therefore, it seems that new efforts to apply the improved techniques to the improved data are justified. Examples of such efforts are: Cavan and Cavan, 1968; Clinard and Abbott, 1973; Gibbens 1966; Jepsen, 1969; Mays, 1963 and Wolf, 1971. The present study fits in this new trend.

2. THE PROBLEM

The problem that lies at the basis of this research can be formulated as follows:

(1) What is the relation between the rates and nature of registered crime and a number of macro-social characteristics?

(2) What is the relation between these two types of variables when studied over a certain period of time?

(3) What differences and similarities in these relations can be found between various countries?

3. THE DATA

Data were collected for 21 countries over a period of 10 years; the data concerned macro-social variables and crime variables.

In selecting the data, countries and years the availability of usable information was the principal limiting condition.

The countries

The main idea was to select a group of industrialized countries that were not too far apart in geographical respect and in socioeconomic structure. The first group that came to mind and was in fact chosen comprised the countries of Western Europe. Apart from these countries it seemed interesting to select a few additional industrialized countries from other continents: United States, Canada, Japan, Australia, New Zealand.

Some of the Western European countries, for instance Greece, had to be rejected on the basis of the impossibility to collect sufficient data. The countries that eventually were included are listed in Table 1.

Table 1: List of countries studied

1. The Netherlands
2. Belgium
3. Luxembourg
4. France
5. Switzerland
6. Austria
7. Federal Republic of Germany
8. Denmark
9. Sweden
10. Norway
11. Finland
12. Great Britain
13. Ireland
14. Italy
15. Spain
16. Portugal
17. United States
18. Canada
19. Japan
20. Australia
21. New Zealand

A further reduction in the number of countries became necessary for the application of some of the statistical techniques. See 4 hereafter.

The period of time studied

In deciding which years to include in the study the following considerations have played a role.

Table 2: List of variables

Predictor variables

Description	*Expressed in*	*Source***
1. Unemployment	unemployed per 10,000 workers	a
2. Government expenditure on education	per 10,000 monetary units of the GNP	b
3. Government expenditure on education, public health and other social services	per 10,000 monetary units of the GNP	a
4. Divorces	divorces per 100,000 inhabitants	c
5. Consumer price index	index: 1963 = 100	a
6. Population density	inhabitants per square kilometer	c
7. Energy consumption	tons coalequivalent energy-consumption per 100 inhabitants	d
8. Population younger than 15 years	per 1,000 inhabitants	c
9. Population older than 65 years	per 1,000 inhabitants	c
10. Deaths caused by traffic accidents	per 1,000,000 inhabitants	e
11. Kilometers covered per car per year	megameters per 10 cars	f
12. Road density	running meters of road per km^2	f
13. Motor cars	per 1,000 inhabitants	f
14. Labor disputes	working days lost per 10,000 inhabitants	g
15. Total tax revenue	taxes paid per 1,000 monetary units of the GNP	h
16. Suicides	per 10,000,000 inhabitants	i
17. Alcohol consumption	litres of 100% alcohol per 100 inhabitants	j
18. Deaths caused by cirrhosis of liver	per 10,000,000 inhabitants	i
19. Hours worked in manufacturing	per 10 inhabitants	g
20. Industrial production	index: 1963 = 100	a
* Total government expenditure		a
* Level of education expressed in school enrollment ratio, first level		b
* Idem, second level		b
* Idem, third level		b
* Estimates of national income, expressed in U.S. dollars		k
* Beds in mental hospitals		k
* Social security contributions as % of GNP		h
* Physicians per inhabitant		m

* These variables were not included in the analyses.

Criterion variables

Description	*Expressed in*	*Source* **
21. Prison population	per 1,000,000 inhabitants	l
22. Murders	per 100,000,000 inhabitants, as registered by W.H.O.	i
23. Murders	per 10,000,000 inhabitants, as registered by Interpol	n
24. Sex offenses	per 1,000,000 inhabitants, idem	n
25. Major larceny	per 100,000 inhabitants, idem	n
26. Minor larceny	per 100,000 inhabitants, idem	n
27. Fraud	per 100,000 inhabitants, idem	n
28. Counterfeit currency offenses	per 10,000,000 inhabitants, idem	n
29. Drug offenses	per 1,000,000 inhabitants, idem	n
30. Total number of offenses	per 10,000 inhabitants, idem	n
31. Murderers	per 10,000,000 inhabitants, idem	n
32. Sex offenders	per 1,000,000 inhabitants, idem	n
33. Major larceny offenders	per 100,000 inhabitants, idem	n
34. Minor larceny offenders	per 100,000 inhabitants, idem	n
35. Fraud offenders	per 100,000 inhabitants, idem	n
36. Total number of offenders	per 10,000 inhabitants, idem	n
* Counterfeit currency offenders		n
* Drug offenders		n

** Sources:
a. Statistical Yearbook, United Nations
b. Statistical Yearbook, UNESCO
c. Demographic Yearbook, United Nations
d. World Energy Supplies, United Nations
e. Statistics of Road Traffic Accidents
f. World Road Statistics
g. Yearbook of Labour Statistics
h. Revenue Statistics of the O.E.C.D.
i. World Health Statistics
j. *Hoeveel alcoholhoudende dranken worden er in de wereld gedronken? Schiedam*
k. Yearbook of National Account Statistics
l. Statistical Yearbook of each country
m. A. S. Banks, *Cross-policy Time Series Data,* 1971
n. International Crime Statistics, Interpol

In general it is assumed that the longer the time period covered by a research project the more reliable and generalizable the results are. It was impossible, however, to go back further than 1950 because international statistics date back no further. The last year had to be 1970 inasmuch as at the time the project was started this was the last year for which sufficient data had become available. The period of 20 years in between, however, seemed too long. There have been so many changes in definitions of data and in data registration that the homogeneity of the data was bound to be too seriously affected. It was decided to cover only the second half of these 20 years. This decision was based on the assumption that international statistics have improved. Therefore, the 10 years between 1961 and 1970 are examined.

The variables

On the basis of literature study and common sense a list of data was composed that could be expected to sufficiently reflect the macro-social structure (predictor variables) and indicate the nature and level of crime in the countries under study (criterion variables). A priori the predictor variables can be divided into five categories, that taken together can be considered to be a reflection of the macro-social structure, insofar as a relation with criminality can be expected:

(1) economic variables, e.g.: energy consumption, consumer price index;

(2) demographic variables, e.g.: population density, population under the age of 15 and population older than 65;

(3) traffic variables, e.g.: car density, road density;

(4) variables indicative for social welfare, e.g. government expenditure on education, public health and other social services;

(5) variables indicative for mental health, e.g. divorces, alcohol consumption.

These categories cannot be seen as independent of each other and may therefore show overlap.

The first set of variables that were originally included, but had to be dropped (first reduction of data) because of their apparent incompleteness, were: length of sentences, police officers, lawyers, car thefts, deaths in industry, and migrant workers. The variables on which data were collected can be found in Table 2.

4. METHODS OF ANALYSIS

Taking the above-mentioned problem statement as the starting point it is natural to analyze the relations between the crime variables and the macro-social variables with the help of multiple regression techniques that will also provide a multiple correlation coefficient. These analyses were done per criterion variable. In order to assess the relative importance of the predictor variables stepwise multiple regression analysis was applied (Nie *et al.*, 1970). With this technique new variables are added to the prediction equation until the point is reached at which a predictor variable does not contribute significantly (F-test) to the total amount of explained variance.

The material was analyzed in yet another way. Factor analysis and canonical discriminant analysis were applied for the purpose of further exploration. Factor analysis makes it possible to find out whether an underlying pattern of relations exists, by which the data might be rearranged to form a smaller set of components called factors (See e.g. van de Geer, 1971). The purpose of canonical discriminant analysis is to find, with the help of a mathematical transformation, significant dimensions that reveal a maximum of differences between groups, in this case the countries (Porebski, 1966).

In the initial efforts to perform these analyses it appeared that there were still too many missing values to meet the needs of the computer programs. A further number of variables had to be eliminated (second reduction). This was done in such a way that a maximum of remaining countries and variables was achieved. For the purpose of factor analysis the following countries and variables were eliminated:

countries: Belgium, Luxembourg, Switzerland, Ireland, Spain, Portugal and the United States of America.

predictor variables (in Table 2 indicated with *):
  total government expenditure
  level of education, expressed in school enrollment ratio, first level
  level of education, expressed in school enrollment ratio, second level
  level of education, expressed in school enrollment ratio, third level
  estimate of national income, expressed in U.S. dollars
  beds in mental hospitals
  social security contributions as % of GNP
  physicians per inhabitant

criterion, variables (in Table 2 indicated with *):
  counterfeit currency offenders
  drug offenders

For the purpose of canonical discriminant analysis the following countries also had to be eliminated: Italy, Japan, New Zealand and Canada. There was an alternative possibility of eliminating 11 variables instead of these four countries. This, however, would certainly have decreased the comparability of the results of this type of analysis with the other results.

5. RESULTS

5.1. The means

The results of the data collection can be represented by a three-dimensional data matrix (14 countries x 36 variables x 10 years). In order to achieve a rough overall picture of the approximately 5,000 data the means over the years per country and per variable are presented in Table 3.

For some countries one variable is missing. In Table 3 this is indicated by –. In Italy divorce (var. 4) was not officially recognized in the years covered and therefore was not registered. For Canada counterfeit currency offenses (var. 28) are absent because they have been registered in one category together with fraud offenses (var. 27). The figures on alcohol consumption (var. 17) in Japan and on tax revenue (var. 15) in New Zealand proved to be inaccessible.

With regard to the crime variables the following remarks are relevant. The data on murder as registered by Interpol (var. 23) do not tally with those registered by the World Health Organization (var. 22). This can probably be explained by a lack of uniformity in the definition of 'murder.' Although the correlation between these two variables for the various countries should have been perfect, this was by no means the case. Problems of definition in all probability also play a role with respect to other crime variables in some countries, such as major larceny (var. 25), drug offenses (var. 29) and total number of offenders (var. 36). One of the most striking examples is the tremendous decrease in the total number of offenders (var. 36) in Japan between the years 1964 (606) and 1965 (89). The mean score of this variable (562) is furthermore unreliable, because it was computed over the years 1961–1964 instead of over the entire 10-year-period. The prison population (var. 21) sometimes includes pre-trial detention and/or forced labor (Sweden, Japan, France, New Zealand). This illustrates again the persisting differences in the definitions of the variables by the various countries.

5.2. Multiple regression analysis of the means

In addressing the first problem statement stepwise multiple regression analysis was performed on the means of the variables. The purpose of this analysis is mainly to gain insight into the relations between the predictor variables and each criterion variable separately. This results in a total of 16 regression equations and 16 multiple correlation coefficients. In Table 4 an overview is presented of the number of predictors that contributed significantly to the prediction of the criterion, together

Table 3: Means over the years per variable per country

(For the description of the 36 variables see Table 2)

Var.	Neth	Fra	Austria	FRG	Denm	Swe	Norw	Finl	Gr Br	Italy	Can	Jap	Austr	N Zeal
1	101	84	273	97	312	143	98	200	200	329	492	99	147	14
2	669	393	427	410	608	716	595	656	530	504	757	505	377	404
3	662	2745	2538	5287	687	1611	298	278	393	178	287	163	92	20
4	551	701	1199	910	1509	1279	723	1022	817	–	456	807	788	777
5	115	109	110	107	114	112	113	110	111	110	109	114	109	112
6	369	89	87	230	111	17	12	14	224	172	2	268	2	10
7	368	306	270	433	424	475	375	283	506	192	723	205	459	251
8	283	247	233	229	238	211	248	270	230	243	327	259	296	328
9	950	1247	1317	1135	1138	1277	1189	800	1223	984	765	642	848	837
10	210	278	270	286	215	160	118	211	139	197	237	159	270	195
11	177	102	135	169	159	140	120	166	125	127	145	205	142	104
12	218	141	108	160	142	41	20	22	140	84	7	268	12	34
13	129	196	120	203	175	239	138	105	176	120	278	40	263	277
14	39	565	157	57	608	98	228	576	817	2936	1772	389	874	392
15	352	355	351	329	314	367	344	317	311	291	276	185	243	–
16	679	1541	2254	2062	1935	1999	762	2066	1020	548	887	1557	1368	921
17	411	1827	983	1052	583	539	307	324	578	1526	589	–	737	682
18	377	3341	2701	2208	807	673	396	356	289	2357	676	1060	514	274
19	458	457	387	438	388	370	376	418	460	475	405	449	436	404
20	128	119	120	119	122	121	120	124	112	119	124	155	117	127
21	286	630	308	820	330	641	467	1407	591	656	1170	606	706	730
22	409	1019	1050	1247	558	766	541	2269	699	967	1481	1484	1473	1027
23	316	365	210	292	118	197	238	211	124	262	241	229	230	168
24	662	285	449	1014	752	457	250	146	445	140	498	140	784	782
25	231	147	683	651	789	1000	372	304	650	449	41	4	365	554
26	711	824	520	1309	2308	2530	636	647	1558	45	1918	1038	1371	1318
27	71	229	180	418	301	557	109	223	117	39	237	117	179	188
28	48	58	150	69	118	190	55	15	2286	42	–	4	135	20
29	20	6	28	49	66	2065	76	339	4	1	253	15	48	37
30	147	199	351	343	322	558	137	394	248	94	483	412	187	497
31	325	298	221	283	35	45	21	183	42	300	191	242	180	76
32	370	282	449	673	88	48	93	99	129	143	206	145	374	507
33	125	43	241	133	61	86	78	146	118	74	17	4	62	215
34	181	194	198	375	26	190	71	222	318	14	357	182	337	463
35	61	197	171	301	27	103	23	144	21	39	67	47	49	125
36	75	104	268	163	16	44	28	274	53	46	148	562	48	207

with the squared multiple correlation coefficient (R^2), i.e. the proportion of the explained variance of the criterion variable.

Table 4: Results of first multiple regression analyses

Criterion variable	Number of predictors	R^2
21	10	.997
22	12	.984
23	10	.995
24	10	.995
25	6	.993
26	7	1.000
27	9	.999
28	8	.999
29	10	1.000
30	13	1.000
31	10	.999
32	9	.999
33	7	.993
34	10	1.000
35	13	1.000
36	10	.998

The outcome seems to be very satisfactory. With a maximum of 13 macro-social variables it was possible to almost fully explain the occurrence of various types of criminality as well as the size of the prison population. To assess the meaning of these relations it is necessary to look at the contents of these predictors. For this purpose major larceny (var. 25) has been chosen as an example. The computed regression formula reads:

B x		(var.)	R^2	
	84.8	(divorces, var. 4)	.58	
−	365.6	(industrial production, var. 20)	.74	
−	9.1	(alcohol consumption, var. 17)	.78	
+	.1	(deaths caused by traffic accidents, var. 10)	.987	
			——	$R^2 \geqslant .95$
+	3.82	(road density)	.992	
−	.001	(suicides)	.993	
+	45,242.6			
=		(major larcency)		

It appears to be impossible to offer a sensible interpretation of the contents of this series of predictors. Scrutiny of the results of the other regression equations reveals a similar picture.

The rank order of the predictor variables appearing in the regression formulas is given per criterion variable in Table 5. This rank order was determined on the basis of the size of the B-values. Not all the predictor variables are mentioned in this table. The line has been drawn at $R^2 = .95$. Also, under F the frequency is given with which the predictor variables figure in the regression equations.

Table 5: Rank order of the predictor variables in the regression equations per criterion variable

Criterion variables	Predictor variables 1	2	3	4	5	6	7	8	9	10	11	12	13	14	15	16	17	18	19	20
21	4	3		5	1	6			2				8							7
22		7	8	3	2	5			1			9	4	6						
23	7	6									2		3		4		1		5	
24			6	4		2	9	5					1	3			7			8
25				1						4							3			2
26				2			1						4							3
27	4	3		6	5								2			1				
28		4	5				1	2								3				6
29	4	1		6								3		5		2			7	
30		4			5		6	3		8	7	9				1		2		
31						3			2						4			1	5	
32		1	2			5		3							6		4			
33	5	2							4						1		3			
34				2	4	7							1	3	5				6	
35		5	1		6		3	2				4		7						
36			5		2								3	4			6			1
F	5	10	6	8	7	6	5	5	4	2	2	4	8	6	5	4	6	2	4	6

Table 5 not only shows that all the predictor variables play a part in the explanation of the crime variables (criterion variables) but demonstrates an absence of any consistent pattern whatsoever as well. This implies, among other things, that the crime indexes used are slightly or not at all predictable by similar macro-social items.

5.3. Factor analysis of the means

Since multiple regression analysis only offers insight into the nature of the relations between the predictor variables and one criterion variable at a time and not between all the predictor and criterion variables conjointly, the next step was to perform factor analysis of all 36 variables. It was hoped that with the help of this type of analysis a clear picture would emerge of the underlying pattern of the relations between all the macro-social and crime variables together.

In Table 6 the results of this analysis are presented. A principal components analysis, followed by rotation according to the varimax principle was executed. The six-factor solution was chosen on the basis of the size of the eigenvalues. Only those loadings whose absolute value was $\geqslant .30$ are shown. Also included in this table are the communalities (h^2). Finally, the amount of explained variance is given.

Table 6: Factor analysis of the means of the 36 variables

	1	2	3	4	5	6	h^2
1					.68		.54
2	.49				.58		.63
3	–.70	.50					.90
4		.80				.33	.80
5	.64		.60				.91
6	–.33		.76	–.39			.86
7					.56	–.73	.93
8		–.63	–.44			–.42	.89
9		.51	.39	.69			.94
10	–.82			–.34			.84
11				–.85			.79
12	–.37		.71	-.53			.95
13			–.32	.43		–.75	.87
14		–.48			.59		.77
15		.37		.67			.69
16		.79					.80
17	–.86						.88
18	–.86					.33	.91
19	.70				–.56		.94
20				–.93			.91
21			–.83				.81
22			–.79	–.42			.84
23	–.78						.68
24					–.35	–.78	.81
25		.69		.47			.81
26	.33	.60			.33	–.57	.90
27		.88				–.33	.95
28			.38		.33	–.30	.43
29		.70					.66
30		.56	–.46	–.36		–.32	.81
31	–.78	–.33					.81
32	–.47				–.67	–.50	.93
33					–.76		.68
34			–.34		–.30	–.81	.89
35	–.66	.36			–.49		.91
36				–.82			.84
Factor Variance	6.56	5.44	4.31	5.20	3.98	4.03	

The six factors that were found cannot be clearly interpreted. As was the case with the results of the multiple regression analysis the variables do not appear to load in an informative way on the six factors, which therefore could not adequately be given a name.

5.4. Analyses per country

In an effort to answer the second problem statement the above described analyses (multiple regression analysis and factor analysis) were subsequently performed per country. The correlation matrices that form the basis of these analyses were computed over the years.

Out of the 226 regression analyses theoretically possible 173 were carried out. This extensive number makes it impossible to present the findings in one table. The outcomes of the 173 analyses are comparable to those of the multiple regression analyses of the means. Here, too, it was found that all the predictor variables play a role, while, moreover, the predictors of importance for each criterion variable, differ per country. A remarkable difference with the previously executed multiple regression analyses of the means is that this time after only a very few steps (an average of 2.41 for all 173 regression analyses) an R^2 of .95 was reached. For instance, for Great Britain the 16 crime indexes can be predicted with the help of 1 variable (7 times), 2 variables (5 times), 3 variables (3 times), and 4 variables (once). These results seem to be even less probable than the results of the previous analyses of the means. Not only were the R^2's extremely high again but the number of steps needed to reach this result was furthermore minimal.

The cause of this phenomenon can be found in the high correlations between the variables per country. As an illustration of this fact the correlations for the Netherlands and Denmark are shown in Table 7. As Törnudd (1969) and probably also Jepsen (1969) found, one is confronted with an extremely large number of correlations greater than .90. As the correlations have been computed over years, a parallel development of the variables must be present for the period of time under study.

In order to test this, those variables for the Netherlands were selected that showed a monotonic decrease or monotonic increase. There proved to be 15 of these variables. It was supposed that at least these 15 variables would demonstrate high loadings on one factor. The mean loading on the first factor in the unrotated eight-factor solution of these 15 variables appears to be .97 (using the absolute values of these loadings). The mean loading of the remaining 21 items – including some variables that showed an almost monotonic trend – was considerably lower: .63. The supposition was thus confirmed by the results of this factor analysis. This single factor explained a great deal of the variance (71%). In fact it appeared that for the various countries one could discern such a factor that explained a large part of the total variance (range 54–77%). With some precaution the suggestion is made to call this factor a 'growth factor.' (Growth in this case also includes negative growth.) This means that in spite of the fact that most of the variables have been indexed on

Table 7: Correlation matrix for the Netherlands (upper right half) and Denmark (lower left half)

	1	2	3	4	5	6	7	8	9	10	11	12	13	14	15	16	17	18
1		47	78	76	76	74	65	–68	78	87	04	82	81	–64	79	–04	55	31
2	02		68	76	66	58	73	–60	74	41	–54	69	61	–55	66	01	40	04
3	49	36		96	99	94	98	–93	97	95	05	99	99	55	97	64	89	52
4	54	45	39		94	83	94	–83	96	90	01	98	95	–41	91	33	69	53
5	44	75	65	84		97	98	–96	97	97	15	97	99	50	99	62	89	48
6	31	79	75	66	96		92	–98	91	97	32	91	97	41	98	53	91	33
7	31	81	51	85	97	91		–95	96	90	–01	96	97	60	95	67	87	49
8	–13	–92	–45	–64	–86	–86	–92		–93	–96	–36	–92	–99	19	–98	–23	–86	–26
9	38	77	63	82	98	95	97	–89		92	10	97	96	–42	98	23	71	46
10	12	27	55	80	92	95	89	–80	94		19	94	97	39	97	56	83	62
11	–93	27	–60	22	15	09	40	–48	20	26		–06	14	–06	17	22	24	01
12	21	08	75	49	80	86	72	–33	64	75	–08		98	46	97	56	82	67
13	34	43	55	87	98	97	93	–81	97	97	20	83		50	99	62	86	65
14	04	–92	–37	–12	–48	–55	–50	74	–44	19	32	–44	02		43	76	54	30
15	19	80	55	80	96	94	98	–91	96	94	46	83	96	–50		52	87	46
16	32	73	28	61	60	50	65	–73	65	29	–04	–34	36	–51	54		61	39
17	33	75	55	89	97	90	97	–83	96	91	34	80	96	–38	97	58		27
18	45	39	20	97	70	48	73	–53	68	70	29	33	78	–03	67	61	78	
19	03	–92	–39	–19	–54	–61	–57	80	–52	–88	–21	–77	–96	99	–56	–55	–45	–09
20	30	50	57	86	96	94	96	–91	98	98	30	71	97	23	98	45	97	75
21	33	43	43	08	52	62	42	–39	43	12	–10	70	24	–42	47	–04	43	–08
22	50	59	18	42	42	35	48	–57	43	–04	–14	–25	05	–46	40	43	34	35
23	32	–67	16	–22	–29	–28	–40	34	–26	–21	–61	–18	–24	23	–39	–22	–42	–29
24	–50	–58	–53	–88	–91	–79	–82	69	–83	–86	–07	–74	–94	09	–81	–51	–89	–82
25	56	64	34	95	95	82	97	–92	93	84	34	69	91	15	93	58	96	89
26	65	69	31	97	93	76	94	–88	90	79	29	61	88	10	89	64	94	92
27	58	45	26	88	87	75	91	–92	90	77	31	29	81	41	85	65	85	81
28	–03	66	–24	30	–03	–29	–03	16	–15	57	16	04	65	–10	–12	27	–01	44
29	–33	–17	93	70	95	93	95	–58	70	78	90	94	93	10	95	–58	91	–44
30	70	14	92	93	89	79	72	–57	84	58	–72	50	75	–12	61	37	75	42
31	53	–54	–19	–22	–31	–35	–34	22	–26	–56	–51	–55	–49	18	–40	–03	–42	–23
32	-51	–67	–70	–74	–93	–89	–87	82	–88	–78	09	–72	–86	57	–87	–50	–85	–58
33	72	27	55	75	84	77	74	–50	80	78	–02	74	88	–04	73	34	78	60
34	61	50	51	86	98	90	92	–84	94	86	15	80	94	04	92	44	94	75
35	49	63	27	94	84	66	87	–75	80	73	32	45	81	–35	81	71	87	92
36	60	67	49	89	97	87	95	–82	94	82	21	71	91	–37	92	64	95	78

19	20	21	22	23	24	25	26	27	28	29	30	31	32	33	34	35	36	
–89	74	–35	49	80	58	77	68	57	–03	47	77	82	–26	76	34	32	63	1
–60	62	–72	72	60	05	74	65	72	37	95	70	61	–42	63	–05	24	56	2
–97	99	–79	82	95	33	99	99	70	63	98	99	96	–65	90	55	31	85	3
–93	98	–81	85	88	54	98	95	67	55	98	97	88	–40	90	50	34	90	4
–95	99	–73	83	96	34	98	98	63	65	97	99	96	–68	87	50	23	82	5
–89	93	–56	73	96	40	92	92	46	59	97	93	94	–72	76	35	04	70	6
–94	99	–82	83	93	21	98	99	69	69	99	99	94	–74	85	49	24	80	7
88	–96	48	–65	–94	–56	–92	–93	–25	–54	–96	–93	–92	72	–61	–20	21	–57	8
–93	96	–68	79	91	51	98	96	55	49	89	98	91	–57	79	37	12	76	9
–93	94	–65	77	97	51	92	92	63	49	91	94	95	–61	93	76	70	91	10
05	06	32	–03	05	41	02	03	–54	25	–67	03	–02	–02	01	–02	–51	–02	11
–96	97	–84	83	95	42	96	96	81	53	90	98	95	–62	98	79	87	96	12
–95	99	–75	83	95	44	97	97	70	58	96	98	95	–67	98	77	76	94	13
–64	59	–51	43	43	–23	61	61	51	43	77	57	51	–46	55	41	25	38	14
–92	97	–67	78	96	37	95	95	59	57	90	96	95	–71	82	43	15	75	15
–62	71	–61	55	50	–07	69	71	48	65	71	67	53	–45	67	39	28	61	16
–84	85	–57	59	89	48	84	88	42	63	70	86	88	–62	71	38	05	67	17
–51	68	–80	53	36	34	50	53	54	40	67	53	38	–04	62	88	57	69	18
	–96	74	–80	–94	–25	–97	–95	–75	–52	–96	–97	–97	62	–90	–59	–38	–81	19
–93		–83	85	94	34	99	99	76	64	99	99	94	–74	99	79	80	95	20
–40	28		–77	–64	–11	–80	–82	–87	–65	–88	–81	–67	41	–83	–72	–58	–87	21
–50	16	12		79	07	85	82	62	77	83	84	79	–48	83	61	42	85	22
27	–34	–22	43		35	93	93	58	58	87	94	99	–69	80	44	17	76	23
90	–83	–29	–10	20		20	24	–04	15	–49	26	29	20	31	42	13	41	24
–97	91	25	31	–31	–90		99	74	63	99	99	95	–68	91	51	33	84	25
–95	87	20	34	–29	–91	99		70	68	99	99	94	–71	87	53	27	83	26
–90	85	11	43	–17	–78	94	93		23	91	73	64	–31	80	52	74	74	27
–07	–13	–51	08	14	–29	13	22	12		61	63	55	–44	55	46	06	64	28
–95	84	68	–14	–61	27	78	39	24	–64		98	91	–83	97	88	87	85	29
–85	70	68	–05	01	–83	94	99	78	–32	03		96	–68	90	53	32	85	30
18	–38	–11	52	71	32	–22	–19	–04	–09	–51	10		–70	82	47	22	76	31
63	–81	–55	–63	–09	84	–83	–82	–77	–02	–32	–74	08		–33	08	36	–23	32
–10	82	55	27	–15	–84	85	83	82	–08	83	92	–07	–75		69	66	94	33
–96	90	47	26	–21	–93	95	93	88	00	84	91	–18	–91	95		68	76	34
–41	75	14	49	–26	–86	93	96	88	45	–66	69	–22	–76	66	82		67	35
–44	89	45	47	–25	–90	98	98	93	08	71	96	–18	–89	87	98	91		36

the size of the population, thereby eliminating the influence of population growth, nevertheless some other kind of growth (perhaps economic growth) seems to be involved. A remarkable fact in this case is that these so-called growth factors differ per country in composition, as is also the case with the other factors, incidentally.

Summing up this section on the analyses per country it can be seen that the countries show great differences, not only in absolute values of the variables included in this study but just as much in the direct relations between these variables and consequently also in the underlying relation patterns.

5.5. *Analysis per year*

In addressing the third problem statement multiple regression analysis was performed per year per criterion variable over the countries. The years 1961 and 1970 had to be omitted because there were too many missing values. One hundred twenty-eight regression formulas were computed. In 1962, e.g., the total number of offenses (var. 30) was almost entirely explained by only four predictor variables, with the help of the following regression equation:

B ×	(var.)	R^2	rank order
33.9	(motor cars, var. 13)	.43	1
—8118.8	(consumer price index, var. 5)	.90	2
—155.9	(population under 15 years old, var. 8)	.9954	3
			——— $R^2 \geqslant .95$
—8.5	(divorces)	.9955	
+809,251.6			
=	(total number of offenses)		

Just like the previous results, this equation cannot be interpreted in a meaningful manner, especially when one also looks at the distribution over the years of the various predictor variables. By way of illustration the predictor variables and their rank order per year for the total number of offenses are given in Table 8.

Table 8: Rank order of incidence of predictor variables in regression equations per year ($R^2 \geqslant .95$) for criterion variable 30

Years	Predictor variables																			
	1	2	3	4	5	6	7	8	9	10	11	12	13	14	15	16	17	18	19	20
1962					2			3					1							
1963						3	4	5	6					2	1					
1964		6		5			7				3				2	4			8	1
1965			6								7	2			5	3		8	4	1
1966		3				1				8		6	4			2	7			5
1967											5	6		3		1		2		4
1968								5		4			2			1				3
1969				1									2							

When one examines these results it appears that the previously noted absence of some sort of systematic occurrence of predictors (compare Table 4) remains constant. The variables that play an important role differ per year. Variables that do play a role in more than one year are not always of relatively equal importance, as can be judged by their rank order. Also the contents of the variables show little coherence, making interpretation impossible.

In order to gain some insight into the distribution of the occurrence of predictor variables per criterion variable, the frequencies of occurrence in 8 years (2 years had to be dropped because there were too many missing values) were determined and are presented in Table 9. Here, too, as was pointed out in the discussion of the results of multiple regression analysis per country (see Table 5), the results are inconclusive.

Table 9: Incidence of predictor variables in regression equations ($R^2 \geqslant .95$) *per year over eight years*

Criterion	Predictor variables																			
variables	1	2	3	4	5	6	7	8	9	10	11	12	13	14	15	16	17	18	19	20
21	1	3	5	0	3	1	1	2	7	2	3	3	0	2	2	2	0	1	2	1
22	1	1	1	3	2	0	1	0	8	0	4	1	1	2	1	5	1	0	0	1
23	0	0	1	1	1	1	2	4	2	2	2	2	2	3	4	1	5	1	5	0
24	2	3	2	4	1	4	0	1	0	0	2	1	7	2	2	1	1	1	3	0
25	0	2	2	7	1	0	0	2	4	0	1	0	6	1	2	4	1	1	1	1
26	2	1	0	6	0	0	7	2	2	1	0	0	3	2	0	3	0	1	1	3
27	0	5	5	2	1	1	0	4	1	1	2	2	1	7	0	0	6	1	1	4
28	0	5	3	0	0	3	7	4	2	0	4	0	2	0	3	1	2	1	1	0
29	3	3	0	5	2	0	0	0	0	0	1	2	2	1	3	2	1	0	1	2
30	0	2	1	2	1	2	2	3	1	2	3	3	4	2	3	5	1	2	2	5
31	0	1	3	2	0	2	1	5	1	1	3	0	4	2	1	0	2	3	2	0
32	1	5	4	2	1	2	0	5	1	0	2	0	1	2	4	3	0	0	2	1
33	4	1	2	2	2	3	4	1	2	0	2	3	2	2	3	5	1	3	5	3
34	1	4	1	5	2	1	2	3	1	1	2	0	5	3	1	5	0	1	4	2
35	0	1	7	2	1	0	4	0	2	1	2	0	0	1	1	2	1	2	2	1
36	1	0	2	4	4	0	2	0	0	2	2	2	3	0	3	3	1	0	1	1

5.6. Analyses of the data after the third reduction

Apart from the 'growth factor' the material has thus far yielded only a few clear findings. Inasmuch as this could very well be due to the quality of the investigated variables, for instance to a too great similarity between the variables (such as between alcohol consumption and liver cirrhosis) or to too great a difference between the variables (as is the case with murder [WHO] and murder [Interpol]), a further twelve variables were eliminated (third reduction):

the predictor variables:
var. 18 (deaths caused by liver cirrhosis)
var. 11 (kilometers covered per car per year)
var. 12 (road density)
the criterion variables:
var. 22 (murders – WHO)
var. 28 (counterfeit currency offenses)
var. 29 (drug offenses)
vars. 31–36 (offenders per group of offenses committed)

The variables 31–36 were eliminated because there were perhaps too many crime variables, which may have affected the chances of finding clear structures, especially when using factor analysis, and also because of a presumed low reliability of these data.

On this reduced set of variables the greater part of the analyses was executed once again (e.g. factor analysis and multiple regression analysis of means). These analyses too produced no meaningful information whatsoever.

5.7. Canonical discriminant analysis

Finally, because it was supposed that the greatest source of variance could be the countries themselves, canonical discriminant analysis was performed on the original 36 variables and on the variables remaining after the third reduction. The results of the latter analysis are presented in Table 10. The 10 countries showed significant differences in 9 dimensions, i.e. the greatest possible number of dimensions. Once again the dimensions that were found could not clearly be characterized by one concept or name.

6. CONCLUSIONS AND DISCUSSION

The following general conclusions can be drawn from the results presented above:

(1) The countries are too diverse to justify the formulation of statements valid for more than one country.

(2) General statements concerning the relations between variables can be made only for very limited time periods.

(3) Insofar as relations between the variables exist, they seem to be connected mainly with a general 'growth factor' which is independent from the population growth.

Some of the findings of Jepsen and Pal (1969) and Törnudd (1969) and of this study show similarities. In contrast with Jepsen ans Pal and Törnudd the authors consider these findings 'unsatisfactory.'

The negative results, that are nonetheless results, may have been caused by any of the decisions taken in the course of the research project, e.g. the choice of number and type of countries, predictor and criterion variables and time period, the choice

Table 10: Canonical structure (absolute values ⩽ .30 are omitted)

Variable	1	2	3	4	5	6	7	8	9	Proportion variance
1				–.34		.43	–.43	.34		.70
2		–.49	.33	–.32				–.46		.83
3		.77					.39			.89
4	.34			–.69		.42				.87
5										.03
6	–.97									.999
7		–.39	–.51		–.34					.65
8				.82						.93
9		.30	–.47	–.50	.52					.94
10		.71				.50				.90
13			–.66		–.42					.73
14										.21
15					–.47	–.34				.61
16	.45	.50		–.53		.32				.97
17		.83	–.45							.98
19	–.54	.31		.53	–.38					.92
20										.05
21	.31		.47		–.71	–.32				.98
23		.61		.30				–.30	.30	.74
24	–.40		–.33		–.33	.63	.31			.93
25				–.81						.78
26			–.49	–.59						.93
27				–.59				–.42		.73
30				–.71					.30	.82
percentages of contribution to variance	9.2	14.0	8.9	18.9	8.5	7.0	3.5	4.1	1.4	

of official statistics as a source of information, the way of operationalization and indexing, the choice of analyzing techniques and computer programs.

Nevertheless, the importance of this type of research is still considered to be very great, not only from a scientific point of view, but also with respect to policymaking. A better insight into and grip on the conjuncture of criminality seems to be urgently needed.

This study was executed in an explorative manner. It has acted like sonar brought into a huge mountain in order to find out what that mountain is made of and what tools must be used to master it. From this study the interested researcher can derive information about the pitfalls of this type of research. If this leads in any way to a better approach to criminological problems the authors have been rewarded enough.

Culemborg, November 1975

REFERENCES

A short manual on sampling, Vols. I and II. New York: United Nations, 1972 and 1973.

Banks, A. S., *Cross-policy time series data*. Cambridge, Mass., 1971.

Bonger, W. A., *Criminality and economic conditions*. Boston: Little, Brown and Co., 1916.

Cavan, R. and J. Cavan, *Delinquency and crime: cross-cultural perspectives*. Philadelphia: J. B. Lippincott, 1968.

Clinard, M. B. and D. J. Abbott, *Crime in developing countries: A comparative perspective*. New York: Wiley, 1973.

Clinard, M. B., 'Criminological Research,' in R. K. Merton (ed.), *Sociology today*. New York: Basic Books, 1959, pp. 509–536.

Clinard, M. B., 'Research frontiers in criminology,' *British Journal of Delinquency* (1956), pp. 110–122.

Compendium of social statistics. New York: United Nations, 1968.

Demographic Yearbook. New York: United Nations, *1960–1972*.

Durkheim, E., *Suicide*. Translated by Spaulding and Simpson. New York: the Free Press, 1966.

Friday, P. C., 'Problems in comparative criminology: comments on the feasibility and implications of research,' *International Journal of Criminology and Penology*, 1 (1973), pp. 151–160.

Gercenzon, A. A. (ed.), *Prestupnost' v kapitaliceskom mire posle vtoroj mirovoj vojny*. Moscow: Academy of Sciences of the USSR, 1963.

Gibbens, T. C. N. and R. H. Ahrenfeldt, *Culture factors in delinquency*. London: Tavistock, 1966.

Guerry, A., *Essai sur la statistique morale de la France*. 1833.

Harries, K. D., *The geography of crime and justice*. New York: MacGraw Hill, 1974.

Henry, L., 'Forecasting the trend of criminality,' in *Collected Studies in Criminological Research*, 4 (1969), Strasbourg: Council of Europe.

Hoeveel alcoholhoudende dranken worden er in de wereld gedronken? Schiedam: Productschap voor Gedistilleerde Dranken, 1974.

International Crime Statistics. Paris: Interpol, *1960–1970*.

Jepsen, J. and L. Pal, 'Forecasting the volume and structure of future criminality,' in *Collected Studies in Criminological Research*, 4 (1969), Strasbourg: Council of Europe.

Lynn, R., *Personality and national character*. Oxford: Pergamon Press, 1971.

Mays, J. B., *Crime and the social structure*. London: Faber and Faber, 1963.

Methodology and evaluation of population registers and similar systems. New York: United Nations, 1969.

Nie, N., D. H. Bent and C. H. Hull, *Statistical package for the social sciences*. New York: McGraw-Hill, 1970, p. 180.

Porebski, O. R., 'Discriminatory and canonical analysis of technical college data,' *British Journal of Mathematical and Statistical Psychology*, 19 (1966), pp. 215–236.

Quetelet, A., *Recherches sur le penchant au crime aux différents ages*. Brussels, 1831.

Radcliff-Brown, A. R., *A natural science of society*. New York: The Free Press, 1957.

Revenue Statistics of O.E.C.D. member countries 1965–1971. Paris: O.E.C.D., 1974.

Rummel, R. J., *The dimensions of nations*. Beverly Hills/London: Sage Publications, 1972.

Schuyt, C. J. M., *Rechtvaardigheid en effectiviteit in de verdeling van de levenskansen. Een rechtssociologische beschouwing*. Rotterdam: Universitaire Pers, 1973.

Statistical Yearbook. Paris: Unesco, *1960–1972*.

Statistical Yearbook. New York: United Nations, *1960–1972*.

Statistics of Road Traffic Accidents in Europe. New York: Economic Commission for Europe of the United Nations, *1960–1970*.

Törnudd, P., 'Forecasting the trend of criminality,' in *Collected Studies in Criminological Research*, 4 (1969), Strasbourg: Council of Europe.

Towards a system of social and demographic statistics. New York: United Nations, 1975.

Van de Geer, J. P., *Introduction to multivariate analysis for the social sciences*. San Francisco: Freeman, 1971, p. 128.

Van Weringh, Jac., *Heeft de maatschappij de kriminaliteit die zij verdient?* Amsterdam: De Arbeiderspers, 1971.
Wolf, P., 'Crime and development – an international comparison of crime rates,' in *Scandinavian Studies in Criminology*, 3 (1971), Strasbourg: Council of Europe, pp. 107–120.
Wootton, B., *Social science and social pathology*. London: Allen and Unwin, 1959.
World Energy Supplies 1960–1970. New York: United Nations, 1973.
World Health Statistics Annual, 1, 2, and 3 (1960–1972), Geneva: World Health Organization.
World Road Statistics. Geneva: International Road Federation, *1960–1972*.
Yearbook of Labor Statistics. New York: United Nations, *1960–1972*.
Yearbook of National Account Statistics. New York: United Nations, *1960–1972*.

SELECTED BIBLIOGRAPHY OF WILLEM H. NAGEL

1949

De criminaliteit van Oss (The Criminality of Oss), Dissertation, The Hague: D. A. Daamen's Uitgeversmij 1949.

1951

De Meineed (Perjury), Amsterdam: De Bezige Bij 1951.
'Verzoening als element in het herstel der rechtsorde.' *Tweede studiedag Nederlands Gevangeniswezen 1951* (Reconciliation as an element in the restoration of the legal order. Second Study-day of the Dutch prison system 1951), Studie- en documentatiecentrum van de afdeling Gevangeniswezen, Ministerie van Justitie, Den Haag (Research and Documentation Center, Prison Department, Ministry of Justice, The Hague), 1951 pp. 45–76.

1952

'Enige beginselbeschouwingen bij de ordening van het ordeningsstrafrecht' (A few basic considerations with regard to regulating social-economic regulatory penal law), *Soc.-Econ. Wetgeving* (1952), pp. 65–78.
'De Derde Weg, opheffing van een dodelijk alternatief' (The Third Way, abolition of a fatal alternative), *Socialisme en Democratie, Maandblad van de Partij van de Arbeid,* June (1952) pp. 345–350.

1953

'Lezend over misdaad' (Reading about crime), *T. Strafr.* 62 (1953), pp. 1–25.

1955

'In Memoriam Prof. M. P. Vrij,' *T. Strafr.* 64 (1955), pp. 1–26.

1956

'Het strafrecht en de onmens.' Inaugurele rede op 2-11-1956, (Criminal law and the monster. Inaugural address November 2, 1956), The Hague: Bert Bakker-Daamen N.V.

1958

'La délinquance sexuelle du point de vue de la sociologie du droit' (Sexual offenses from the perspective of the sociology of law), Working Paper No. 6 of the European Advisory Committee on Crime Prevention and Treatment of Offenders, prepared for the U.N., July (1958).
'Penologische beschouwing over 5 jaren Wet Economische Delikten (1952 t/m 1956)', (Penological considerations of five years of the Economic Offenses Act (1952–1956)), *Soc Econ. Wetgeving* 6, Nos. 3, 4, 5 (1958), pp. 79–99.
'Sociologische criminologie' (Sociological criminology), *Jaarboek Ned. Soc. Ver.* (1958), pp. 58–102.

1959

'Klassische und Moderne Kriminologie' (Classical and modern criminology), *Z.ges. Strafrechtswiss.* 71 (1959), pp. 114–136.
'Victimologie' (Victimology), *T. Strafr.* 68 (1959), pp. 1–26.

1960

'Criminality and Religion', *T. Strafr.* 69 (1960), pp. 263–291.

1961

'Onzedelijke onmaatschappelijkheid' (Immoral antisociality), *T. Strafr.* 70 (1961) pp. 252–267).

1963

'The notion of victimology in criminology', *Excerpta Criminologica* 3 (1963), pp. 245–247.
'De Utrechtse School' (The Utrecht School), *T. Strafr* 72 (1963), pp. 322–355.

1965

'International collaboration in the field of criminology' in: *Le droit pénal international, recueil d'études en hommage à J. M. van Bemmelen* (International criminal law, collection of studies in honor of J. M. van Bemmelen), Leiden: Brill, 1965, pp. 193–222.
Het voorspellen van krimineel gedrag. Rapport uitgebracht aan het Ministerie van Justitie (Prediction of criminal behavior. Report to the Ministry of Justice), The Hague: Staatsuitgeverij, 1965.

1966

'De Groningse School I' (The Groningen School I), *Ned. T. Criminol.* 8 (1966), pp. 81–93.
'De Groningse School II' (The Groningen School II), *Ned. T. Criminol.* 8 (1966), pp. 122–134.
PTK, Rapport over het begeleidingsonderzoek Penitentiair Trainingskamp (Zeeland, N-B), *fase I*, uitgebracht aan Min. van Just., Den Haag, (PTK, Report on the evaluative research Penitentiary Training Camp (Zeeland, N-B), phase I, made to the Ministry of Justice, The Hague), July 1966, stencil.

1967

Juvenile Delinquency in Thailand, Rapport als expert van de United Nations Technical Assistance (Report made as United Nations Technical Assistance expert) 1967, stencil.

1968

'Wat is strafbaar?' (What is punishable?), *Wijsgerig Perspectief* 8 (1968), pp. 192–206.
'On Criminologists', in: *Crime and Culture, Essays in honor of Thorsten Sellin.* M. E. Wolfgang (ed.), New York: John Wiley and Sons, Inc. 1968.
'Beccaria en Calkoen' (Beccaria and Calkoen), *T. Strafr.* 77 (1968), pp. 67–84.

1969

'Pönitentiäre Behandlung und die gusseiserne Tautologie' in *Festschrift A. Krebs, Erziehung zur Freiheit durch Freiheitsentzug. Internationale Probleme des Strafvollzugs an jungen Menschen* (Prison treatment and the cast iron tautology, in 'Festschrift' for A. Krebs, Development toward freedom through detention. International problems of corrections for juveniles), Darmstadt: Druck- und Verlags-GmbH, 1969, pp. 121–127.
'Religion', in: *Handwörterbuch der Kriminologie*, R. Sieverts and H. -J. Schneider (eds.) (Pocket dictionary of Criminology), second edition 3, No. 1/2. Berlin: Walter de Gruyter & Co. 1969.
'Verkehrskriminalität und Strafe in den Niederländen', 6. Tagung für Richter und Staatsanwälte. Bund gegen Alkohol im Strassenverkehr e.v. (Traffic offenses and punishment in the Netherlands. Proceedings of the sixth conference for Judges and Public Prosecutors), Freiburg i.Br.: Landessektion Südbaden, April 25 1969, pp. 50–74.

1970

Critical Criminology, Paper presented at the VIth Congress of the International Society of Criminology, Madrid, Spain, Sept. 24, 1970, reprinted in 1971.
PTK, Rapport over het begeleidingsonderzoek Penitentiair Trainingskamp (Zeeland, N-B) *fase II*, uitgebracht aan Min. van Just. Den Haag, (PTK, Report on the evaluative research Penitentiary Training Camp (Zeeland, N-B), phase II, made to the Ministry of Justice, The Hague), 1970, stencil.

1971

'L'Avocat du Diable en ce qui concerne le "Terrorisme"' (The devil's advocate in matters of 'terrorism'). Paper presented at the meeting of the Société Internationale de Prophylaxie Criminelle, Paris, 17 December 1971.

1972

'Terrorisme' (Terrorism), *T. Soc. Wetensch.* 2 (1972), pp. 135–156.

1973

The Utilization of research as a basis for social defence policy and planning, Paper presented at the United Nations Inter-regional Seminar on the Use of Research as a Basis for Social Defence Policy and Planning, Copenhagen, 20-31 Aug. 1973.
'De "True Believer" en het probleem van de vergelding' (The 'True Believer' and the problem of retribution), in: *Speculum Langemeijer; 31 rechtsgeleerde opstellen*, Zwolle: W. E. J. Tjeenk-Willink, 1973, pp. 365–386.
'Mode en Model' (Fashion and Model), *Ned. Juristenblad* 48 (1973), pp. 1311–1316.

1974

'Structural Victimisation', *Int. J. Criminol. Penol.* 2 (1974), pp. 99–132.
'Politiek en Kriminologie,' in: *Waarde, Macht, Kriminologie* (Politics and criminology, in: Value, power, criminology), The Hague: Nijhof, 1974, pp. 3–24.
'Plaisir et Déplaisir en Matière de Delinquance Sexuelle (Eléments inséparables de l'appréciation)' (Pleasure and disgust in the matter of sexual crime (Inseparable elements of appreciation)), Paper presented at congress 15-18 March 1972 in Brussels, in: *Les Frontières de la Répression* (Limits to repression), Brussels: Editions Université de Bruxelles, 1974, pp. 113–133.
'Om de kwaliteit van ons strafrechtelijk systeem, of: opnieuw op de overloop' (The quality of our criminal justice system, or 'on the landing' once again), *Ned. Juristenblad* 49 (1974), pp. 1205–1220.
The subject-matter of criminology reconsidered. The importance Erasmus, More and Vives should have had for the development of criminology. Paper presented at the

Anglo-Dutch Criminology Colloquium, Keele, 7-8 Sept. 1974; stencil.

1975

De immateriële schade van slachtoffers van misdrijven (The non-material damage to victims of crimes). Paper presented at the Colloquium 'Het Slachtoffer' (the Victim) in Ghent, Belgium, Febr. 1975.
'Terrorisme' (Terrorism), Ministry of Justice, The Hague (eds.), *Justitiële Verkenningen* 4, (1957), pp. 150–156.
'De dialektiek: jouw vrijheid/mijn vrijheid' (The dialectic: your freedom/my freedom), in: *Bundel 4e eeuwfeest, Fakulteit der Rechtsgeleerdheid* (Book commemorating 400th anniversary, Law Faculty), Leiden, 1975.
The Impact of Technological Progress on Penal Law, Paper presented at the Colloquium on Social Change and Social Control through Law, Aswan, Egypt, 19-23 Dec. 1975.

1976

Het werkschuwe tuig, De Nederlandse Kriminologie (Work-shy scum, Dutch Criminology series), Arnhem: Van Loghum Slaterus, 1976.

NAME INDEX

SUBJECT INDEX

GPSR Compliance

The European Union's (EU) General Product Safety Regulation (GPSR) is a set of rules that requires consumer products to be safe and our obligations to ensure this.

If you have any concerns about our products, you can contact us on ProductSafety@springernature.com

In case Publisher is established outside the EU, the EU authorized representative is:

Springer Nature Customer Service Center GmbH
Europaplatz 3
69115 Heidelberg, Germany

Batch number: 10844669

Printed by Printforce, the Netherlands